T0319944

Career Dynamics in a Global World

NEW HORIZONS IN ORGANIZATION STUDIES

Books in the New Horizons in Organization Studies series make a significant contribution to the study of organizations and the environment and context in which they operate. As this field has expanded dramatically in recent years, the series will provide an invaluable forum for the publication of high-quality works of scholarship and show the diversity of research on organizations of all sizes around the world. Global and pluralistic in its approach, this series includes some of the best theoretical and analytical work with contributions to fundamental principles, rigorous evaluations of existing concepts and competing theories, stimulating debate and future visions.

Career Dynamics in a Global World

Indian and Western Perspectives

Edited by

Premarajan Raman Kadiyil

Professor of Organizational Behaviour and Human Resources Management, XLRI Jamshedpur, India

Anneleen Forrier

Professor, Department of Work and Organisation Studies, KU Leuven, Belgium

Michael B. Arthur

Emeritus Professor, Suffolk University, Boston, USA and Visiting Professor, Cranfield University, UK

NEW HORIZONS IN ORGANIZATION STUDIES

Cheltenham, UK • Northampton, MA, USA

Published by
Edward Elgar Publishing Limited
The Lypiatts
15 Lansdown Road
Cheltenham
Glos GL50 2JA
UK

Edward Elgar Publishing, Inc.
William Pratt House
9 Dewey Court
Northampton
Massachusetts 01060
USA

A catalogue record for this book
is available from the British Library

Library of Congress Control Number: 2019956714

This book is available electronically in the **Elgar**online
Business subject collection
DOI 10.4337/9781789901504

ISBN 978 1 78990 149 8 (cased)
ISBN 978 1 78990 150 4 (eBook)

Printed and bound by CPI Group (UK) Ltd, Croydon CR0 4YY

Premarajan: To the memory of my parents, Kallyani Amma and Govindan Nair, who taught me the importance of being grounded, to my wife Sugi and children Avneeth and Anaswara for making me cherish life

Anneleen: For my father, Edward Forrier, and my mother, Hilda de Grave, who taught me the joy of travelling and the richness of an open mind

Michael: For my wife, Patricia Keck, and my daughter, Victoria Arthur, who keep me going and bring purpose to my life

Contents

Figures

Tables

Contributors

Michael B. Arthur is Emeritus Professor of Management at Suffolk University, Boston, USA, and Visiting Professor at Cranfield University, UK. His co-authored/edited works include the *Handbook of Career Theory* (1989), *The Boundaryless Career* (1996), *The New Careers* (1999), *Knowledge at Work* (2006) and most recently *An Intelligent Career: Taking Ownership of Your Work and Your Life* (2017, with Svetlana Khapova and Julia Richardson). He is co-developer of the ICCS® Career Exploration System and a contributor to Forbes.com.

Anna Katharina Bader is Senior Lecturer in International Human Resource Management at Newcastle Business School, Northumbria University, UK. Her research focuses on diversity management and expatriate management and most of her studies are based on international, comparative research. Her work has been published in international, peer-reviewed journals such as *Human Resource Management* and *The International Journal of Human Resource Management* and she has received several international awards for her research. Before her academic career, she worked in the private sector as a leadership development manager and trainer.

Sharmistha Banerjee is Professor of Business Management at the University of Calcutta, India. Her teaching areas include management, human resource management and organizational behaviour and her research areas spread across interdisciplinary themes covering small business management, microfinance and entrepreneurship, which is evident in her national and international publications and PhD supervision. In addition to Indian public and privately sponsored research, she has been part of international interdisciplinary research projects.

Yehuda Baruch (DSc Technion, Israel), Fellow of the Academy of Social Sciences and of the British Academy of Management, is Professor of Management at Southampton Business School, University of Southampton, UK. His research focus on careers and global human resource management. He has published over 145 papers, including in the *Journal of Management*, *Academy of Management Annals*, *Human Resource Management*, *Journal of Vocational Behavior*, *Human Relations* and *Organization Studies* and 50 books and book chapters. He was formerly Vice-President Research at EURAM,

Associate Editor of *Human Resource Management* (US), Editor of *Group & Organization Management* and *Career Development International* and past Chair, Careers Division at the Academy of Management.

Anil K. Bhat (B.E Mechanical Engineering, Regional Engineering College, NIT Srinagar and Fellow, Indian Institute of Management [IIM] Bangalore) is Professor of Management in the Department of Management, Birla Institute of Technology and Science (BITS) Pilani, India. He has held memberships of the Academy of Management, American Marketing Association, Academy of International Business, British Academy of Management and is also a Fellow of the Institution of Engineers (India). He has been certified as an Entrepreneur Educator by Stanford Technology Ventures Program, National Entrepreneurship Network and IIM Bangalore. He has more than 100 publications to his credit and has co-authored a book on management published by Oxford University Press.

John Blenkinsopp is Professor of Work & Organisational Psychology and co-convenor of the Sustainable Working Futures (SWiFt) research group at Newcastle Business School, Northumbria University. His research examines how people experience and make sense of work and the workplace, particularly in relation to careers and ethical issues, often with a comparative element to the studies. His work has been published in outlets such as the *Journal of Business Ethics*, *The International Journal of Human Resource Management* and the *Journal of Occupational and Organizational Psychology*. Prior to becoming an academic he worked as a human resources professional in healthcare.

Chris Brewster is Professor of International Human Resource Management (HRM) at Henley Business School, University of Reading, UK and is a frequent speaker at universities around the world. The first half of his working life he spent as a practitioner but now he researches international and comparative HRM. He has published 30 books and well over 200 articles. He has a doctorate from the London School of Economics and an honorary doctorate from Vaasa University, Finland.

Pawan Budhwar is the 50th Anniversary Professor of International Human Resource Management (HRM) at Aston Business School, Aston University, Birmingham, UK. He is also the Associate Pro-Vice Chancellor International, the Director of the Aston Indian Centre for Applied Research and the Co-Editor-in-Chief of the *British Journal of Management*. Pawan's research interests are in the field of strategic HRM, international HRM and emerging markets with a specific focus on India. He has published over 120 articles in leading journals and has also written and/or co-edited 20 books. Pawan is a Fellow of the Higher Education Academy, British Academy of Management, the Academy of Social Sciences and the Indian Academy of Management.

Leena Chatterjee is a Professor at the Indian Institute of Management (IIM) Calcutta, India in the area of Organizational Behaviour. Her current research interests include understanding career choices, career management and diversity management in the Indian context. She has over 35 years of experience in teaching, training and consulting in organizational behaviour. She received her bachelor's and master's degrees in psychology from Delhi University and a PhD in social/organizational psychology from the Indian Institute of Technology (IIT) Kanpur.

Mary Conway Dato-on is Professor of International Business and Social Entrepreneurship, George D. & Harriet W. Cornell Chair, Crummer Graduate School of Business, Rollins College, USA. She is a Fulbright Garcia-Robles Scholar whose research covers social entrepreneurship, non-profit branding, social marketing, cross-cultural consumer behaviour, gender and ethics. She has published 20+ peer-reviewed journal articles, five book chapters, 10+ cases and 40+ professional conference papers. Additionally, Mary leads efforts to promote social entrepreneurship, including a board position on Rally: The Social Enterprise Accelerator, as the inaugural Faculty Director for Rollins's Social Innovation & Entrepreneurship Hub, and as a leader in developing the Global Links Program – a public–private partnership with reach in four countries.

Sumita Datta is Professor (Adjunct) of Organizational Behaviour (OB) & Human Resource Management (HRM) and Advisor, Women Leadership Programme at S P Jain Institute of Management and Research (SPJIMR), Mumbai, India. She is also post-doctoral scholar at Interdisciplinary Centre for Gender Studies of ISCSP, University of Lisbon, Portugal. She has prior experience of more than 15 years in the corporate sector and has served in senior positions in human resources. At SPJIMR she started a first of its kind full-time accelerated MBA programme in 2016 for returning women. She has curated women leadership development programmes for large corporates as well as coached more than 100 women entrepreneurs and corporate leaders. Sumita has published her research in international journals as well as presented at top international conferences.

Amit Dhiman is Associate Professor of Human Resource Management (HRM) at the Indian Institute of Management Calcutta, India. He teaches HRM and strategic HRM in services. His research interests are performance appraisals, strategic HRM in IT and healthcare services and evolving challenges in management education.

Srinivas Ekkirala is a Professor in the Organizational Behavior and HRM Area at the Indian Institute of Management Bangalore (IIMB). Earlier he worked as faculty at XLRI Jamshedpur and Indian School of Business (ISB). He has published his research in leading scholarly journals such as the *Academy of Management Journal*, *Journal of Applied Psychology*, *Journal of Occupational and Organizational Psychology* and the *International Journal of Human Resource Management*, among others. He has designed and delivered executive education programmes for over 50 leading organizations. His research interests include leadership, proactivity, emotions, well-being, and mindfulness. He was one of the Guest Editors for a special issue on Indian Psychology and guided doctoral research in this area.

Margie J. Elley-Brown is a Senior Lecturer in Management in the Faculty of Business, Economics and Law at AUT University, Auckland, Aotearoa New Zealand. She had extensive experience in education and management prior to joining academia. Her doctoral research used a phenomenological approach to explore women's lived experiences of career and what career means to them at different career stages. Margie is particularly invested in creating opportunities for women to tell their career stories, giving voice to their lived experience.

Anneleen Forrier is Full Professor at the Faculty of Economics and Business of the KU Leuven, Belgium, where she is a member of the Department of Work and Organisation Studies. Her research interests include employability, careers, labour market attachment, the potential additional labour force, (re) employment and ageing policies. She has published her research in leading scholarly journals such as *Journal of Occupational and Organizational Psychology*, *Journal of Vocational Behavior*, *Human Resource Management Journal* and *Journal of Management Studies*, among others.

Sara Haviland, PhD, is a Research Scientist in the Academic to Career Research Center at Educational Testing Service (ETS), Princeton, New Jersey, USA. Her body of work examines how educational interventions and career development can improve post-secondary educational access and opportunities for movement into higher socio-economic statuses. Sara currently conducts research on career and technical education, community colleges, career pathways and development, employer engagement, and skill acquisition for adult learners.

Elizabeth Houldsworth is Associate Professor of Leadership, Organisations and Behaviour at Henley Business School, University of Reading, UK. She has considerable practical experience, having worked in international human resource management (HRM) and in management consulting. She is now Programme Director for the MSc in International HRM and involved in research on careers, adult learning, and comparative aspects of HRM practice. She has a doctorate from Brunel University, UK.

Chetan Joshi is Associate Professor in Organizational Behaviour at the Indian Institute of Management Calcutta, India. He holds an MBA from the University of Roorkee, India and a doctorate in management from Richard Ivey Business School, Western University (formerly University of Western Ontario), Canada. His research has been published in *The International Journal of Human Resource Management* and presented at international conferences such as the Administrative Sciences Association of Canada, Society for Industrial and Organizational Psychology, International Congress of Psychology, Eastern Academy of Management and the Academy of Management. His co-authored case studies and teaching notes are available from Harvard Business School Publishing.

Premarajan Raman Kadiyil is a Full Professor of Organizational Behaviour and Human Resource Management at Xavier School of Management (XLRI) Jamshedpur, India. His teaching, research and consulting interests include careers, alternate methodology in assessment centres and competency assessment. He is the chairperson of the Centre for Human Resource Development at XLRI. He has also occupied the L&T Scholar of Human Resource – a chair position at XLRI in the Competency Assessment and Development area.

Pavni Kaushiva is an Assistant Professor of Organizational Behaviour at the Indian Institute of Management Lucknow, India. She holds a BTech from the Jaypee Institute of Information Technology, Noida, India, and completed her PhD on Gender and Diversity in Management at the Indian Institute of Management Calcutta, India. Her research has been presented at the Annual Conference of the Administrative Sciences Association of Canada, 2015, 2016 and 2017, VII International Conference of Work and Family, 2017 and the British Academy of Management, 2019.

Ravishankar Venkata Kommu is a Doctoral Candidate in the group area of Human Resource Management at the Indian Institute of Management (IIM) Calcutta, India. His research interests include careers, economic sociology and critical management studies. He is currently working on a dissertation studying academic careers in the context of the IIMs in India.

Anupama Kondayya is a Doctoral Student of Organizational Behaviour and Human Resource Management at the Indian Institute of Management Bangalore, India. Her current research interests include Eastern perspectives in management, indigenous institutions and diversity and inclusion.

Angela Stephanie Mazzetti is a Senior Lecturer at Newcastle University Business School, Newcastle University, UK. Angela's research focuses on how individuals and groups cope with stressful life and career events. Angela has conducted a number of research projects focusing on appraisal and coping and has published in a range of research journals. Angela also has a keen interest in research methodology and in particular how the adoption of a more diverse range of research methodologies can advance our understanding of stress and coping.

Richard McBain is an Academic Fellow at Henley Business School, University of Reading, UK, having previously been Associate Professor of Leadership, Organisations and Behaviour and Head of Post-Experience Postgraduate Programmes. Prior to joining Henley, he was Head of Group Training and Development for a financial services organization. He has a doctorate from Brunel University, UK and has undertaken research in careers, coaching and mentoring and employee engagement.

Yasmin Mesbah, MBA, is an Adjunct Professor of Social Entrepreneurship at Rollins College, USA. Yasmin is also the Program Manager for the Global Links Program, a partnership among founding partners: Crummer Graduate School of Business at Rollins College, Tupperware Brands, and the U.S. Secretary of State's Office of Global Women's Issues that encourages aspiring female entrepreneurs' success in developing countries. In her position, Yasmin oversees strategy development and scaling opportunities, and serves as project planning lead.

Jennifer Craft Morgan is an Associate Professor with the Gerontology Institute at Georgia State University, USA. Her research focuses on jobs and careers, attempting to understand how policy, population, workplace and individual-level factors shape how work is experienced and how work is organized across settings. She is a US expert on recruitment, training and retention of frontline healthcare workers, highlighting the impact of good jobs and high-quality training on worker and organizational outcomes.

Vivek G. Nair is a Doctoral Student of Organizational Behaviour at the Indian Institute of Management (IIM) Calcutta, India. His current research interests include studying the role of contextual factors in contemporary Indian careers. He has close to five years of corporate work experience across companies such as Oracle, Mahindra & Mahindra and T.I.M.E. He received his BTech in Electrical and Electronics Engineering from the National Institute of Technology Calicut and Postgraduate Diploma in Management from IIM Bangalore.

Mousumi Padhi is Associate Professor at Xavier School of Human Resource Management (HRM), Xavier University, Bhubaneswar, India, has more than a decade of experience in teaching. She has experience of teaching at the National Institute of Technology Rourkela, Indian Institute of Management Ranchi and Indian Institute of Management Lucknow. As a member of faculty in HRM, she has teaching expertise in talent management, industrial relations and employment relations. Her research interests lie in gender, work–family interface, work values, neuroscience, and employment relations, among others. Her research has been published in a number of international and national journals of repute.

Tania Saritova Rath is Associate Professor, Xavier School of Human Resource Management (HRM), Xavier University, Bhubaneswar, India, has 27 years of managerial experience at the State Bank of India, spanning various fields in banking. She was a national-level trainer in the bank, being part of various management development and change management programmes. Her research interests lie in women's careers, gender studies, values in management, responsible leadership and learning and development. Her research papers have been published in reputed Indian and international journals.

Snehal Shah is Professor of Organizational Behaviour (OB), Chairperson of the Doctoral Programme and Head of Research at S P Jain Institute of Management and Research, India. Her research interests include diversity and inclusion, Eastern wisdom traditions and intersectionality of OB concepts in other management disciplines. Snehal has published papers in journals such as the *Journal of Applied Psychology*, *Journal of Organizational Behavior*, *Journal of Management Information Systems*, and others. She has presented papers at top international conferences and invited to write book chapters. Snehal has served as a reviewer for top journals in the field of organizational behaviour.

Jyoti Tikoria obtained her PhD from the Department of Management Studies, Indian Institute of Technology Delhi in 2009. Her primary areas of interest in teaching and research are strategy and entrepreneurship, technology management, R&D management and intellectual property rights management. Currently, she is Associate Professor in the Department of Management at the Birla Institute of Technology and Science (BITS), Pilani, India. She served as Faculty-in-Charge at the Centre for Innovation, Incubation & Entrepreneurship (CIIE) and Center for Entrepreneurial Leadership (CEL), India. She has guided and mentored more than 100 budding entrepreneurs and has facilitated more than 30 faculty members in their patent filing process.

Preeti Tiwari is Assistant Professor of Strategy at T. A. Pai Management Institute, India. She completed her PhD in the area of Entrepreneurship at Birla Institute of Technology and Science (BITS), Pilani, India in 2017. Her area of interests are entrepreneurship, strategy, social start-ups and management practices. At the T. A. Pai Management Institute she is also involved in sustainability courses and initiatives. She has published in more than 20 international journals and presented at conferences of high repute. She is also involved in various social entrepreneurial activities like working towards the development of health of tribal women in Orissa, India.

Gunjan Tomer is an Assistant Professor of Decision Sciences and Information Systems at the Indian Institute of Management (IIM) Nagpur. She holds a doctoral degree in Information Systems from IIM Indore. She has published in reputed journals in her area. Her research interests are socio-technical systems and digital transformation. Her papers have been selected for top international conferences such as Academy of Management, European Conference on Information Systems, Pacific Asia Conference on Information Systems and European Group for Organizational Studies.

Marijke Verbruggen is a Professor at the Department of Work and Organisation Studies at KU Leuven, Belgium. Her main research interests include career counselling, career transitions, flexible work arrangements and work–home balance. She has published in the *Academy of Management Review*, *Journal of Management*, *Journal of Organizational Behavior*, *Journal of Vocational Behavior*, *European Journal of Work and Organizational Psychology* and *Human Resource Management Journal*, among others.

Acknowledgements

This book had its genesis in an invitation from Premarajan Raman Kadiyil to Michael Arthur and Anneleen Forrier to visit Xavier School of Management (XLRI), Jamshedpur, India, in December 2018. We are deeply grateful to that institution for its generous support of those visits, and the conversations they initiated that ultimately led to the publication of this book.

Writing a book is taxing, but editing one can be harder. Things can go beyond the editors' control, but at the same time they can provide a richness of experience. This book would not have been possible without the unstinted support of the wonderful group of scholars who contributed its 16 chapters. Those scholars consistently rose to our challenging demands and occasionally also allowed us to influence – and to be influenced. The entire process was a deep source of cross-cultural learning.

Alan Sturmer, Executive Editor at Edward Elgar Publishing was a constant source of support and guidance in completing this work. His promptness and encouragement went a long way toward the final product. Munish Thakur deserves a special mention for his support during the conversations of December 2018. Saggurthi Suneetha and Subhasree Pan Lahiri worked painstakingly to see us through those discussions and help us in the follow-up.

1. Introduction to *Career Dynamics in a Global World*

Premarajan Raman Kadiyil, Anneleen Forrier and Michael B. Arthur

An important question for researchers and practitioners in human resource management in general, and career development in particular, is this: are existing knowledge and practice developed in the West directly applicable to non-Western and particularly collectivistic societies? Or, to put it more specifically, does a predominant one-way influence of Western career concepts interfere with our understanding of careers in other parts of the world? There is good reason to ask these questions. Differences in national context, governance and culture have been widely shown to co-vary with people's career-related attitudes, orientations and behaviours across countries (Khapova, Briscoe and Dickmann, 2012; Tlaiss, 2014; Tsai et al., 2019).

In this book we take up the challenge to look beyond an emphasis on Western careers research. Specifically, we set out to compare ideas from a distinctly Eastern society, India, with related ideas from recognized Western societies. We hope that this comparison will not only serve careers research and practice across the two kinds of society, but also set an example for other international initiatives. We further hope that this will lead to a greater appreciation of career phenomena in a turbulent, substantially globalized economy.

We have also tried to position this book to encourage a conversation among and between career theorists and practitioners. In doing so we have created something very different from a typical comparative study, where matching research samples and methodologies are applied across geographies. Instead, we present eight pairs of chapters, with each pair involving one contribution from an Indian perspective and one from a Western perspective. Each pair also addresses a different topic, and each chapter offers a specific view of its subject within the topic area. In this way, we left greater scope for each authorship team to investigate and discuss phenomena of their own choosing within their adopted topic area. In every case, you are reading about something the authors consider to be important, and worth their time and energy in delivering their chapter to you.

We have also chosen to provide a brief preview of each topic, suggesting some of the differences you may notice as you read along. However, they are only suggestions, intended to stimulate rather than restrict your further response to the material presented. We simply ask that you give yourself the opportunity to see deeper contrasts between the Indian and Western perspectives addressed, which in many cases carry over to other topics in the book. Our commitment to the adopted approach grew through successive stages in which we three editors spent time in India, conferred with other scholars and practitioners, developed our ideas, joined up with our publisher, and reached out to a wide range of both Indian and Western authors.

HOW DID THE BOOK COME ABOUT?

The inspiration for the book came from Premarajan Raman Kadiyil's invitation to Anneleen Forrier and Michael Arthur to visit the Centre for Human Resource Development, Xavier School of Management (XLRI), in Jamshedpur, India, in December 2018. During that visit, the three of us interacted with scholars from India and abroad and discussed their research. One of two kinds of research papers we saw focused on the distinctive circumstances of a country, in this case India, from which the paper originated. A second kind of papers were those such as those relating personality to career decision-making, that claimed broader applicability outside their country of origin.

We further noticed that it was the first kind of papers that promoted the liveliest conversation among the scholars we met. When we spoke with practitioners, they were also stimulated to talk about cultural differences underlying Indian and Western careers. As the three of us reflected on this, we asked ourselves what range of topics could we identify that would promote the kind of conversation and comparisons we were witnessing? At that point we reached out to Edward Elgar Publishing and went back and forth between the broader literature on careers and potential areas for comparison between India and the West. We ended up identifying four broad drivers giving rise to the evolution of careers today, and across which we might profitably look for contrasting insights. Those drivers are globalization, national culture, convergence/divergence and gender roles, each of which is discussed below.

DRIVERS OF THE EVOLUTION OF CAREERS

Globalization

Globalization has both an economic and a sociological meaning. An economic meaning comes from former Harvard Business School professor, Theodore Leavitt (1983), who argued that technology had 'proletarianized communication, transport, and travel' and global markets had emerged 'on a previously unimagined scale of magnitude'. A sociological meaning from London School of Economics sociologist Anthony Giddens (1990, p. 64) refers to 'the intensification of worldwide social relations which link distant localities in such a way that local happenings are shaped by events occurring many miles away, and vice versa'. These voices of the West resonated with conversations already under way in India, where the minority government of Prime Minister P.V. Narasimha Rao and Finance Minister Dr Manmohan Singh introduced 'Liberalization, Privatization and Globalization' (LPG) reforms in 1991 to qualify for a much-needed loan from the International Monetary Fund (Wikipedia, 2019a).

Both economic and sociological globalization began to change Indian careers. The proletarianization of communication was encouraged by the release of the first commercial web browser in 1994. Web browsing capability combined with email to enhance the coordination and movement of goods and the outsourcing of services. Further reforms were introduced in India from 1998 to 2004 (Wikipedia, 2019a). In the following year, Nandan Nilekani, CEO of the Indian software company Infosys, showed *New York Times* reporter Thomas L. Friedman his global video-conferencing room, and inspired Friedman to famously declare 'The world is flat' – in the sense that the business playing field had become levelled and that careers would never be the same (Friedman, 2005). India subsequently emerged as the second fastest growing economy in the world (Paul and Gupta, 2014) and perhaps the fastest growing economy in the world in 2018 based on GDP growth.

Culture

National culture reflects the underlying system of values, beliefs and preferences that are common among residents of a country (Hofstede, 2010) and is an important determinant of how people think and behave. Various studies have focused on cultural dimensions and variations as factors influencing career choice (Özbilgin, Küskü and Erdoğmuş, 2005; Shen et al., 2015). A popular although controversial view is that Asians are collectivistic, the self being identified with an in-group, while Westerners are individualistic, the self being distinct from the in-group (Noordin, Williams and Zimmer, 2002). Research suggests that parental expectations and adherence to traditional values have more influence on career development among the Indian population (Sandhu, 2014). National culture also provides a reference point for regional differences, where, for example, variability in cultural dimensions like individualism/collectivism may have an effect on people's career choices (Agarwala, 2008).

A prominent cultural theme in India is spiritualism. In that, *moksha* (salvation) depends on an individual's *karma* (action or duty) based on his or her *dharma* (placement in the social order). In Gandhi's (1932) interpretation, work over time can be a means of self-realization. This contrasts sharply with Western views on enlightenment or rationalism (Wikipedia, 2019b). National cultures can also influence whether entrepreneurship becomes a career choice (Stephan and Uhlaner, 2010; Wennberg, Pathak and Autio, 2013) and can serve as a catalyst for globalization and its career consequences (Paul and Shrivastava, 2015). In addition, the existence of diverse national cultures challenges the common Western attribution of career behaviour to the inner person, rather than to cultural influences (Gibbons, Hughes and Woodside, 2015).

Convergence/Divergence

The overall idea of convergence is that globalization will blur differences between nation states. Convergence also has an economic and a sociological meaning. The economic meaning refers to the tendencies of societies 'to develop similarities in structures, processes and performances' (Kerr, 1983, p. 3) if the conditions of investment – such as a stable political system, dependable workers and relatively low wage rates – are favourable. With the introduction of the LPG reforms in 1991, India's greater openness to foreign investment, the availability of educated English language speakers, and pockets of expertise in technology and medicine have spurred convergence with the West. The sociological meaning comes from looking more deeply into political and social consequences of convergence. For example, sociologists raise concerns about increasing risks for employees. They also point to political and sociological arrangements to understand why convergence may not occur. For example, it may be argued that many Western countries have converged through their promotion of free trade arrangements over the last 40 years, allowing for the spread of manufacturing and service work around the globe. The shoes you wear, the cars you buy and the help to run your computer may now be sourced from anywhere around the globe (Encyclopedia.com, 2019).

Divergence occurs when nation states remain distinct and tailor changes to their own needs (Mills et al., 2008). That is where a nation's political history, different institutions and distinct values and norms come into play. There are concerns, though, that the apparent growth of political extremism, recent US scepticism toward free trade, and greater international tensions over global warming will herald an overemphasis on divergence (Mills et al., 2008). We need to better understand global career dynamics to better understand how individual careers will both influence and be influenced by larger geopolitical forces.

Gender Roles

Gender role expectations and gender-based socializations across cultures are another set of key variables that can influence the career journey of individuals. The World Economic Forum's Gender Gap Economic Participation and Opportunity Subindex reports the following data from the three countries represented by the editors of this book: India ranked 139 in 2013, 136 in 2015 and 142 in 2018 (out of 149 countries). In contrast, the US went from 43 (2012) to 53 (2015) to 52 (2018) and Belgium went from 34 to 37 to 49 (World Bank, 2019). In terms of political representation, women stand at 11 per cent of the total parliamentary representatives in India, 24 per cent in the US and 40 per cent in Belgium (Inter-Parliamentary Union, 2019). The percentage of female CEOs in India is 3 per cent (Verma and Basu, 2019), around 5 per cent in US leading companies (Desilver, 2018) and 10 per cent in Belgium (Page Group, 2019). The key question, of course, is what is holding women back?

The limited levels of women's participation in executive and political life prevail despite the widespread attention the subject has received over the past 30 years (Frear et al., 2019). Much of the literature has focused on the challenges that women face in entering the workforce generally, and particularly the professions, as well as the difficulties they face in advancing to higher levels within organizations or professions (Triana et al., 2019; Wille et al., 2018). It also seems clear that women continue to face stereotyping, biases in performance appraisal, promotion and salary and difficult work–life trade-offs (Cohn, 2019). A further key question is whether a combination of cultural and family circumstances leads to women being 'pushed out' of successful careers (Kossek, Su and Wu, 2017).

TOPICS AND CHAPTERS

With the above four drivers in mind, we built on what we had learned and made a list of topics that we anticipated could respond to the energy we had witnessed, and signed on with Edward Elgar Publishing. As noted earlier, we came up with the idea of explicitly pairing Indian and Western chapters, reached out to scholars we knew about and searched widely for further scholars with expertise on the topics selected. As a result, we came up with the eight topics and 16 authorship teams represented in this book. Upon receiving draft chapters, we encouraged each authorship team to consider and cite the work of its paired chapter. The eight topics, with associated chapters and author teams, are indicated below.

Self and Career

This topic responds to the globalization and cultural drivers identified above. Anupama Kondayya and Srinivas Ekkirala in Chapter 2, 'An incongruence-driven approach to careers: insights from Ayurveda', present a distinctive approach to person–environment fit derived from an ancient Indian science. In a volatile, uncertain, complex and ambiguous world, individuals are advised to respond through adaptability, versatility and flexibility. Specifically, career variety is highlighted as a way to develop adaptability. In contrast, Marijke Verbruggen in Chapter 3 on 'Self-awareness in career development: meaning, importance and malleability', explores Western literature on self-awareness, asserting that people ought to emphasize who they already are, and what strengths they already have. However, her ideas about malleability as an important career competence connect back to the Ayurvedic approach.

Social Entrepreneurship as a Career Choice

This topic also responds to both the globalization and cultural drivers. Preeti Tiwari, Anil K. Bhat and Jyoti Tikoria provide Chapter 4, 'A field research of nascent social entrepreneurs' intention formation', and look at how social entrepreneurial education, social entrepreneurial self-efficacy, empathy and moral obligation in India influence social entrepreneurs' intention toward launching a business. Mary Conway Dato-on, Sharmistha Banerjee and Yasmin Mesbah in Chapter 5, 'Individual factors in predicting and encouraging social entrepreneurship as a career choice', offer a similar study from the US. Their work finds common ground with their Indian counterparts on social entrepreneurial education and social entrepreneurial self-efficacy. However, they find separate ground for empathy and moral obligation, which show no influence over their subjects' entrepreneurial intentions.

Stepping Off the Career Ladder

This topic responds to both cultural and gender roles drivers underlying decisions to either step off or stay on a career ladder. Sumita Datta and Snehal Shah in Chapter 6, 'Satisficing career choices of Indian women managers', observe the interaction with changing family structures and career choices of women. A common outcome is that women 'satisfice' and adjust their careers downwards to adapt to family responsibilities. Angela Stephanie Mazzetti's chapter, Chapter 7, 'Stepping off the career ladder: exploring the impact of career shocks on women's career decisions in the UK', investigates career shocks that women experience. Positive shocks can turn negative, and vice versa, and negative shocks can create downward spirals of resource loss. However, the development of 'resource-enhancing environments' can benefit both women and organizations.

MBA Careers Across the Globe

This topic responds primarily to the drivers, globalization and convergence/ divergence. Vivek G. Nair and Leena Chatterjee contribute Chapter 8, 'Economic structural changes and subjective career success of MBAs in India'. They study two groups of MBA students largely educated either before or after the liberalization of the Indian economy in the early 1990s and show how the two groups differ in their perceptions of career success. Elizabeth Houldsworth, Chris Brewster and Richard McBain deliver Chapter 9, 'How an MBA contributes to the unfolding of careers: a comparative analysis'. They look at the outcomes for alumni of the same Western MBA programme offered in different parts of the world. Context clearly matters a great deal in the career development of these MBA alumni.

Breaking and Re-entry

Our next topic responds directly to the gender roles driver, and also explores how different cultures reinforce those roles. Pavni Kaushiva and Chetan Joshi's chapter, Chapter 10, is titled 'Women's careers: starting a new chapter post career break'. They describe an experimental study that revealed a pattern of neosexism over whether to hire a woman returning to work after a career break. Anna Katharina Bader and John Blenkinsopp counter with Chapter 11, 'Can we release the brake on the career re-entry of mothers? A UK perspective'. Their chapter also focuses on women returning to work after a career break, who face challenges despite the robust legal framework that exists to support them. The combination of chapters points to the continuation of privileged career opportunities for men in both situations.

Academic Careers

Our next topic also focuses on the three drivers, globalization, culture and convergence/divergence. Ravishankar Venkata Kommu and Amit Dhiman bring us Chapter 12, 'The changing nature of academic careers in management education in India', and apply the legendary French sociologist Pierre Bourdieu's ideas to the 'career field' of Indian academics in management education. The authors describe how 'winds of change' stemming from globalization, neoliberalism and managerialism have become embedded within the Indian context. Yehuda Baruch in Chapter 13 discusses 'The changing nature of academic careers in management education in Western societies'. He takes an ecological view that sees individuals, institutions and social entities interdependently influencing scholars' emergent career patterns. He observes a dominant Anglo-Saxon model across the global management education arena, with forces of supply and demand shaping and being shaped by academic career paths.

Careers in IT

Our next topic highlights globalization and an industry that has thrived in India since the introduction of economic reforms. Gunjan Tomer and Pawan Budhwar's chapter, Chapter 14, is titled 'Flying high in the turbulent skies: managing careers in the Indian IT industry'. They describe a persistent tension between the IT worker's needs for challenging work and career development and the employer's need to manage resources and sustain competitive advantage. Sara Haviland and Jennifer Craft Morgan respond with Chapter 15, 'Risk allocation, employer dependence and the welfare state: an investigation of IT workers in the US and Canada'. They report how IT workers' perceptions of risk in the US and Canada are affected by the 'welfare regime' they live in, and where US workers look to maintain employer-dependent benefits more than their Canadian counterparts.

Opting Out or Staying In

Our final topic engages with all four drivers: globalization, culture, convergence/divergence and gender roles. Tania Saritova Rath and Mousumi Padhi bring us Chapter 16, 'Integrating care work for sustainable careers of women: an Indian perspective', and highlight a sharp decline in labour force participation of Indian women with children. A focus on highly educated women finds them opting out of the workforce, seeing unpaid caregiving work as more important than paid work. Margie J. Elley-Brown closes with Chapter 17, titled 'Leaning in: why some women are challenging the opt-out model', and focuses on New Zealand women's career decisions to stay in the workforce. The educators she studied made decisions in consultation with their partners, including decisions where the women took a 'front seat' in dual-career partnerships.

* * *

We have had our say. We hope you are interested to read on from here and engage with the topics and chapters as we have suggested. We hope this book leads you – wherever you may live, and whether scholar or practitioner – to a deeper awareness of global career dynamics. We further hope that such awareness will lead to more effective conversation and greatly improved practice. Let the work begin!

REFERENCES

Agarwala, T. (2008), 'Factors influencing career choice of management students in India', *Career Development International*, **13**(4), 362–76.

Cohn, S. (2019), *Race, Gender, and Discrimination at Work*, New York: Routledge.

Desilver, D. (2018), 'Women scarce at top of U.S. business – and in the jobs that lead there', *Pewresearch.org*, 20 April 2018, accessed 14 October 2019 at https://www.pewresearch.org/fact-tank/2018/04/30/women-scarce-at-top-of-u-s-business-and-in-the-jobs-that-lead-there/.

Encyclopedia.com (2019), 'Convergence theories', accessed 14 October 2019 at https://www.encyclopedia.com/social-sciences/encyclopedias-almanacs-transcripts-and-maps/convergence-theories

Frear, K.A., S.C. Paustian-Underdahl, E.D. Heggestad and L.S. Walker (2019), 'Gender and career success: a typology and analysis of dual paradigms', *Journal of Organizational Behavior*, **40**(4), 400–416.

Friedman, T.L. (2005), 'It's a flat world, after all', *The New York Times Magazine*, 3 April 2005, accessed 14 October 2019 at https://www.nytimes.com/2005/04/03/magazine/its-a-flat-world-after-all.html.

Gandhi, M.K. (1932), 'Working and thinking', in *Collected Works of Mahatma Gandhi*, Vol. 57, pp. 22–3, accessed 28 January 2020 at https://www.gandhiashramsevagram.org/gandhi-literature/collected-works-of-mahatma-gandhi-volume-1-to-98.php.

Gibbons, M., M.A. Hughes and M. Woodside (2015), 'Exploring the influence of culture on career through the career-in-culture interview', *Adultspan*, **14**(2), 77–89.

Giddens, A. (1990), *The Consequences of Modernity*, Cambridge, UK: Polity Press.

Hofstede, G. (2010), 'The GLOBE debate, back to relevance', *Journal of International Business Studies*, **41**(8), 1331–46.

Inter-Parliamentary Union (2019), 'Women in national parliaments', accessed 14 October 2019 at http://archive.ipu.org/wmn-e/classif.htm.

Kerr, C. (1983), *The Future of Industrial Societies: Convergence or Continuing Diversity?*, Cambridge, MA: Harvard University Press.

Khapova, S.N., J.P. Briscoe and M. Dickmann (2012), 'Careers in cross-cultural perspective', in J.P. Briscoe, D.T. Hall and W. Mayrhofer (eds), *Careers Around the World: Individual and Contextual Perspectives*, New York: Routledge, pp. 15–38.

Kossek, E.E., R. Su and L. Wu (2017), '"Opting out" or "pushed out"? Integrating perspectives on women's career equality for gender inclusion and interventions', *Journal of Management*, **43**(1), 228–54.

Leavitt, T. (1983), 'The globalization of markets', *Harvard Business Review*, May, accessed 14 October 2019 at https://hbr.org/1983/05/the-globalization-of-markets.

Mills, M., H.P. Blossfeld, S. Buchholz, D. Höfacker, F. Bernardi and H. Hofmeister (2008), 'Converging divergences? An international comparison of the impact of globalization on industrial relations and employment careers', *International Sociology*, **23**(4), 561–95.

Noordin, F., T. Williams and C. Zimmer (2002), 'Career commitment in collectivist and individualist cultures: a comparative study', *The International Journal of Human Resource Management*, **13**(1), 35–54.

Özbilgin, M., F. Küskü and N. Erdoğmuş (2005), 'Explaining influences on career "choice": the case of MBA students in comparative perspective', *The International Journal of Human Resource Management*, **16**(11), 2000–2028.

Page Group (2019), 'The position of women in companies and female leadership in Belgium' [media release], accessed 14 October 2019 at https://www.michaelpage .be/sites/michaelpage.be/files/Media%20release_gendergap_EN.pdf.

Paul, J. and P. Gupta (2014), 'Process and intensity of internationalization of IT firms – evidence from India', *International Business Review*, **23**(3), 594–603.

Paul, J. and A. Shrivastava (2015), 'Comparing entrepreneurial communities: theory and evidence from a cross-country study in Asia', *Journal of Enterprising Communities: People and Places in the Global Economy*, **9**(3), 206–20.

Sandhu, G. (2014), 'The influence of family and cultural values on the career develop- ment of Asian Americans', Doctor of Philosophy (Counselling Psychology) disser- tation, August 2014, accessed 14 October 2019 at https://digital.library.unt.edu/ark:/ 67531/metadc799461/.

Shen, Y., B. Demel, J. Unite, J.P. Briscoe, D.T. Hall and K. Chudzikowski (2015), 'Career success across 11 countries: implications for international human resource management', *The International Journal of Human Resource Management*, **26**(13), 1753–78.

Stephan, U. and L. Uhlaner (2010), 'Performance based vs. social supportive culture: a cross national study of descriptive norms and entrepreneurship', *Journal of International Business Studies*, **41**, 1347–64.

Tlaiss, H.A. (2014), 'Between the traditional and the contemporary: careers of women managers from a developing Middle Eastern country perspective', *The International Journal of Human Resource Management*, **25**(20), 2858–80.

Triana, M.D.C., M. Jayasinghe, J.R. Pieper, D.M. Delgado and M. Li (2019), 'Perceived workplace gender discrimination and employee consequences: a meta-analysis and complementary studies considering country context', *Journal of Management*, **45**(6), 2419–47.

Tsai, C.-J., C. Carr, K. Qiao and S. Supprakit (2019), 'Modes of cross-cultural lead- ership adjustment: adapting leadership to meet local conditions and/or changing followers to match personal requirements?', *The International Journal of Human Resource Management*, **30**(9), 1477–504.

Verma, P. and S.D. Basu (2019), 'At only 3%, corporate India is still struggling to bring women to the top', *Economic Times*, 27 March 2019, accessed 14 October 2019 at https://economictimes.indiatimes.com/news/company/corporate-trends/at -only-3-corporate-india-is-still-struggling-to-bring-women-to-the-top/articleshow/ 68589499.cms.

Wennberg, K., S. Pathak and E. Autio (2013), 'How culture moulds the effects of self-efficacy and fear of failure on entrepreneurship', *Entrepreneurship & Regional Development*, **25**(9–10), 756–80.

Wikipedia (2019a), 'Economic liberalisation in India', accessed 14 October 2019 at https://wikipedia.org/wiki/Economic_liberalisation_in_India.

Wikipedia (2019b), 'Rationalism', accessed 14 October 2019 at https://en.m.wikipedia .org/wiki/Rationalism.

Wille, B., B.M. Wiernik, J. Vergauwe, A. Vrijdags and N. Trbovic (2018), 'Personality characteristics of male and female executives: distinct pathways to success?', *Journal of Vocational Behavior*, **106**, 220–35.

World Bank (2019), 'Global Gender Gap Economic Participation and Opportunity Subindex', accessed 14 October 2019 at https://tcdata360.worldbank.org/indicators/.

PART I

Self and career

We begin with a pair of chapters that reflect on how the self may influence an individual's career decision-making. They are both grounded in different cultural paradigms, revealing an interesting contrast in thinking.

Anupama Kondayya and Srinivas Ekkirala's chapter is titled 'An incongruence-driven approach to careers: insights from Ayurveda', where Ayurveda literally means 'The Science of Life'. Ayurveda thinking was developed in the Indian subcontinent 3000 years ago and is based on the idea that balance between mind and body is crucial for health and well-being. In recounting their approach, the authors take you to familiar ground if you are an Indian reader, and to what may be entirely fresh ground if you are a Western reader. Applying Ayurvedic thinking to careers, the authors argue that people should seek out *in*congruence, rather than congruence, in their careers to promote further personal growth and well-being. Their thinking turns the conventional person–environment fit idea upside down.

In her chapter 'Self-awareness in career development: meaning, importance and malleability', Marijke Verbruggen, in turn, offers a series of Western perspectives on the self that draw on entirely different underpinnings, where self is mainly 'in the mind' and where the final aim is to match what is in the mind to one's career situation – that is, to seek congruence. She sketches the main conceptualizations of self-awareness in existing Western career theories. While these conceptualizations differ fundamentally, they all start from the idea that the self is in the mind and self-awareness is needed to achieve congruence.

Taken together, these two chapters provide a stimulating introduction to the design of this book – to look at and learn from contrasting Indian and Western perspectives on the career. We could not have imagined a better way to begin. The contrast between both chapters points to the implicit assumptions we take for granted in our thinking about careers, influencing both research and practice. Looking at well-known concepts and practices from different perspectives makes us reconsider their actual meaning. We invite you to open your mind, reflect, and enjoy the learning opportunity as you proceed.

2. An incongruence-driven approach to careers: insights from Ayurveda

Anupama Kondayya and Srinivas Ekkirala

No step in life, unless it may be the choice of a husband or wife, is more important than the choice of a vocation.
(Parsons, 1909, p. 3)

INTRODUCTION

Americans spend 8.5 hours a day on average at work, according to the American Time Use Survey 2018 (Bureau of Labor Statistics, 2018). We spend a third of our productive years at work, making the choice of a career of paramount importance indeed, as noted by Parsons (1909). This choice has been explained by the concept of person–environment fit for over a century. Pioneered by Frank Parsons (1909) and furthered by the likes of John Holland (1959), one of the central tenets of the approach is the concept of fit or congruence, where individuals are advised to seek environments that allow them to manifest their traits. However, with the rise of post-industrialist knowledge-based economies that are characterized by volatility, uncertainty, complexity and ambiguity (VUCA) (Shaffer and Zalewski, 2011), the notion of achieving fit or congruence may need to be reconsidered in a changing career environment.

Scholars have underlined the importance of adaptability, versatility and flexibility for career development within a VUCA world, with self-awarenesses the starting point for developing these characteristics (Kaplan and Kaiser, 2003; O'Connell, McNeely and Hall, 2008). In addition, career variety has been suggested as one of the ways to develop these characteristics (Karaevli and Hall, 2006). Efforts to enhance career management skills also aim at increasing awareness of one's strengths and interests (Wang and Wanberg, 2017). Thus, a VUCA world necessitates considering alternative approaches to career planning other than the dominant paradigms.

We look eastward for one such alternative approach, in line with Chen's (2014) call to synthesize perspectives from the East and the West and enlighten organizations, managers and scholars from different countries and cultural backgrounds to highlight the ambicultural promise of not only transcending but also synthesizing opposites. We explore the concept of personality with a psychophysiological basis as laid out in the ancient Indian system of Ayurveda through the concept of *doshas*. We then introduce an Ayurveda prescription to maintain balance for well-being and health by pursuing *incongruence* between individual preferences and environmental inputs. We then extend this concept to the arena of careers and suggest incongruence as a way of achieving well-being while answering the call of career management in a VUCA world. By suggesting the pursuit of balance instead of fit while choosing careers that are incongruent with individual preferences, we offer an alternative perspective to the dominant person–environment fit approach to career planning.

THE PERSON–ENVIRONMENT FIT APPROACH TO CAREERS

Career planning remains dominated by person–environment fit theories, which are based on the assumptions that people actively seek out environments that allow them to manifest their traits, and that the environments in turn shape the person. John Holland is a prominent scholar who has shaped this stream with his theory of vocational choice (Holland, 1959).

The idea of person–environment fit propounds that a higher fit between the environment and the person leads to better outcomes (Su, Murdock and Rounds, 2015). Holland's RIASEC theory posits that individuals as well as work environments can be categorized into six types – realistic (doers), investigative (thinkers), artistic (creators), social (helpers), enterprising (persuaders) and conventional (organizers) – that 'people search for environments that will let them exercise their skills and abilities, express their attitudes and values, and take on agreeable problems and roles' (Holland, 1992, p. 4) and that the interaction between the individual and the environment is the primary driver of behaviours (Holland, 1992).

The key concept in this theory is congruence, which forms the basis of the governing principle of the person–environment fit approach to career counselling with an emphasis on the need to achieve congruence while choosing careers to achieve optimal job satisfaction and performance. Congruence is when individuals are in an environment that is conducive to their personality, preferences and abilities. Conversely, and important for our discussion, 'Incongruence occurs when a type lives in an environment that provides opportunities and rewards foreign to the person's preference and abilities' (Holland, 1992, p. 5). To maintain clarity in the discussion, we will use this definition of incongruence that emphasizes the aspect of foreignness to the individual's preferences and abilities.

We live in a post-industrial knowledge era characterized by a progressive loss of control over the environment and an age of strategic surprises, leading to the transformation of stable environments into a world that is characterized as VUCA – volatile, uncertain, complex and ambiguous – with rapid change being its hallmark (Shaffer and Zalewski, 2011). Consequently, workers and employees need to deal with this changing landscape and protect themselves from uncertainty by adopting a similar stance. Where once careers were characterized by long engagement with one organization or industry, today individuals build careers across multiple organizations (Callanan, Perri and Tomkowicz, 2017). A VUCA environment demands that individuals demonstrate continuous learning attitudes and embrace change as the opportunity to reinvent themselves (Shaffer and Zalewski, 2011). While notions of fit or congruence encourage the development of expertise, they can lead to an individual settling into comfort zones. These comfort zones inhibit the continuous learning needed to deal with the changing environment (Amundson, Mills and Smith, 2014) and may only ensure short-term success. Comfort zones are also detrimental in as much as the increased consolidation of organizations around the world reduces opportunities for vertical growth and necessitates lateral growth (Amundson et al., 2014). Further, comfort zones may inhibit the development of 'paradox savviness', which Waldman and Bowen (2016) have mentioned as a requirement for a leader in an increasingly complex and uncertain environment. Thus, a changing VUCA world necessitates alternative approaches to career planning compared to notions of person–environment fit.

We look eastward for one such alternative approach and explore the Ayurvedic argument for pursuing incongruence in life before synthesizing an incongruence-based approach to career planning.

AYURVEDA AND THE CONCEPT OF PERSONALITY

Ayurveda is an ancient Indian life science. The word derives from two Sanskrit words: *ayu* – meaning age or life, and *veda* – meaning science (Mishra, Singh and Dagenais, 2001). Thus, Ayurveda is the science of life or longevity. This longevity, or health and well-being, is achieved through the principle of balance in the body. Balance helps to prevent disease and restore health; imbalance leads to disease in the body.

The body is said to be composed of five fundamental physical elements of matter that also compose the universe – earth, fire, water, air and space (Chopra and Doiphode, 2002; Rhoda, 2014). These elements combine to form three primary humours or *doshas* in the body – *Vata* (air + space), *Pitta* (fire + water) and *Kapha* (earth + water) (Lad, 2002; Shilpa and Venkatesha Murthy, 2011b) – which are manifestations of an individual's physical, mental and emotional characteristics. *Vata*, composed of air and space, manifests as the energy of movement in the body and is responsible for the movement of blood through the arteries, food through the intestines, thoughts through the mind and so on. *Pitta*, composed of fire and water, manifests as the energy of digestion and transformation in the body, and the processing of thoughts in the mind. *Kapha*, composed of earth and water, manifests properties of water as lubrication and accumulation and governs accumulation of thoughts in the mind, lubricates the joints, promotes cohesion in the body, and so on (Chopra and Doiphode, 2002). Since each *dosha* is composed of physical elements, physical qualities of matter manifest in each *dosha* accordingly. Material qualities associated with *Vata* are dryness, lightness, cold, roughness, subtlety, mobility and clarity. Material qualities associated with *Pitta* are heat, sharpness, lightness, liquidity, mobility and oiliness. Material qualities associated with *Kapha* are heaviness, slowness, dullness, coldness, oiliness, liquidity, smoothness, sliminess, density, softness, static nature, stickiness, cloudiness, hardness and so on (Chopra and Doiphode, 2002; Lad, 2002).

Every individual is born with a certain proportion of *Vata*, *Pitta* and *Kapha* in their body, where one *dosha* may be usually dominant at birth and the other two less dominant (Lad, 2002; Rhoda, 2014). This combination or constitution of *Vata*, *Pitta* and *Kapha* in a certain proportion is unique to an individual and does not change during one's lifetime, nor does it deteriorate (Lad, 2002; Mukherjee, 2007; Waghulade, 2013). The differences in the nature of *Vata*, *Pitta* and *Kapha* manifest in the characteristics of the individual; the individual demonstrates properties and preferences as per the nature of their dominant *dosha* and the material qualities of the *dosha* (Rhoda, 2014). For example, at the physical level, a *Vata*-dominant individual has a small or lean body frame and does not gain weight easily (weight moves and does not accumulate); a *Pitta*-dominant individual has a medium body frame and can both gain and lose weight easily (the metabolism principle allows for this to happen); and a *Kapha*-dominant individual has a large body frame and gains weight easily but does not lose it easily (accumulation happens easily but not movement or transformation). In terms of preferences, for example, a *Vata*-dominant individual prefers physical activity such as outdoor sports; a *Pitta*-dominant individual prefers moderate activity; and a *Kapha*-dominant individual does not like physical activity. A *Vata*-dominant individual absorbs information quickly but also forgets quickly; a *Pitta*-dominant individual has moderate absorption and retention; and a *Kapha*-dominant individual takes time to absorb information but retains it well for the long term. In terms of work, for example, a *Vata*-dominant individual prefers jobs that involve less or no routine; a *Pitta*-dominant individual prefers jobs with moderate routine but also some flexibility; and a *Kapha*-dominant individual prefers jobs that are routine in nature and highly structured. *Vata*-dominant individuals are capable of coming up with creative ideas (driven by the movement principle);

Pitta-dominant individuals are capable of analysis and critique (driven by digestion and transformation of thoughts); and *Kapha*-dominant individuals are capable of maintaining the continuity of execution (driven by the cohesion principle).

Thus, the combination of *Vata*, *Pitta* and *Kapha* at birth can be approximated to the individual's constitution and personality since it governs their physical and psychological characteristics and responses (Shilpa and Venkatesha Murthy, 2011b). The interaction and dominance of *Vata*, *Pitta* and *Kapha* in the human body may determine an individual's physiology, cognitive capabilities, as well as psychological dispositions and preferences. A summary of the physical and psychological characteristics related to the *Vata*, *Pitta* and *Kapha* are summarized in Table 2.1.

It is important to note that the descriptions include physiological as well as psychological characteristics (Jayasundar, 2010; Travis and Wallace, 2015), supporting the link between psychological and physiological characteristics as manifested through the *doshas*. Rizzo-Sierra (2011) has supported this view by drawing comparisons between the three extreme body types in Ayurveda with Western constitutional psychology. Shilpa and Murthy (2011a) have pointed out studies that establish this link between physiology and psychology, while Travis and Wallace (2015) have devised a neural model of individual differences based on their mapping of the three *doshas* to brain types.

THE AYURVEDIC ARGUMENT FOR INCONGRUENCE

The principal approach towards maintaining health and well-being in Ayurveda is to maintain balance and harmony among the *doshas*, *Vata*, *Pitta* and *Kapha* (Chopra and Doiphode, 2002). Balance in *Vata*, *Pitta* and *Kapha* (in the proportion constituted at birth) leads to harmony in the psychology and physiology of the individual and drives the individual's response to their environment, but imbalance leads to corruption of the bodily functions at both levels (Lad, 2002). Disease is said to result from the *doshas* being disturbed and out of balance (Jayasundar, 2010; Mishra et al., 2001) and the curative approach of Ayurveda is thus to restore balance between the *doshas* through medical intervention (Jayasundar, 2010; Joshi, 2004). The preventive approach is also aimed at maintaining the balance of the *doshas* (Dey and Pahwa, 2014; Joshi, 2004).

Doshas can become out of balance and disturb well-being through the process of accumulation, which is the first step of disease formation in Ayurveda. As Lad (2002, p. 32) states:

> In Ayurveda there is a law which states that like increases like. When similar qualities come together, their quantitative expression increases. For example, the

Table 2.1   *Physical and psychological characteristics of the three doshas*

	Vata	*Pitta*	*Kapha*
Principle	Movement	Metabolism	Lubrication and accumulation
Body frame	Thin	Medium	Broad
Muscles	Less developed	Moderately developed	Well developed
Skin	Dry, rough	Oily, smooth, thin, acne-prone	Thick, smooth, clear
Hair	Dry, thin breaks easily	Oily, smooth, early greying	Thick, smooth, strong
Weight	Gains weight with difficulty	Gains and loses weight easily	Gains weight easily, loses weight with difficulty
Movements	Quick, erratic	Moderate-paced	Slow
Communication	Talkative but incoherent	Sharp, focused, purposeful	Slow, good communication skills
Memory	Quick to grasp and forget	Moderate to grasp and retain	Slow to grasp but good retention
General characteristics	Easily excited, quick to act without much thinking, alert, wakeful, good imagination, enjoys daydreaming, does not like sitting idle, seeks constant action, flexible, highly creative, changeable, unsteady, impulsive, energetic, enthusiastic	Highly disciplined, excellent and passionate leader, steadfast, excellent learner, good concentration, capability for analytical thinking, judgmental, critical, perfectionist, direct, irritable, short-tempered, intelligent, courageous, brave	Deep stable faith, slow to act and react, loving, compassionate, can be greedy, attached, possessive, given to laziness, calm, usually conservative, self-controlled, forbearing, unselfish, strong, virtuous, obedient, righteous, foresighted

Source: Dey and Pahwa (2014); Lad (2002); Mukherjee (2007); Travis and Wallace (2015); Waghulade (2013).

summer season has attributes similar to those of pitta – hot, liquid, light, mobile, and penetrating. Therefore, in the summer pitta in the body will be increased.

The qualities referred to here are the material qualities of entities. Anything that can be experienced through the five senses and belongs to the material world has material qualities. Thus, smells, tastes, temperatures, visuals and sounds generate material qualities that the body encounters through food, environment and lifestyle. By the additive principle, when two entities possessing similar material qualities come together, their material qualities add up and increase. Thus, when an individual encounters food or environments, they increase *doshas* in the body as per their material qualities. Thus, spicy food, which has properties of heat, will increase *Pitta* in the body. Similarly, getting angry generates chemicals in the body that have properties of heat and can increase *Pitta*. An air-conditioned cold environment may increase *Kapha* as well as *Vata* in the body. An environment promoting movement will increase *Vata* in the body, and so on. We must note that because of the close link between physiology and psychology through the *doshas*, the physical environment of an individual such as the work environment as well as the mental demands of the work and work environment can affect the *doshas* in the body.

When minor *doshas* accumulate, they can manifest as acute conditions and be balanced by effects of the dominant *dosha*. For example, when a *Pitta*-dominant person has an increase of *Kapha* due to cold, the property of heat in *Pitta* can help counter it. By extension, exposing *Pitta*-dominant individuals to *Kapha* environments may help keep *Pitta* in balance to an extent since a complementary *dosha* is increasing. However, if the accumulating *dosha* is the dominant *dosha* of the individual, it will lead to an increase in the dominant *dosha* from birth constitution without the minor *doshas* being able to counter it to the full extent. Thus, when a *Pitta*-dominant individual is exposed to foods or environments that have properties of heat (such as prolonged time spent in the sun), *Pitta* accumulates in the body and *Kapha* or *Vata* may not be able to counter it to maintain balance, resulting in manifestations of increased *Pitta* such as acidity, heat rashes, and so forth. Thus, disease can result from the process of accumulation by exposure to environments that are aligned with a person's dominant *dosha*.

As a result, the Ayurvedic prescription to maintain well-being is to maintain balance and avoid accumulation or aggravation of *doshas* by pursuing diets, lifestyles and environments that help balance the *doshas* (Dey and Pahwa, 2014). This involves actively seeking diets, lifestyles and environments that are dissimilar to the constitution of the individual (as expressed through their preferences) since having an environment congruent to a person's preferences will increase the related *dosha*, leading to accumulation and disturbance of well-being.

AN INCONGRUENCE-DRIVEN APPROACH TO CAREERS

Viewing the above discussion from the point of view of Holland's definitions of congruence and incongruence, an individual preferring and seeking environments aligned with their dominant *doshas* comprises the individual seeking congruence between their preference and environment, while the Ayurvedic prescription for seeking environments foreign to the individual's preference and dominant *dosha* comprises a prescription for *in*congruence. Thus, we can see that, as with Ayurveda, seeking congruence leads to imbalance between *doshas* and can be detrimental to the individual, while seeking incongruence leads to maintenance of balance of *doshas* and, hence, well-being. For example, a *Pitta* individual engaged in a job requiring constant analysis and debate may be at risk of accumulation of *Pitta* in the body and burn out as a result. Thus, an individual must choose environments incongruent with one's disposition in order to maintain health and well-being.

This is in line with prescriptions that allow individuals to deal with rapidly changing environments. Attaining fit with the environment in the face of rapid change and complexity is a challenge. Rather, in contexts distinguished by change and development, long-term career success is characterized by versatility, adaptability and flexibility. Versatility is the absence of imbalance, in terms of opposing pairs of qualities and skills and as 'a wide and flexible range of behaviours' (Kaplan and Kaiser, 2003, p. 23), and adaptability is 'dealing with uncertain and unpredictable work situations' (Karaevli and Hall, 2006, p. 361) and has been found to be a critical component for building protean careers driven by individual values (O'Connell et al., 2008).

Amundson (2014) calls for new forms of career development that will support such a flexible, adaptable and versatile approach to careers. Career variety has been said to be an important way to build adaptability especially for those with ambitions to ascend the ladder and handle managerial positions (Karaevli and Hall, 2006). Important aspects of adaptability for personal learning and change are awareness of one's self and one's developmental needs. Kaplan and Kaiser (2003) point out that overdoing what one is good at can lead to blind spots regarding what the environment truly demands, and the first step to correcting imbalance is to be aware of it. Thus, self-awareness combined with adaptability, versatility and flexibility are advocated as ways to approach career planning in a VUCA world.

The implication of the above for career planning is for an individual to pursue careers that offer physical and mental environments incongruent with their preference instead of static fits in order to maintain balance of *Vata*, *Pitta* and *Kapha*, in the process preparing oneself to deal with changing environments in a VUCA world. This can be done by starting with an assessment of the demands that a work environment is likely to place on an individual and creating an inventory of these demands and corresponding skills required to fulfil them. Counter to predominant approaches, as the next step we suggest a mapping of careers that are incongruent with the individual's personality, in order to maintain balance for overall health and well-being, as well as for being better prepared for the challenges of navigating careers in a VUCA world. This includes an assessment of incongruent jobs that allow the individual to reskill themselves fast and achieve relevance for the current demands. This model of career planning may ensure readiness for a VUCA world as well as personal well-being that may lead to longevity of the individual, and hence, of their careers.

CONCLUSION

In a VUCA world, adaptability, versatility and flexibility are paramount for individuals to craft careers. Continuous learning attitudes are necessary to avoid the trap of comfort zones, which can inhibit long-term growth in constantly changing career environments.

As the field of business management looks at expanding horizons and incorporating Eastern perspectives into management literature, we have the opportunity to explore the rich and ancient knowledge traditions of the East in order to look at things afresh. The ancient Indian science of Ayurveda propounds how individuals can attain well-being by aligning their diet, lifestyle and environment to maintain balance in their mind–body complex. The Ayurvedic prescription of seeking a diet, lifestyle and environment that counterbalances one's *doshas* implies a pursuit of incongruence to maintain balance for well-being and health.

Combining this prescription with the demands of a VUCA environment, we make the case for an incongruence-based approach to careers that can meet environmental demands while allowing the individual to take control of their careers and overall well-being, and offer a perspective in contrast to the dominant person–environment fit approach to career planning. We suggest a pursuit of balance as opposed to fit while planning careers, such that individuals can fulfil demands of a changing environment, keep themselves relevant, while also lengthening their lives and careers.

REFERENCES

Amundson, N.E., L.M. Mills and B.A. Smith (2014), 'Incorporating chaos and paradox into career development', *Australian Journal of Career Development*, **23**(1), 13–21.

Bureau of Labor Statistics (2019), 'American Time Use Survey – 2018 results', June 2019 [news release], accessed 14 January 2020 at https://www.bls.gov/news.release/pdf/atus.pdf.

Callanan, G.A., D.F. Perri and S.M. Tomkowicz (2017), 'Career management in uncertain times: challenges and opportunities', *The Career Development Quarterly*, **65**(4), 353–65.

Chen, M.-J. (2014), '2013 presidential address. Becoming ambicultural: a personal quest, and aspiration for organizations', *Academy of Management Review*, **39**(2), 119–37.

Chopra, A. and V.V. Doiphode (2002), 'Ayurvedic medicine: core concept, therapeutic principles, and current relevance', *The Medical Clinics of North America*, **86**(1), 75–89.

Dey, S. and P. Pahwa (2014), 'Prakriti and its associations with metabolism, chronic diseases, and genotypes: possibilities of newborn screening and a lifetime of personalized prevention', *Journal of Ayurveda and Integrative Medicine*, **5**(1), 15–24.

Holland, J.L. (1959), 'A theory of vocational choice', *Journal of Counseling Psychology*, **6**(1), 35–45.

Holland, J.L. (1992), *Making Vocational Choices: A Theory of Vocational Personalities and Work Environments* (2nd edition), Odessa, FL: Psychological Assessment Resources.

Jayasundar, R. (2010), 'Ayurveda: a distinctive approach to health and disease', *Current Science*, **98**(7), 908–14.

Joshi, R.R. (2004), 'A biostatistical approach to Ayurveda: quantifying the tridosha', *The Journal of Alternative and Complementary Medicine*, **10**(5), 879–89.

Kaplan, R.E. and R.B. Kaiser (2003), 'Developing versatile leadership', *MIT Sloan Management Review*, Summer, 19–26.

Karaevli, A. and D.T. Hall (2006), 'How career variety promotes the adaptability of managers: a theoretical model', *Journal of Vocational Behavior*, **69**(3), 359–73.

Lad, V. (2002), *Textbook of Ayurveda*, Albuquerque, NM: Ayurvedic Press.

Mishra, L., B.B. Singh and S. Dagenais (2001), 'Ayurveda: a historical perspective and principles of the traditional healthcare system in India', *Alternative Therapies in Health and Medicine*, **7**(2), 36–42.

Mukherjee, R. (2007), 'Concept of personality type in West and in Ayurveda', *IJTK*, **6**(3), 432–8.

O'Connell, D.J., E. McNeely and D.T. Hall (2008), 'Unpacking personal adaptability at work', *Journal of Leadership & Organizational Studies*, **14**(3), 248–59.

Parsons, F. (1909), *Choosing a Vocation*, Boston, MA: Houghton Mifflin Co.

Rhoda, D. (2014), 'Ayurvedic psychology: ancient wisdom meets modern science', *International Journal of Transpersonal Studies*, **33**(1), 158–71.

Rizzo-Sierra, C.V. (2011), 'Ayurvedic genomics, constitutional psychology, and endocrinology: the missing connection', *Journal of Alternative and Complementary Medicine*, **17**(5), 465–8.

Shaffer, L.S. and J.M. Zalewski (2011), 'Career advising in a VUCA environment', *NACADA Journal*, **31**(1), 64–74.

Shilpa, S. and C.G. Venkatesha Murthy (2011a), 'Development and standardization of Mysore Tridosha scale', *Ayu*, **32**(3), 308–14.

Shilpa, S. and C.G. Venkatesha Murthy (2011b), 'Understanding personality from Ayurvedic perspective for psychological assessment: a case', *Ayu*, **32**(1), 12–19.

Su, R., C. Murdock and J. Rounds (2015), 'Person–environment fit', in P.J. Hartung, M.L. Savickas and W.B. Walsh (eds), *APA Handbook of Career Intervention, Volume 1: Foundations*, Washington, DC: APA, pp. 81–98.

Travis, F. and R. Wallace (2015), 'Dosha brain-types: a neural model of individual differences', *Journal of Ayurveda and Integrative Medicine*, **6**(4), 280–85.

Waghulade, H. (2013), 'A review on role of Prakruti in vocational guidance', *International Journal of Advanced Ayurveda, Yoga, Unani, Siddha and Homeopathy*, **2**(1), 46–53.

Waldman, D.A. and D.E. Bowen (2016), 'Learning to be a paradox-savvy leader', *Academy of Management Perspectives*, **30**(3), 316–27.

Wang, M. and C.R. Wanberg (2017), '100 years of applied psychology research on individual careers: from career management to retirement', *Journal of Applied Psychology*, **102**(3), 546–63.

3. Self-awareness in career development: meaning, importance and malleability

Marijke Verbruggen

INTRODUCTION

This chapter explores the (mainly Western) literature on the role of self-awareness in career development. The career literature has always considered self-awareness – and related constructs, such as self-knowledge, self-reflection and self-exploration – as a key career competence, important for people to make successful career decisions and to manage their career (Tang, 2018). Self-awareness refers to a clear view on who one is (DeFillippi and Arthur, 1994), on one's strength and weaknesses (Cabral and Salomone, 1990) and on one's interests, values and needs (Cabral and Salomone, 1990; DeFillippi and Arthur, 1994; Hall, 1996). Self-awareness is believed to be important for individuals to find career direction, to be motivated to invest in one's career and to sense one's learning needs (Hall, 2004).

Although there is general agreement on the importance of self-awareness for people's career development, different theories seem to attach different meanings to the construct, largely dependent on the philosophical paradigm that underlies the theory. In the first part of this chapter, I explore the main conceptualizations of self-awareness in existing career theories. I continue by examining the empirical literature on the role and importance of self-awareness for people's career development. Finally, I reflect on the malleability of this important career competence.

SELF-AWARENESS IN CAREER THEORIES

Self-awareness is a central feature in almost all career theories. Career theories, as attempts to unravel career development dynamics, point to different aspects that (might) intervene in the career development process and are therefore highly valuable guides for career counsellors (Leung, 2008; Tang, 2018). Although most career theories agree that self-awareness is a crucial career competence (Tang, 2018) – which is necessary to make satisfying and sustainable career decisions – they differ somewhat in how they conceptualize and understand this competence. We can roughly distinguish three conceptualizations across the different career theories, linked with the different philosophical perspectives underlying them.

Trait-and-Factor Theories and Their Logical Positivist View on Self-awareness

A first main conceptualization of self-awareness can be found in the traditional trait-and-factor theories, which were developed from the early twentieth century onwards and are primarily concerned with the choice of vocation (for example, Parsons, 1909; Williamson, 1939). According to these theories, a career choice can best be made by matching the traits of the individual with the factors – or characteristics – of the work environment (Brown, 2002). An individual's traits include their aptitudes, personality traits, interests and values (Brown, 2002). Factors initially referred to characteristics of specific jobs or occupations (Brown, 2002), but over time, theories widened their focus and stressed the importance of looking at the entire working environment, including the co-workers, the supervisor and the company's values and policies (for example, Holland's 1973 RIASEC theory[1]). The main claim of trait-and-factor theories is that the better the achieved fit between an individual's traits and the characteristics of the work environment, the more successful (for example, satisfying, sustainable) the career choice will be (Brown, 2002). Trait-and-factor theories further assume that both individual traits and characteristics of the work environment can be measured validly and reliably (Brown, 2002). Once traits are assessed and knowledge of the world is gained, these should be matched through cognitive processes or – as Parsons (1909), the pioneer of the trait-and-factor theories, stated – 'through true reasoning'. Career counselling in this spirit hence involves helping clients gather and analyse information about the self and the world of work (Rounds and Tracey, 1990; Super, 1957).

Trait-and-factor theories thus conceptualize self-awareness as people's knowledge about their general, internal traits, such as their aptitudes and personality traits. Less emphasis is put on an understanding of people's temporary needs – for instance, needs related to their current family situation or life stage. In addition, people's traits are believed to be measurable in a valid and reliable way, which shows a belief in an objective 'true' self that people should try to understand. Also, trait-and-factor theories treat self-awareness as an emotion-free competence: these theories assume that individuals accept the characteristics of themselves and that they base their career decisions upon these 'given facts'.

This conceptualization of self-awareness as an emotion-free understanding of one's true internal traits is largely related to the philosophical paradigm that underlies trait-and-factor career theories – that is, logical positivism. According to logical positivism, the only meaningful forms of knowledge are statements that can be verified logically – which reveals logical positivism's faith in humans as rational beings – or empirically (Bem and Looren de Jong, 1997; O'Hear, 1989). Empirical verification should be done by dividing a complex phenomenon into its elementary components and then studying these components separately (reductionism; Bem and Looren de Jong, 1997). As such, for people to understand themselves, it suffices that they understand – that is, measure – their general traits. And as long as valid and reliable measurements are used, people – as rational beings – will accept these measured characteristics as true and use these as the basis for their career decisions.

Systemic Perspective to Self-awareness

A second philosophical stance that, from the mid-1980s onwards, influenced the career domain is the systemic perspective (Chartrand, Strong and Weitzman, 1995). The systemic perspective, like logical positivism, asserts that neutral knowledge can be derived from neutral observations. The main difference between both perspectives lies in the conceptualization of the person–environment relationship: rather than seeing the person and the environment as independent (cf. reductionism), the systemic perspective conceives both as interdependent, as mutually affecting each other and dynamically interacting over time (Walsh and Osipow, 1995). This implies that to understand oneself, it does not suffice to have knowledge of one's general internal traits, but it is also important to understand one's (fluctuating) needs in relation to the environment. This is, for instance, clear in Super's (1984) 'life span, life-space' approach to career development, which acknowledges that at each point in their career, people occupy various roles (for example, parent, husband/wife and worker) that interact with each other in a complex way and trigger time-varying and person-specific needs. Similar views can be found in other systemic career theories, such as the life-span developmental approach (Vondracek, Lerner and Schulenberg, 1986) and the systems theory framework (STF) of career development (Patton and McMahon, 2006). As such, from a systemic perspective, self-awareness implies more than understanding one's general traits; it is also important that people understand their personal and time-varying needs in relation to the roles they occupy and the environments they are embedded in.

Constructivist Career Theories and Their View on Self-awareness

A third philosophical paradigm that has been influential in the career field is constructivism. Constructivism asserts that the world cannot be known objectively since all observations are mediated (constructed) by the person who is observing and, thus, knowledge is not objective but constructed in a rhetorical and interactional process (Young and Collin, 2004). This starting point is completely opposite from the objectivist viewpoint (logical positivism and systemic perspective), which asserts that neutral observations are possible and lead to general (objective) knowledge. According to the constructivist paradigm, observations are channelled and limited by the foreknowledge, values, norms, abilities, and so on, of the observer and through social interactions with others (Chartrand et al., 1995). As such, self-awareness is a constructed understanding of oneself, influenced by past interpretations, norms and values, and formed through reflections and social interactions.

Savickas's (2002) career construction theory is probably the best-known example of constructivist career theory. Career construction theory states that individuals build their careers by imposing meaning on their career behaviour (Savickas, 2002). The process of meaning-making is an active process – that is, not simply a discovery of pre-existing facts. This active process can be facilitated by social interactions and conversations. The personal meaning people find in – or construct by building upon – their past memories, present experiences and future aspirations may then guide and regulate their future career behaviour. As such: 'Careers do not unfold; they are constructed' (Savickas, 2002, p. 154). Career counselling according to Savickas's career construction theory uses the client's career narrative as the main instrument. This narrative is the person's present story of his or her career up till now. This story reveals important life themes, accords meaning to past events and shows connections between elements. In that way, people's career narrative provides a valuable guide for their future career decisions. Self-awareness in this perspective refers to a (constructed) personal understanding of the life themes that bind past memories, present experiences and future aspirations.

RELEVANCE OF SELF-AWARENESS

Despite the differences in how self-awareness is conceptualized across different career theories (that is, emotion-free knowledge of one's true internal traits, an understanding of one's traits and situation-specific needs, or constructed personal understanding of the life themes that bind one's past, present and aspired future), there is considerable agreement in the career field about the importance of this competence for people's career development. In particular, being self-aware is expected to help people find career direction and judge whether or not a specific career option or opportunity is likely to be satisfying (Brown, 1995; Hall, 1996). In addition, self-awareness is believed to be particularly relevant in turbulent and complex times when there is a lot of information and plenty of options to consider (Bright and Pryor, 2005; Cabral and

Salomone, 1990; Hall, 1996). This is because high self-awareness is believed to make it easier for people to filter and process information in a consistent way (Morin, 2011). As such, self-awareness is believed to be an important adaptive competence (Morin, 2011).

Empirical research generally supports the importance of self-awareness for people's career development. First, research has found that increasing people's self-awareness facilitates career decision-making (Sauermann, 2005). Several studies, for instance, found that self- (and environmental) exploration is associated with more confidence in one's ability to make career decisions (Betz and Voyten, 1997; Brown et al., 1999; Creed, Patton and Prideaux, 2007). Relatedly, increased self- (and environmental) exploration has been shown to relate to increased career decision-making (Cheung and Jin, 2016; Park et al., 2017), thus, when people gain self-awareness through self-exploration, they seem to be better able to specify an educational or occupational choice. In addition, self-awareness may motivate people to work towards their career goals. In my own research, for instance, I have found that employees who enhanced their self-awareness through career counselling made more progress towards their career goals in the six months following the end of the career counselling (Verbruggen and Sels, 2009).

Research further seems to support the importance of self-awareness as an adaptive competence necessary to navigate and steer one's career. Verbruggen and Sels (2008), for instance, found that employees who increased their self-awareness through career counselling experienced an increase in career self-direction afterwards, which was in turn related to – among others – undertaking additional training and making a job transition. Relatedly, Guan and colleagues (2015) found a positive association between self- (and environmental) exploration and career adaptability – that is, the ability to approach one's career tasks with concern for the future, a sense of control over one's careers, curiosity to experiment with possible selves, and the confidence to engage in career planning (Savickas and Porfeli, 2011).

Furthermore, self-awareness has been associated with better career outcomes (Sauermann, 2005). For instance, people with more self-awareness have been found to perceive more career opportunities. Indeed, Praskova, Creed and Hood (2015) found that self- (and environmental) exploration was associated with higher perceived employability. Similarly, Forrier, Verbruggen and De Cuyper (2015) found that movement capital – which includes, among others, self-awareness – was positively related to both perceived internal and perceived external employability. Self-awareness has also been linked with other (career) benefits. In my own research, I, for instance, found that increased self-awareness was related to increased self-esteem, increased career satisfaction and increased life satisfaction among employees who followed career counselling (Verbruggen and Sels, 2009; Verbruggen, Dries and Van

Laer, 2017); however, the latter associations were only found when employees had expected to increase their self-awareness through career counselling (Verbruggen et al., 2017).

Despite these general benefits associated with self-awareness, research has also pointed to some potential dark sides of this competence. For instance, Praskova and colleagues (2015) found a positive association between self-exploration and career distress. So, people who engaged more in self-exploration – which probably resulted in increased self-awareness – experienced more distress about their career. Praskova and colleagues (2015) thought that this finding could perhaps be due to the fact that people who are exploring themselves may sometimes receive feedback that challenges the image they have of themselves (Morin, 2011). Such discrepancies may trigger self-doubt and lead to distress (Praskova et al., 2015; Zikic and Klehe, 2006). Relatedly, when self-awareness is combined with low levels of self-esteem, it may trigger self-rumination (Morin, 2011) – that is, a form of anxious rumination about oneself and one's self-worth. This has been associated with other negative consequences, such as depression and insomnia (Joireman, 2004; Leary, 2004; Mor and Winquist, 2002). Furthermore, Storme and Celik (2018) found that when self-exploration was related to low confidence in one's ability to solve original and complex problems, students experienced more rather than less career indecision. Overall, these studies show that for self-awareness to be a true career competence, it is important that people also feel positive about themselves and their abilities.

MALLEABILITY OF SELF-AWARENESS

Given the general importance of self-awareness for people's career development, an important question is whether people can enhance this career competence. Career practitioners seem to be convinced that this is possible. Indeed, McMahon, Arthur and Collins (2008) showed that almost all career development practitioners in their study reported that their clients experienced increased self-awareness after the career intervention. Also, research among career counselling clients seems to support the malleability of self-awareness. For instance, Verbruggen and Sels (2008) found that employees who underwent career counselling reported higher levels of self-awareness immediately after the counselling as well as six months later. Also, Cheung and Jin (2016) found that a group of students who followed a career exploration course reported a higher increase in self-exploration during one semester than a control group who did not follow this course.

However, increased self-awareness may not always be achieved or experienced after a career intervention. For instance, while the career practitioners in McMahon and colleagues' study (2008) reported increased self-awareness after the intervention, not all clients mentioned this outcome. This could perhaps be explained by the above-mentioned finding of Verbruggen and colleagues (2017), who showed that counsellees mainly report increased self-awareness as an outcome of career counselling when they *expected* to improve their self-awareness through the counselling. Another explanation may lie in the methods used during the career counselling or in the quality of the counsellor–counsellee relationship. Verbruggen and Sels (2009), for instance, found that counsellees reported a higher increase in self-awareness when the quality of the intake interview was better and when the career counsellor had stimulated them to consult important others (for example, partner or colleagues) for feedback about themselves. In addition, Elad-Strenger and Littman-Ovadia (2012) found that counsellees who were more positive about their counsellor–client working alliance reported higher levels of self- (and environmental) exploration.

Self-awareness may not only be enhanced purposefully in career interventions such as career counselling. Other environmental and situational features may also nurture or trigger self-reflection and, as such, enhance self-awareness. Research has, for instance, found that parental support (Guan et al., 2015), as well as support from peers and supervisors (Gamboa, Paixão and de Jesus, 2013), are positively related to self-exploration. These forms of support may provide a safe environment in which to accept feedback about oneself. In addition, specific situations may also lead to momentary increases in self-awareness. For instance, situations in which the first person singular is used often (Davis and Brock, 1975) as well as social environments in which a person's unique characteristics are emphasized (for example, being the only person with a disability in a workgroup) have been found to temporarily enhance self-focus and, consequently, self-reflection and self-awareness (Morin, 2011; Phemister and Crewe, 2004). However, the latter situations may also trigger an evaluation of oneself compared to others, which may entail the risk of self-doubt and distress, as described above.

Finally, there seem to be individual differences in (the malleability of) people's self-awareness and self-exploration. For instance, Verbruggen and Sels (2009) found in particular that open and agreeable people realized an increase in self-awareness through career counselling. Also, Fan and colleagues (2012) found a link between specific personality traits and self- (and environmental) exploration, but the exact link was found to depend on the cultural context. Finally, Creed and colleagues (2007) found that people who have more confidence in their career decision-making ability engaged more in self- (and environmental) exploration compared to people low on career decision-making self-efficacy.

CONCLUSION AND SUGGESTIONS FOR FUTURE RESEARCH

This chapter showed that even though the exact conceptualization of self-awareness differs somewhat across different career theories, all theories agree that self-awareness is highly important for people's career development. This is largely supported by empirical research, which has found self-awareness to relate to a range of (career) benefits. At the same time, however, several studies point to an important risk of self-awareness: when people have a hard time accepting their strengths and weaknesses, high self-awareness may lead to self-doubt, self-rumination and distress (Morin, 2011; Praskova et al., 2015). As such, it seems important for career practitioners who are trying to help people improve their self-awareness to also pay attention to people's emotions related to their personal characteristics and situation as these emotions may point to relevant career development challenges.

To further advance our understanding of self-awareness, the following directions for future research may be interesting. First, this chapter showed that the dominant conceptualizations of self-awareness are strongly linked with the underlying philosophical perspective. As such, it may be interesting to explore alternative (non-Western) philosophical traditions that have not yet been so influential in the career field and reflect on what these perspectives may imply for the meaning of self-awareness. For instance, the Ayurveda-based approach, as explained in Chapter 2 by Kondayya and Ekkirala, could be inspirational. In particular, this approach could help us to better understand the link between people's interests and strengths on the one hand and their physiology on the other, which may shed novel light on how to improve our self-awareness.

Second, research on the effects of self-awareness often integrates self-awareness (or self-exploration) into a broader construct, such as movement capital (for example, Forrier et al., 2015) or career exploration (for example, Guan et al., 2015; Praskova et al., 2015). As such, these studies do not always attribute the effects found to self-awareness. Future research may therefore study the effects of different competences separately. Third, while extant research on the malleability of self-awareness offers some important guidelines for practitioners, some important questions remain. For instance, what are the best intervention tools with which to increase people's self-awareness? And are there risks involved when offering self-awareness interventions too early – for example, at high school (e.g., foreclosure of certain career options; Luken, 2014)?

NOTE

1.   Holland's RIASEC theory is one of the best-known and most widely used theories of career choice in the Western world. This theory identifies six personality types: realistic, investigative, artistic, social, enterprising and conventional and argues that when people can find a work environment that fits their personality type they are more likely to feel satisfied and successful in their career.

REFERENCES

Bem, S. and H. Looren de Jong (1997), *Theoretical Issues in Psychology: An Introduction*, London: Sage.
Betz, N. and K. Voyten (1997), 'Efficacy and outcome expectations influence career exploration and decidedness', *Career Development Quarterly*, **46**, 179–89.
Bright, J. and R. Pryor (2005), 'The chaos theory of careers: a user's guide', *Career Development Quarterly*, **53**, 291–305.
Brown, C., E.E. Darden, M.L. Shelton and M.C. Dipoto (1999), 'Career exploration and self-efficacy of high school students: are there urban/suburban differences?', *Journal of Career Assessment*, **7**, 227–37.
Brown, D. (1995), 'A values-based approach to facilitating career transitions', *Career Development Quarterly*, **44**, 4–8.
Brown, D. (ed.) (2002), *Career Choice and Development* (4th edition), San Francisco, CA: Jossey-Bass.
Cabral, A. and P. Salomone (1990), 'Chance and careers: normative versus contextual development', *Career Development Quarterly*, **39**, 5–17.
Chartrand, J., S. Strong and L. Weitzman (1995), 'The interactional perspective in vocational psychology: paradigms, theories and research practices', in W. Walsh and S. Osipow (eds), *Handbook of Vocational Psychology: Theory, Research and Practice*, Mahwah, NJ: Lawrence Erlbaum Associates, pp. 35–65.
Cheung, R. and Q. Jin (2016), 'Impact of a career exploration course on career decision making, adaptability, and relational support in Hong Kong', *Journal of Career Assessment*, **24**, 481–96.
Creed, P.A., W. Patton and L. Prideaux (2007), 'Predicting change over time in career planning and career exploration for high school students', *Journal of Adolescence*, **30**, 377–92.
Davis, D. and T.C. Brock (1975), 'Use of first person pronouns as a function of increased objective self-awareness and prior feedback', *Journal of Experimental Social Psychology*, **11**, 381–8.
DeFillippi, R. and M. Arthur (1994), 'The boundaryless career: a competency-based perspective', *Journal of Vocational Behavior*, **15**, 307–24.
Elad-Strenger, J. and H. Littman-Ovadia (2012), 'The contribution of the counselor–client working alliance to career exploration', *Journal of Career Assessment*, **20**, 140–53.
Fan, W., F.M. Cheung, F.T. Leong and S.F. Cheung (2012), 'Personality traits, vocational interests, and career exploration: a cross-cultural comparison between American and Hong Kong students', *Journal of Career Assessment*, **20**, 105–19.
Forrier, A., M. Verbruggen and N. De Cuyper (2015), 'Integrating different notions of employability in a dynamic chain: the relationship between job transitions,

movement capital and perceived employability', *Journal of Vocational Behavior*, **89**, 56–64.

Gamboa, V., M.P. Paixão and S.N. de Jesus (2013), 'Internship quality predicts career exploration of high school students', *Journal of Vocational Behavior*, **83**, 78–87.

Guan, Y., F. Wang and H. Liu et al. (2015), 'Career-specific parental behaviors, career exploration and career adaptability: a three-wave investigation among Chinese undergraduates', *Journal of Vocational Behavior*, **86**, 95–103.

Hall, D.T. (1996), 'Protean careers of the 21st century', *Academy of Management Executive*, **10**, 8–16.

Hall, D.T. (2004), 'The protean career: a quarter-century journey', *Journal of Vocational Behavior*, **65**, 1–13.

Holland, J.L. (1973), *Making Vocational Choices: A Theory of Careers*, Englewood Cliffs, NJ: Prentice-Hall.

Joireman, J.A. (2004), 'Empathy and the self-absorption paradox II: self-rumination and self-reflection as mediators between shame, guilt, and empathy', *Self and Identity*, **3**, 225–38.

Leary, M.R. (2004), *The Curse of the Self: Self-awareness, Egoism, and the Quality of Human Life*, New York: Oxford University Press.

Leung, S.A. (2008), 'The big five career theories', in J.A. Athanasou and R. van Esbroeck (eds), *International Handbook of Career Guidance*, Dordrecht: Springer, pp. 115–32.

Luken, T. (2014), 'Are we on the right track with career learning?', *Journal of Counsellogy*, **2**, 299–314.

McMahon, M., N. Arthur and S. Collins (2008), 'Social justice and career development: views and experiences of Australian career development practitioners', *Australian Journal of Career Development*, **17**, 15–25.

Mor, N. and J. Winquist (2002), 'Self-focused attention and negative affect: a meta-analysis', *Psychological Bulletin*, **128**, 638–62.

Morin, A. (2011), 'Self-awareness part 1: definition, measures, effects, functions, and antecedents', *Social and Personality Psychology Compass*, **5**, 807–23.

O'Hear, A. (1989), *Introduction to the Philosophy of Science*, Oxford: Oxford University Press.

Park, K., S. Woo, K. Park, J. Kyea and E. Yang (2017), 'The mediation effects of career exploration on the relationship between trait anxiety and career indecision', *Journal of Career Development*, **44**, 440–52.

Parsons, F. (1909), *Choosing a Vocation*, Boston, MA: Houghton Mifflin Co.

Patton, W. and M. McMahon (2006), 'The systems theory framework of career development and counseling: connecting theory and practice', *International Journal for the Advancement of Counselling*, **28**, 153–66.

Phemister, A.A. and N.M. Crewe (2004), 'Objective self-awareness and stigma: implications for persons with visible disabilities', *Journal of Rehabilitation*, **70**, 33–8.

Praskova, A., P.A. Creed and M. Hood (2015), 'Career identity and the complex mediating relationships between career preparatory actions and career progress markers', *Journal of Vocational Behavior*, **87**, 145–53.

Rounds, J. and T. Tracey (1990), 'From trait-and-factor to person–environment fit counseling: theory and process', in W.B. Walsh and S.H. Osipow (eds), *Career Counseling: Contemporary Issues in Vocational Psychology*, Hillsdale, NJ: Lawrence Erlbaum Associates, pp. 1–44.

Sauermann, H. (2005), 'Vocational choice: a decision making perspective', *Journal of Vocational Behavior*, **66**, 273–303.

Savickas, M. (2002), 'Career construction: a developmental theory of vocational behavior', in D. Brown (ed.), *Career Choice and Development*, San Francisco, CA: Jossey-Bass, pp. 149–205.

Savickas, M.L. and E.J. Porfeli (2011), 'Revision of the career maturity inventory: the adaptability form', *Journal of Career Assessment*, **19**, 355–74.

Storme, M. and P. Celik (2018), 'Career exploration and career decision-making difficulties: the moderating role of creative self-efficacy', *Journal of Career Assessment*, **26**, 445–56.

Super, D. (1957), *The Psychology of Careers*, New York: Harper & Row Publishers.

Super, D. (1984), 'A life-span, life-space approach to career development', in D. Brown and L. Brooks (eds), *Career Choice and Development*, San Francisco, CA: Jossey-Bass, pp. 192–234.

Tang, M. (2018), *Career Development and Counseling: Theory and Practice in a Multicultural World*, Thousand Oaks, CA: Sage.

Verbruggen, M. and L. Sels (2008), 'Can career self-directedness be improved through counseling?', *Journal of Vocational Behavior*, **73**, 318–27.

Verbruggen, M. and L. Sels (2009), *Loopbaanbegeleiding in Vlaanderen: De instroom in en effecten van loopbaanbegeleiding onder de loep genomen* [Career Counselling in Flanders: An Examination of the Participants and the Effects], Leuven: Steunpunt Werk en Sociale Economie.

Verbruggen, M., N. Dries and K. van Laer (2017), 'Challenging the uniformity myth in career counseling outcome studies: examining the role of clients' initial career counseling goals', *Journal of Career Assessment*, **25**, 159–72.

Vondracek, F., R. Lerner and J. Schulenberg (1986), *Career Development: A Life-Span Developmental Approach*, Hillsdale, NJ: Lawrence Erlbaum Associates.

Walsh, B. and S. Osipow (1995), *Handbook of Vocational Psychology: Theory, Research and Practice*, Mahwah, NJ: Lawrence Erlbaum Associates.

Williamson, E.G. (1939), *How to Counsel Students: A Manual of Techniques for Clinical Counsellors*, New York: McGraw-Hill.

Young, R. and A. Collin (2004), 'Introduction: constructivism and social constructivism in the career field', *Journal of Vocational Behavior*, **64**, 373–88.

Zikic, J. and U.-C. Klehe (2006), 'Job loss as a blessing in disguise: the role of career exploration and career planning in predicting reemployment quality', *Journal of Vocational Behavior*, **69**, 391–409.

PART II

Social entrepreneurship as a career choice

Both chapters on this topic address the importance of social entrepreneurship for society. They try to figure out what drives the intention to develop a career as a social entrepreneur, in India and the US respectively.

Preeti Tiwari, Anil K. Bhat and Jyoti Tikoria's chapter is 'A field research of nascent social entrepreneurs' intention formation'. This Indian study reveals that social entrepreneurial education, social entrepreneurial self-efficacy, empathy and moral obligation all predict social entrepreneurial intentions. These relationships are, moreover, mediated by perceived desirability and perceived feasibility of social entrepreneurship.

At first glance, Mary Conway Dato-on, Sharmistha Banerjee and Yasmin Mesbah's chapter, titled 'Individual factors in predicting and encouraging social entrepreneurship as a career choice', seems very similar. In this US study, social entrepreneurial intention is positively influenced by educational background, entrepreneurial self-efficacy and collective self-efficacy. Surprisingly so, however, and in contrast to the findings of Tiwari and colleagues, neither empathy nor moral obligation influenced the respondents' social entrepreneurial intention.

Both chapters examine similar variables using similar scales. As a result, a first opportunity is to use the chapters to make a traditional cross-cultural comparison. Most striking here is that empathy and moral obligation are only significant in the Indian sample and not in the US sample. Both empathy and moral obligation are related to the purpose of social entrepreneurship. This raises questions for future research. Are empathy and moral obligations stronger drivers toward social entrepreneurship in contexts that are facing more urgent social problems? Or, are individuals more driven by empathy and moral obligation in collective cultures? The questions invite further investigation.

We further invite you, the reader, to reflect on and apply the two chapters' conclusions to your own life space, and ask, what do you want to do, and what does society want to do, with these findings? Does it make sense to draw a sharp line between straightforward entrepreneurship and social entrepreneur-ship? Or might you consider all entrepreneurship as social, in as much as it seeks to fill a gap in people's needs?

4. A field research of nascent social entrepreneurs' intention formation

Preeti Tiwari, Anil K. Bhat and Jyoti Tikoria

INTRODUCTION

Social entrepreneurship is critical to the development and well-being of an economy, contributing significantly to job creation and innovation. In addition to the creation of employment opportunities, it also leads to an increase in technical innovations required for new business creation. Social entrepreneurial activities speed up the structural changes in an economy by introducing new competition, thereby contributing to productivity. It is, thus, a catalyst for economic growth. Given the importance of social entrepreneurship for the overall economy, social entrepreneurship research is increasing and, in particular, social entrepreneurial intention is a rapidly evolving field of research. A growing number of studies use social entrepreneurial intention as a powerful theoretical framework (Liñán and Fayolle, 2015). The purpose of this study is to analyse the relationship between individual-level antecedents and social entrepreneurial intentions in an Indian context.

Similar to various other parts of the world, the term social entrepreneurship has gained increasing importance in India in recent years. India has started developing an environment that is supporting social entrepreneurs with incubators, mentoring and financial support (Ghani, Kerr and O'Connell, 2013). Social entrepreneurship culture in India is young but very aggressive at present. The Indian social entrepreneurial sector has experienced tremendous growth in the last couple of years (British Council, 2016).

Considering the lack of employment opportunities and poverty in India and the benefits of social entrepreneurship, the young population intends to create its own ventures. Yet, in spite of its necessity, the present-day situation of social entrepreneurship in India is highly discouraging. This invokes the obvious question: how can the level of social entrepreneurship in India be increased? As suggested by Krueger (2007), entrepreneurship in general can only develop if the entrepreneurs evolve in terms of both quality and quantity, which is possible only when there is an upsurge of entrepreneurial thinking.

Hence, we study the previously mentioned question in an Indian context and follow a theory-based approach to social entrepreneurship. We follow the approach of Biraglia and Kadile (2017) in seeking to identify antecedents helpful in predicting social entrepreneurial intention, in this case among a young Indian population. Specifically, we try to discover the factors that lead a person to go for new venture creation. We study this question among a sample of nascent social entrepreneurs enrolled in the universities in India.

Nascent entrepreneurs are a group of people whose intentions are some-what converted into behaviour. These entrepreneurs have already started working on their business/social business idea. Reynolds and White (1997) defined venture creation as four stages (conception, gestation, infancy and adolescence) with three transition processes. The very first transition process starts when one or more individuals begin to devote time and other resources for the inception of a new venture. If they carry this out on their own and if the new enterprise can be considered as a start-up, they are called nascent entrepreneurs (Wagner, 2006). According to Wagner (2006, citing the Global Entrepreneurship Monitor, pp. 2415–19), a nascent entrepreneur is defined as a person who is now trying to start a new business, who expects to be the owner or part-owner of the new firm, who has been active in trying to start the new firm in the past 12 months and whose start-up did not yet have a positive monthly cash flow that covers expenses and the owner-manager salaries for more than three months. Given the purpose of this research, we used this defi-nition as a base to select the sample.

Most of the literature available in the field of social entrepreneurial intention comes from Europe and other Western countries. Social set-up and environ-mental factors affecting the process of entrepreneurship are very different in India. Tiwari, Bhat and Tikoria (2017a, 2017b) argued that socio-cultural factors like education, religion, caste, family support and social background are important in the Indian environment for starting a business. Therefore, this chapter tries to bridge the gap by validating the social entrepreneurial intention model in the Indian context.

THEORY AND HYPOTHESES

Various studies emphasize the importance of intention as one of the crucial constructs in predicting planned behaviour (Krueger and Brazeal, 1994). Entrepreneurial intention is an indispensable tendency towards the formation of an enterprise and is also an emerging research area that attracts a substantial number of researchers. The prerequisites contributing to motivating people to act as a social entrepreneur are not yet fully explored (Ziegler, 2009). We build on Shapero and Sokol's (1982) theory of entrepreneurial event as the research framework measuring entrepreneurial educational background, entrepreneurial self-efficacy, empathy and moral obligation towards social entrepreneurial intention. We also include perceived desirability and perceived feasibility as mediators in the model (Fitzsimmons and Douglas, 2011).

Perceived desirability is defined as the degree to which one finds the viewpoint of starting a business to be striking. It reflects one's effect towards entrepreneurship. Perceived feasibility, in contrast, refers to the level or degree of personal capability to start an enterprise as experienced by the person. Various prominent researchers in the field of entrepreneurship proved that perceived desirability and perceived feasibility have a positive impact on entrepreneurial intentions (Engle et al., 2010; Iakovleva, Kolvereid and Stephan, 2011; Krueger, 2007; Segal, Borgia and Schoenfeld, 2005; Shepherd and Patzelt, 2011; Wilson, Kickul and Marlino, 2007) and social entrepreneurial intentions (Segal et al., 2005). Below, we develop arguments for the relationship between the antecedents and social entrepreneurial intentions and for the mediating role of perceived desirability and feasibility in this relationship.

Entrepreneurial Educational Background

Entrepreneurship education can be defined as 'the whole set of education and training activities – within the educational system or not – that try to develop in the participants the intention to perform entrepreneurial behaviours, or some of the elements that affect that intention, such as entrepreneurial knowledge, desirability of the entrepreneurial activity, or its feasibility' (Liñán, 2004, p. 11). Entrepreneurial education is often categorized into two broad categories, namely: entrepreneurial awareness education (tutors who do not really aim to convert students into entrepreneurs, but act as advisors to facilitate their future professional career selection) and education for start-ups (centred on the explicit realistic aspects related to the start-up phase). Scholars have empirically provided evidence that entrepreneurship education is an effective means of inspiring students' intentions towards an entrepreneurial career (Fayolle, Gailly and Lassas-Clerc, 2006; Lee, Chang and Lim, 2005; Matlay, 2008). In his longitudinal study conducted over a ten-year period, Matlay (2008) found that all the 64 graduates in his research sample who had undergone entrepreneurship education became entrepreneurs. In the field of social entrepreneurship, there are a handful of research studies that have tried to measure the effect of education on social entrepreneurial intentions. Studies show that an increase in education increases social entrepreneurial activity (Harding and Cowling, 2006; Penner et al., 2005). A study by Nabi et al. (2011) in Egyptian universities revealed that although governments provide a lot of initiatives to promote social entrepreneurship, changes had to be made in the education system to encourage students to think and behave more entrepreneurially, at the same time equipping them with the skills to start their own ventures on graduation.

Perceived desirability and perceived feasibility may mediate this relationship between entrepreneurial education and social entrepreneurial intention. Ernst's (2011) study on exposure to social entrepreneurial courses showed a positive relationship with perceived desirability and perceived feasibility. Although there are various types of entrepreneurship education programmes projected toward particular stages of development (Bae et al., 2014), an entrepreneurship education programme may prove helpful in developing a student's attitudes and intentions as well as the beginning of a new venture (Liñán, 2011). Entrepreneurship education is assumed to enhance an 'awareness of entrepreneurship as an alternative career path to employment' (Slavtchev, Laspita and Patzelt, 2012, p. 3, cited in Bae et al., 2014, p. 220).

Based on the above discussion we propose the following hypotheses:

H1: Perceived desirability of social entrepreneurship mediates the positive relationship between social entrepreneurial educational background and social entrepreneurial intention.

H2: Perceived feasibility of social entrepreneurship mediates the positive relationship between social entrepreneurial educational background and social entrepreneurial intention.

Entrepreneurial Self-efficacy

Bandura (1999) defined self-efficacy as a person's belief regarding his or her ability to accomplish a certain task. Entrepreneurial self-efficacy is the degree to which a person believes that he or she is able to successfully start a new business venture (Sánchez, 2010). Self-efficacy is considered one of the best predictors of career selection (Bandura, 1971) and it is often included in studies on entrepreneurial intentions (Krueger and Brazeal, 1994). In a meta-analysis conducted by Armitage and Conner (2001), self-efficacy emerged as one of the most influential factors in predicting entrepreneurial intentions. Self-efficacy has also repeatedly been identified as the significant antecedent variable in influencing feasibility perceptions (Guzmán-Alfonso and Guzmán-Cuevas, 2012).

Specifically, in a developing country like India, social enterprises face a lot of problems due to lack of resources and limited opportunities. In such a scenario, self-efficacy is considered as a motivational antecedent that has been shown to persuade an individual's choice of activities, goal levels, persistence and performance in a range of contexts. A high level of self-efficacy may allow an individual to perceive becoming a social entrepreneur as feasible and desirable and may thus lead to a high social entrepreneurial intention (Mair and Noboa, 2006).

The following hypotheses are formed on the basis of the above explanation.

H3: Perceived desirability of social entrepreneurship mediates the positive relationship between social entrepreneurial self-efficacy and social entrepreneurial intention.

H4: Perceived feasibility of social entrepreneurship mediates the positive relationship between social entrepreneurial self-efficacy and social entrepreneurial intention.

Empathy

Empathy is defined as a person's ability to access another person's state of mind in particular circumstances (McDonald and Messinger, 2011). Bandura (1999) divides empathy into two parts: emotional and cognitive. Emotional empathy deals with the emotional response that a person has towards others, whereas, in cognitive empathy, an empathetic person imaginatively acquires the role of the other and is able to estimate the feelings and actions of others.

In the literature on social entrepreneurship, empathy acquires an important place. Social entrepreneurship is all about understanding the difficulties faced by other people and converting that social problem as an opportunity for the betterment of the people (Prahalad, 2008). Mair and Noboa (2006) pointed out that empathy is a personality trait that differentiates a social entrepreneur from business entrepreneurs. An empathic connection is a strong force in deciding to help someone.

Studies by Harding and Cowling (2006) and Forster and Grichnik (2013) have identified empathy as an antecedent for social entrepreneurship. Yet, empirical results on the relationship between empathy and social entrepreneurial intentions are mixed, showing positive (Hockerts, 2015), negative (Ernst, 2011) or no relationship (Hockerts, 2015). Empathy as an antecedent to the social entrepreneurial intention thus requires further investigation. In this study, we use cognitive empathy – that is, capability of understanding others' emotional state of mind – as an antecedent (Hockerts, 2015), as a predictor of social entrepreneurial intention, and we assume a positive relationship. In line with the findings of Mair and Noboa (2006) we assume that perceived desirability and feasibility are mediating this relationship. Research in social entrepreneurship specifies that understanding of others' feelings motivates social entrepreneurs to form social enterprises (Prabhu, 1999). However, not every individual who has the capability to experience empathy is a social entrepreneur. Thus, going by the recommendation of Mair and Noboa (2006) we consider empathy as a necessary but not sufficient condition in the social entrepreneurship process.

We hypothesize that a certain level of empathy is required in order to develop perceived social venture desirability and desirability, which in turn will lead to intentions of creating a social venture:

H5: Perceived desirability of social entrepreneurship mediates the positive relationship between empathy and social entrepreneurial intention.

H6: Perceived feasibility of social entrepreneurship mediates the positive relationship between empathy and social entrepreneurial intention.

Moral Obligation

Moral obligation is defined as the tendency of helping others within religious limits (Bryant, 2009). According to Fishbein (1967), moral elements together with attitudes and subjective norms predict intentions. The moral obligation in relation to social entrepreneurs is related to the extent to which social entrepreneurs are fully committed to their idea and feel morally obliged to pursue it (Beugré, 2016). Mair and Noboa (2006) suggested that the key element that differentiates social entrepreneurs from business entrepreneurs is their moral obligation. Social entrepreneurs have a desire to do good for the betterment of the society and for the development of the nation as a whole (Thompson, 2008).

Moral obligation as an antecedent is very important for a social entrepreneur as it conveys the intention that addressing a particular social problem is an appropriate thing to do. Previous studies emphasize the importance of moral obligation in the development of social entrepreneurial intentions (Ernst, 2011; Hockerts, 2015; Tiwari et al., 2017a). Mair and Noboa (2006) argue that this path from moral obligation to social entrepreneurial intention goes via perceived desirability. Based on the above discussion we next propose the following hypotheses:

H7: Perceived desirability of social entrepreneurship mediates the positive relationship between moral obligation and social entrepreneurial intention.

H8: Perceived feasibility of social entrepreneurship mediates the positive relationship between moral obligation and social entrepreneurial intention.

Table 4.1   Content of the questionnaire

	Antecedents	Sources	# Items	Cronbach's Alpha
1	Entrepreneurial intention (dependent variable)	Liñán and Chen (2009)	5	0.810
2	Perceived desirability	Kolvereid and Isaksen (2006)	5	0.774
3	Perceived feasibility	Ngugi and Gakure (2012)	5	0.701
4	Entrepreneurial educational background	Wu and Wu (2008)	6	0.824
5	Entrepreneurial self-efficacy	Liñán and Chen (2009)	6	0.846
6	Empathy	Ernst (2011)	4	0.712
7	Moral obligation	Hockerts (2015)	3	0.733

RESEARCH METHODOLOGY

Data Collection and Sample

We conducted a quantitative study. We used a sample of nascent social entrepreneurs who have taken the actual behavioural step. No prior Indian study used nascent social entrepreneurs to measure social entrepreneurial intention. Since nascent social entrepreneurs constitute a relatively small group in Indian society, we distributed the questionnaire to the nascent social entrepreneurs across India using a snowball sampling procedure. We personally visited various incubation centres and entrepreneurship cells to collect the sample. We distributed 600 questionnaires, of which 200 were completed (33.33 per cent response rate). Seventy-seven per cent of the respondents were male and 23 per cent were female. These nascent social entrepreneurs were distributed throughout different locations of India.

Questionnaire Development and Measurement

Measures were developed based on an extensive literature review and run through a pre-test before being included in the final questionnaire. Each scale was kept as short as possible – without compromising the validity or reliability of the constructs. Previously tested scales were adapted from existing studies. If no scales existed, they were developed. This study adapted all constructs to social entrepreneurship, both independent and dependent, and chose those items best suited for the measurement of each construct. All scales were seven-point Likert scales. Table 4.1 gives an overview of these scales.

To analyse the data, we conducted structural equation modelling (SEM) using SPSS.[1]

RESULTS

Table 4.2 shows the descriptive statistics. All the antecedents correlate positively with perceived desirability, perceived feasibility and with social entrepreneurial intention. Perceived desirability and perceived feasibility also correlate positively with social entrepreneurial intention. These findings are in line with our hypotheses.

Figure 4.1 contains the results of the SEM analysis. The test showed a reasonable fit of the model. The derived statistics of model fit are CMIN/DF = 1.44, IFI = 0.86, TLI = 0.84, CFI = 0.89 and RMSEA = 0.039. The variables in the model explain 47 per cent of the social entrepreneurial intention.

The results confirm our hypotheses. All antecedents show positive relationships with perceived desirability and perceived feasibility, and these two mediators show positive relationships with social entrepreneurial intention. All the hypotheses are accepted.

DISCUSSION

This study examined the effect of social entrepreneurial educational background, social entrepreneurial self-efficacy, empathy, moral obligation, perceived desirability to become a social entrepreneur and perceived feasibility on social entrepreneurial intention among nascent social entrepreneurs in India. The result shows that the proposed model explains 47 per cent of the variance in social entrepreneurial intention. All the antecedents have a positive statistically significant relationship with social entrepreneurial intention. The findings regarding self-efficacy and social entrepreneurial intention are in line with the findings of a previous study that stated that self-efficacy has been found to be significantly related to state occupational interests and occupational choice among college students (Boyd and Vozikis, 1994). Hockerts (2015) found that social entrepreneurial self-efficacy showed a strong significant relationship with social entrepreneurial intention. Forster and Grichnik (2013) and Ernst (2011) also confirmed the importance of self-efficacy in predicting social entrepreneurial intention.

Empathy and moral obligation showed a strong relationship with both perceived feasibility and desirability to become a social entrepreneur. This is different from the findings of Conway Dato-on, Banerjee and Mesbah in Chapter 5 on a US sample. A feeling of empathy towards others and a desire to help those in need affects the intentions to take a particular career path. In simple

Table 4.2   Descriptive statistics

Variable	Mean	Std Dev.	PD	PF	SEbkd	SESE	EMP	MO	SEI
Perceived desirability	5.23	1.15	(0.59)						
Perceived feasibility	4.64	1.11	0.29	(0.55)					
Entrepreneurial educational background	4.36	1.32	0.77*	0.51*	(0.71)				
Entrepreneurial self-efficacy	5.36	1.08	0.55*	0.59*	0.61*	(0.66)			
Empathy	5.59	1.85	0.32*	0.39*	0.42*	0.49*	(0.69)		
Moral obligation	3.37	1.29	0.29*	0.21*	0.62*	0.36*	0.61*	(0.54)	
Social entrepreneurial intentions	5.09	1.28	0.49*	0.44*	0.57*	0.43*	0.67*	0.32*	(0.68)

Notes: Diagonal values are the square root of average variance extracted (AVE) between the variables and their items and off-diagonal elements are correlations: *$p < 0.05$. To measure discriminant validity, the diagonal values should be higher than off-diagonal values in the same row and column. PD = perceived desirability, PF = perceived feasibility, SEbkd = social entrepreneurial background, SESE = social entrepreneurial self-efficacy, EMP = empathy, MO = moral obligation, SEI = social entrepreneurial intentions.

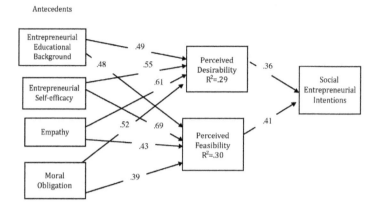

Note: $N = 200$. Arrows indicate standardized regression weights and values in rectangles indicate the variance explained (R^2).

Figure 4.1   Structural model

terms, it is suggested that individuals who want to 'do good' are looking for those career opportunities that enable them to follow this passion.

This research study provides a novel approach toward the development of social entrepreneurial intention by adopting the theory of entrepreneurial event as the research framework. With this study, we have contributed to the growing body of the empirical literature on social entrepreneurship by synthesizing results from the literature on entrepreneurial intentions.

Implications of the Research

In line with similar findings, the academic universities/institutes must also include skill development programmes or specific experiential learning-based courses on entrepreneurship as part of their curriculum so that students may try their hand while studying, only minimizing the risk at later stages of their life. The practical implications of the results of our research study suggest that if policy-makers and universities want to motivate students toward social entrepreneurship, then efforts should be made in the direction of changing their personal attitudes through education and training programmes. This implies that significant efforts must be made to influence the process of creating social enterprises and to conquer the perceived barriers to social entrepreneurship. This has implications for training and development of the young during school and at the university level. Creating a social entrepreneurial culture is thus an imperative in society to enhance personal attitudes and motivation towards social entrepreneurship. Although many of the schools and premier higher education institutes/universities in India are promoting social entrepreneurship through various academic courses, various social entrepreneurial activities – entrepreneurial cells, social incubation programmes and funding support (government as well as non-government grants) – these still need to be strengthened and popularized among the young population.

Based on our findings, efforts should be made by policy-makers and universities to start courses that are helpful in developing social responsibility and belongingness among students. For example, the Ashoka Foundation began an empathy initiative that facilitates schools to collaborate to inculcate in young students a feeling of empathy (Ashoka, 2015). Higher educational institutes should engage in and try to measure the effect of social learning that exposes students to social problems first-hand and introduce programmes that increase empathetic behaviour of the students.

CONCLUSION

The Indian social entrepreneurship culture is quite assertive, characterized by remarkable progress in the past couple of years. Currently, social enterprises in Indian society are playing an active role towards providing affordable basic services like healthcare (Arvind Eye Hospital, Water Health International) and power supply (SELCO, Azure Power Pvt. Ltd.), thus keeping an eye on the 'bottom of the pyramid'. To encourage and support social enterprises, we must closely analyse and understand the factors that affect the perception and thinking process of individuals. Our research study provides a more theory-driven approach, attempting to understand social entrepreneurial intention formation as a whole. To motivate youth toward social entrepreneurship, it is necessary to discover where the desires to 'make a change' or 'do good' come from? Therefore, this research study provides room for further research to investigate how intentions to become social entrepreneurship are formed.

NOTE

1.   More information on the analyses is available from the authors.

REFERENCES

Armitage, C.J. and M. Conner (2001), 'Efficacy of the theory of planned behaviour: a meta-analytic review', *The British Journal of Social Psychology*, **40**(4), 471–99.
Ashoka (2015), 'Start empathy overview', accessed 15 January 2020 at https://startempathy.org/.

Bae, T.J., S. Qian, C. Miao and J.O. Fiet (2014), 'The relationship between entrepreneurship education and entrepreneurial intentions: a meta-analytic review', *Entrepreneurship Theory and Practice*, **38**(2), 217–54.

Bandura, A. (1971), *Social Learning Theory*, Morristown, NJ: General Learning.

Bandura, A. (1999), 'A social cognitive theory of personality', in L. Pervin and O. John (eds), *Handbook of Personality*, New York: Guilford Publications, pp. 154–96.

Beugré, C. (2016), *Social Entrepreneurship: Managing the Creation of Social Value*, London: Routledge.

Biraglia, A. and V. Kadile (2017), 'The role of entrepreneurial passion and creativity in developing entrepreneurial intentions: insights from American homebrewers', *Journal of Small Business Management*, **55**(1), 170–88.

Boyd, N.G. and G.S. Vozikis (1994), 'The influence of self-efficacy on the development of entrepreneurial intentions and actions', *Entrepreneurship Theory and Practice*, **18**, 63–77.

British Council (2016), *Social Value Economy: A Survey of the Social Enterprise Landscape in India*, New Delhi: British Council.

Bryant, P. (2009), 'Self-regulation and moral awareness among entrepreneurs', *Journal of Business Venturing*, **24**(5), 505–18.

Engle, R.L., N. Dimitriadi and J.V. Gavidia et al. (2010), 'Entrepreneurial intent: a twelve-country evaluation of Ajzen's model of planned behaviour', *International Journal of Entrepreneurial Behavior & Research*, **16**(1), 35–57.

Ernst, K. (2011), 'Heart over mind – an empirical analysis of social entrepreneurial intention formation on the basis of the theory of planned behaviour', doctoral dissertation, Universität Wuppertal, Fakultät für Wirtschaftswissenschaft/Schumpeter School of Business and Economics.

Fayolle, A., B. Gailly and N. Lassas-Clerc (2006), 'Assessing the impact of entrepreneurship education programmes: a new methodology', *Journal of European Industrial Training*, **30**(9), 701–20.

Fishbein, M. (1967), *Readings in Attitude Theory and Measurement*, New York: Wiley.

Fitzsimmons, J.R. and E.J. Douglas (2011), 'Interaction between feasibility and desirability in the formation of entrepreneurial intentions', *Journal of Business Venturing*, **26**(4), 431–40.

Forster, F. and D. Grichnik (2013), 'Social entrepreneurial intention formation of corporate volunteers', *Journal of Social Entrepreneurship*, **4**(2), 153–81.

Ghani, E., W.R. Kerr and S. O'Connell (2013), 'Spatial determinants of entrepreneurship in India', *Regional Studies*, **48**, 1071–89.

Guzmán-Alfonso, C. and J. Guzmán-Cuevas (2012), 'Entrepreneurial intention models as applied to Latin America', *Journal of Organizational Change Management*, **25**(5), 721–35.

Harding, R. and M. Cowling (2006), *Social Entrepreneurship Monitor GEM UK*, London: London Business School and The Work Foundation.

Hockerts, K. (2015), 'The Social Entrepreneurial Antecedents Scale (SEAS): a validation study', *Social Enterprise Journal*, **11**(3), 260–80.

Iakovleva, T., L. Kolvereid and U. Stephan (2011), 'Entrepreneurial intentions in developing and developed countries', *Education + Training*, **53**(5), 353–70.

Kolvereid, L. and E. Isaksen (2006), 'New business start-up and subsequent entry into self-employment', *Journal of Business Venturing*, **21**(6), 866–85.

Krueger, N.F. (2007), 'What lies beneath? The experiential essence of entrepreneurial thinking', *Entrepreneurship Theory and Practice*, **31**(1), 123–38.

Krueger, N.F. and D.V. Brazeal (1994), 'Entrepreneurial potential and potential entre-preneurs', *Entrepreneurship Theory and Practice*, **18**, 91–104.

Lee, S.M., D. Chang and S. Lim (2005), 'Impact of entrepreneurship education: a comparative study of the U.S. and Korea', *International Entrepreneurship and Management Journal*, **18**(1), 27–43.

Liñán, F. (2004), 'Intention-based models of entrepreneurship education', *Piccolla Impresa/Small Business*, **3**, 11–35.

Liñán, F. (2011), 'Graduate entrepreneurship in the developing world: intentions, edu-cation and development', *Education + Training*, **53**(5), 325–34.

Liñán, F. and Y. Chen (2009), 'Development and cross-cultural application of a spe-cific instrument to measure entrepreneurial intentions', *Entrepreneurship Theory and Practice*, **33**(3), 593–617.

Liñán, F. and A. Fayolle (2015), 'A systematic literature review on entrepreneur-ial intentions: citation, thematic analyses, and research agenda', *International Entrepreneurship and Management Journal*, **11**(4), 907–33.

Mair, J. and E. Noboa (2006), 'Social entrepreneurship: how intentions to create a social venture are formed', in J. Mair, J. Robinson and K. Hockerts (eds), *Social Entrepreneurship*, London: Palgrave Macmillan, pp. 121–35.

Matlay, H. (2008), 'The impact of entrepreneurship education on entrepreneurial outcomes', *Journal of Small Business and Enterprise Development*, **15**(2), 382–96.

McDonald, N.M. and D.S. Messinger (2011), 'The development of empathy: how, when, and why', in J.J. Sanguineti, A. Ariberton and J.A. Lombo (eds), *Moral Behavior and Free Will: A Neurobiological and Philosophical Approach*, Vatican City: Pontificium Consilium de Cultura, pp. 341–68.

Nabi, G., F. Liñán, D.A. Kirby and N. Ibrahim (2011), 'The case for (social) entrepre-neurship education in Egyptian universities', *Education+ Training*, **53**(5), 403–15.

Ngugi, J.K. and P.R.W. Gakure (2012), 'Application of Shapero's model in explain-ing entrepreneurial intentions among university students in Kenya', *International Journal of Business and Social Research*, **2**(4), 125–48.

Penner, L.A., J.F. Dovidio, J.A. Piliavin and D.A. Schroeder (2005), 'Prosocial behav-ior: multilevel perspectives', *Annual Review of Psychology*, **56**, 365–92.

Prabhu, G.N. (1999), 'Social entrepreneurial leadership', *Career Development International*, **4**(3), 140–45.

Prahalad, C.K. (2008), *The Fortune at the Bottom of the Pyramid: Eradicating Poverty through Profits*, Upper Saddle River, NJ: Pearson Education.

Reynolds, P.D. and S.B. White (1997), *The Entrepreneurial Process: Economic Growth, Men, Women, and Minorities*, Westport, CT: Praeger.

Sánchez, J.C. (2010), 'University training for entrepreneurial competencies: its impact on intention of venture creation', *International Entrepreneurship and Management Journal*, **7**(2), 239–54.

Segal, G., D. Borgia and J. Schoenfeld (2005), 'The motivation to become an entrepre-neur', *International Journal of Entrepreneurial Behavior & Research*, **11**(1), 42–57.

Shapero, A. and L. Sokol (1982), 'The social dimensions of entrepreneurship', *Encyclopedia of Entrepreneurship*, Englewood Cliffs, NJ: Prentice-Hall, pp. 72–90.

Shepherd, D. and H. Patzelt (2011), 'The new field of sustainable entrepreneurship: studying entrepreneurial action linking "what is to be sustained" with "what is to be developed"', *Entrepreneurship Theory and Practice*, **35**, 137–63.

Thompson, J.L. (2008), 'Social enterprise and social entrepreneurship: where have we reached? A summary of issues and discussion points', *Social Enterprise Journal*, **4**(2), 149–61.

Tiwari, P., A.K. Bhat and J. Tikoria (2017a), 'An empirical analysis of the factors affecting social entrepreneurial intentions', *Journal of Global Entrepreneurship Research*, **7**(1), 1–25.

Tiwari, P., A.K. Bhat and J. Tikoria (2017b), 'Predictors of social entrepreneurial intention: an empirical study', *South Asian Journal of Business Studies*, **6**(1), 53–79.

Wagner, J. (2006), 'Are nascent entrepreneurs "Jacks-of-all-trades"? A test of Lazear's theory of entrepreneurship with German data', *Applied Economics*, **38**(20), 2415–19.

Wilson, F., J. Kickul and D. Marlino (2007), 'Gender, entrepreneurial self-efficacy, and entrepreneurial career intentions: implications for entrepreneurship education', *Entrepreneurship Theory and Practice*, **31**(3), 387–406.

Wu, S. and L. Wu (2008), 'The impact of higher education on entrepreneurial intentions of university students in China', *Journal of Small Business and Enterprise Development*, **15**(4), 752–74.

Ziegler, R. (2009), *An Introduction to Social Entrepreneurship*, Cheltenham, UK and Northampton, MA, USA: Edward Elgar Publishing.

5. Individual factors in predicting and encouraging social entrepreneurship as a career choice

Mary Conway Dato-on, Sharmistha Banerjee and Yasmin Mesbah

INTRODUCTION

Social entrepreneurship as a research topic has increased in popularity over the past decades (for example, Bacq and Janssen, 2011; Conway Dato-on and Kalakay, 2016; Mair and Martí, 2006), including investigation on the relative importance of social entrepreneurship for society (Zahra et al., 2009) and career choice for graduating students (Mueller, Brahm and Neck, 2015). Much has also been written on the millennial generation's interest in 'doing good while doing well', which seems to drive motivations and intentions to become involved with social entrepreneurship as well as its relative importance as an actionable path toward doing good for society (Zahra et al., 2009).

Parallel to these movements has been a growing availability of coursework in social entrepreneurship (Ashoka and Brock, 2011; Smith and Woodworth, 2012). Underpinning these courses are a variety of pedagogical approaches that identify skills (Mueller, Chambers and Neck, 2013) and encourage self-identity to assist future social entrepreneurs in bridging the inherent organizational competition between increasing social value while sustaining financial health (Pache and Chowdhury, 2012; Smith and Woodworth, 2012).

Global statistics appear to substantiate strong regional and national differences in social entrepreneurial activities. Specifically, the social early-stage entrepreneurship activity rate (SEA) indicates the percentage of individuals between 18 and 64 years of age currently starting or who own a social enterprise. This SEA is highest in the USA (4.15 per cent), closely followed by the developing regions of the Caribbean (3.05 per cent) and Latin America (2.39 per cent) (see Lepoutre et al., 2013; Terjesen et al., 2009). While these statistical differences generate interesting macro-level discussions regarding correlations between higher levels of SEA and economic development, analogous dialogue comparing individual factors that predict social entrepreneurship as a career choice may be more fruitful for nascent social entrepreneurs.

With this motivation in mind, this chapter investigates individual-level drivers for two groups: (1) current students and (2) self-identified social entrepreneurs in the USA on intention to be social entrepreneurs. The work offers a partner discussion to Chapter 4 by Tiwari and colleagues, who explore similar factors in Indian respondents.

To achieve our goal, we begin with a brief theoretical background on social entrepreneurial intention, including potential influences of entrepreneurial self-efficacy, collective self-efficacy, moral obligation and empathy; from this basis, hypotheses are offered. We then compare the hypothesized relationships across sample demographic differences (for example, current students compared to self-identified social entrepreneurs). We conclude with implications of the research as well as suggesting next steps while acknowledging limitations.

THEORETICAL BACKGROUND

Research suggests that all entrepreneurship is a process that combines risk and uncertainty to create innovations, thus making the construct devoid of ethics, context, or considerations of success (Tan, Williams and Tan, 2005). When we add the word 'social' to 'entrepreneurship', however, the term becomes idiosyncratic and is based on prevailing shared community norms (Blount and Nunely, 2014). Furthermore, 'social' is distinct from 'private', the latter of which has a clear owner who controls the process and keeps the generated output and captured value (Dees, 2001). Thus, social entrepreneurship refers to actions whose purpose is to benefit those 'others' who are not owners of the organization or its output (Prabhu, 1999). Social entrepreneurs, therefore, start with a different mission than commercial entrepreneurs. The former desire to create an enterprise focused on conquering a societal challenge (Neck, Brush and Allen, 2009) or enhancing social wealth (Zahra et al., 2009), while the latter emphasize generating personal, economic wealth. Given this understanding of differences between social and commercial entrepreneurship, why would an individual pursue social entrepreneurship as a career choice?

Dependent Variable: Social Entrepreneurial Intention

According to Krueger and Brazeal (1994), intention indicates a commitment toward a future behaviour. Entrepreneurial intentions direct that pledge toward starting a business or an organization. Intuitively, then, possessing entrepreneurial intentions would be a good indicator of eventually performing entrepreneurial behaviours (Kolvereid, 1996). Social learning theory and theory of planned behaviour (TPB) (Ajzen, 1991, 2001; Fishbein and Ajzen, 1975) support this logic. Considering social entrepreneurship intention specifically, Mair and Noboa (2006) suggest three antecedents: self-efficacy, empathy and moral obligation. The following subsections look at these variables and hypothesize the influence of each on social entrepreneurial intent.

Independent Variables

Entrepreneurial self-efficacy
Selecting a career path can be influenced by one's perception about the anticipated outcome or likelihood of success. This is particularly true in the case of social entrepreneurs, because social and environmental problems may seem overwhelming and beyond an individual's ability to exert influence or get results. As such, understanding social entrepreneurs' self-efficacy, or belief in one's ability to succeed, merits investigation.

Boyd and Vozikis (1994) proposed that belief in one's ability, or self-efficacy, plays an important role in the likelihood to create a new venture. In the context of social entrepreneurship, 'a high level of self-efficacy allows a person to perceive the creation of a social venture as feasible, which positively affects the formation of the corresponding behavioural intention' (Mair and Noboa, 2006, p. 130). Since entrepreneurial self-efficacy (ESE) develops over time and through experiences that improve self-confidence, incorporating social ESE into social entrepreneurship education is imperative (Smith and Woodworth, 2012). Empirical research also suggests that national or regional contexts may influence both the opportunity for experiential learning and thus level of ESE (Mueller and Conway Dato-on, 2011).

Taking previous empirical results and theoretical support outlined above into account, we offer the following hypothesis regarding the influence of entrepreneurial self-efficacy on social entrepreneurial intentions:

H1: Entrepreneurial self-efficacy (ESE) will be positively related to social entrepreneurial intentions (SEI).

Collective entrepreneurial self-efficacy
In the context of social entrepreneurship, additional beliefs about self-efficacy may drive one's intentions to start a social venture (Hockerts, 2015). Recalling that social enterprises, by definition, attempt to tackle 'wicked', complex social problems, it is worthwhile to consider feasibility in addition to one's self-efficacy in entrepreneurial tasks. To succeed, a social entrepreneur must work at the intersection of social and economic goals. Previous researchers suggest that to accomplish this balance, social entrepreneurs must rely on input from societal actors to support their work while simultaneously believing

in their ability to make a difference in the face of a large problem (Hockerts, 2015). Therefore, when assessing antecedents to social entrepreneurial intentions, measuring one's belief that individual action on a social issue will have a positive impact should also be considered. Hockerts (2015) labelled this as collective self-efficacy, which captures the conviction that each of us can make a difference if we act.

Considering these studies, we offer the following hypothesis regarding the influence of collective self-efficacy on social entrepreneurial intentions:

H2: Collective self-efficacy (CSE) will be positively related to SEI.

Empathy

In addition to one's belief in the potential success of personal actions, social entrepreneurs are said to be driven by empathy (Dees, 2012; Sullivan Mort, Weerawardena and Carnegie, 2003). This idea is intuitively appealing given that the purpose of social entrepreneurship is to create value to benefit those 'others' who do not own the enterprise or its output (Prabhu, 1999). Hockerts (2015), citing Miller, Grimes et al. (2012) suggests that empathy will only influence social entrepreneurial intent if the pro-social trait is felt towards a specific group of marginalized people.

The ideas proposed by Mair and Noboa (2006) as to antecedents of social entrepreneurial action have been tested; however, empirical evidence to support the claims of empathy as an antecedent to social entrepreneurial intentions are mixed. Ayob and colleagues (2013) tested empathy as a precursor to perceived feasibility and desirability, rather than as a direct effect on social entrepreneurial intentions. They determine that empathy is a significant determinant to perceived feasibility of creating a social enterprise and thus encourage social entrepreneurial educators to focus on feasibility of a social enterprise in a particular context rather than trying to inculcate empathy. Bacq and Alt (2016) found no empirical evidence to support the relationship between empathic concern and social entrepreneurial intentions.

Perhaps these mixed empirical results express the diverse thoughts on teaching empathy to future social entrepreneurs. For example, studies of social entrepreneurial education found that empathy is not considered an important skill to teach. Miller, Grimes and colleagues (2012) ranked empathy as 32nd out of 35 competencies needed for successful social entrepreneurship results. Nor is empathy found in the syllabi of many university social enterprise courses (Miller, Wesley and Williams, 2012).

Taking the suggested relationships and the mixed empirical results into consideration, we propose the following hypothesis regarding the influence of empathy on social entrepreneurial intentions:

H3: Empathy will be positively related to SEI.

Moral obligation

Perhaps empathy is not enough for a person to act. Perhaps one must feel a moral imperative or obligation to do something in order to act. The findings of Miller, Grimes et al. (2012) support this idea, suggesting that practising social entrepreneurs rated a sense of moral imperative high, notwithstanding low coverage of the topic in social entrepreneurship courses (39 per cent).

Researchers suggest that emotional connections to others through empathetic feelings and thoughts may create a moral compulsion to alleviate the others' suffering, thus stirring an individual to take risks and act on behalf of others (Miller, Grimes et al., 2012). Empathy must combine with the compulsion to act for a social enterprise to be formed. Koe Hwee Nga and Shamuganathan (2010) support this idea when they argue that a strong commitment to enable another to fulfil basic human needs drives social entrepreneurs, while an enduring commitment keeps the work going through tough times. Similarly, Mair and Noboa (2006) proposed moral obligation as a defining difference separating commercial and social entrepreneurial intentions.

These combined results prompt us to suggest the following hypothesis regarding the influence of moral obligation on social entrepreneurial intentions:

H4: Moral obligation will be positively related to SEI.

Previous Experience as Moderator

The suggestion that previous experience may influence social entrepreneurial intentions bears investigation. For example, studies by Basu and Virick (2008) conclude that family and direct experience with entrepreneurship tend to be influential in entrepreneurial intention formation. With this in mind, we hypothesize previous experience to positively moderate between entrepreneurial self-efficacy and social entrepreneurial intentions as well as between collective self-efficacy and social entrepreneurial intentions. The final hypotheses represent these thoughts:

H5a: Previous experience with a social enterprise start-up will moderate the relationship between ESE and SEI.

H5b: Previous experience with a social enterprise start-up will moderate the relationship between CSE and SEI.

The relationships described in the previous sections and hypotheses offered above (H1–H5b) are depicted in Figure 5.1.

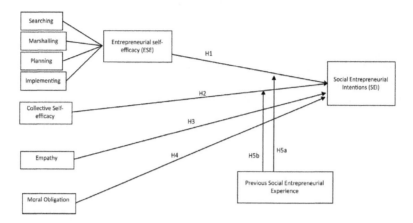

Figure 5.1   Research model

METHODOLOGY

Measurement Instruments

After conducting a thorough literature review, the questionnaire was designed by combining pretested scales from prior studies: Liñán and Chen (2009), Sequeira, McGee and Mueller (2005) and Hockerts (2015). Research data were then collected by administering and distributing a Qualtrics survey to a sample of social entrepreneurs and university students. (Table 5.1 reports descriptive statistics for the sample used to test the hypotheses.)

The reliability of all scales used in the research was tested to ensure their validity. Table 5.2 summarizes the scales' sources, constructs and reliability.[1]

RESULTS

To test the first four hypotheses, a step-wise regression was run to ascertain the influence of entrepreneurial self-efficacy (EFE), empathy, moral obligation and collective self-efficacy (CSE) on the dependent variable: social entrepreneurial intentions (SEI). The results are shown in Table 5.3.

Entering the independent variables one at a time found a regression model with ESE and CSE positively influencing SEI. However, neither empathy nor moral obligation as independent values were significant. Related to the hypotheses, support was found for H1, which predicted a positive influence of ESE on SEI. Similarly, H2 was supported with a significant coefficient and an increase in the R^2 (Table 5.3) indicating that model 2 (with both ESE and CSE

Table 5.1   *Sample characteristics*

	Frequency	Valid %
Employment status		
Employed	77	38.3
Unemployed	19	9.5
Student	101	50.2
Education level		
Less than high school	5	2.5
High school graduate	47	23.4
Some college	58	28.9
College degree	57	28.4
Professional/doctorate degree	34	16.9
Started a social enterprise		
Yes	62	30.5
No	136	67.0
Age		
18–24	77	38.3
25–34	45	22.4
35–44	38	18.9
45–54	20	10.0
55–64	16	8.0
65 or older	2	1.0
Gender		
Male	54	26.9
Female	141	70.1
Transgender	2	1.0

Table 5.2   *Construct measurement and reliability*

Scale	Source	Number of items	Cronbach's Alpha
Entrepreneurial self-efficacy (ESE)	Sequeira et al. (2005)	20	0.969
Collective self-efficacy (CSC)	Hockerts (2015)	3	0.842
Empathy	Hockerts (2015)	3	0.873
Moral obligation	Hockerts (2015	3	0.905
SEI: social entrepreneurial intentions (DV)	Liñán and Chen (2009)	6	0.946

Table 5.3   *Stepwise regression – ESE, CSE as independent variables on*
                    SEI (excluded variable: empathy and moral obligation not
                    reported)

	Model 1[c]		Model 2[c]	
Variable	Unstandardized B	Standardized ß	Unstandardized B	Standardized ß
ESE	0.530	0.488**	0.431	0.397**
CSE			0.269	0.231**
R^2	0.239[a]		0.284[b]	
F-change in R^2	62.95**		12.63**	

Notes:
a. Predictors: (Constant), ESE.
b. Predictors: (Constant), ESE, CSE.
c. Dependent variable: SEI.
** $p < 0.01$.

as predictor variables) has higher capacity to determine SEI. The robustness of the regression equations is also satisfied. The beta values corresponding to ESE and CSE have positive signs, which leads to the inference that an increase in the independent variables brings an increase in SEI, with ESE having higher influence than CSE. Neither H3 nor H4 were supported. The variables of empathy and moral obligation added no predictive value to the regression equation.

Prior to testing the final two hypotheses, we note that 62 respondents (30 per cent) indicated they had started a social enterprise, while 136 (67 per cent) respondents indicated no previous experience. Five respondents selected prefer not to answer for 2.5 per cent of sample, bringing the total to 100 per cent. Comparing SEI means for those with previous social enterprise start-up experience (3.65) and the mean of those without start-up experience (2.77) results in a significant mean difference ($t = 5.66$, df: 196, $p < 0.01$). Similarly, those with previous start-up experience had higher ESE means (3.63) than those without (3.24). Regarding CSE means, those with previous experience also had higher means (3.94) than those without (3.77). The mean difference is significant for ESE means ($t = 2.63$, df: 196, $p < 0.01$), but not for mean difference on CSE ($t = 1.13$, df: 196, $p > 0.10$).

A regression equation with previous experience as a moderator was run to test its influence on the relationship between ESE and SEI (H5a) and CSE and SEI (H5b). Regression analysis was examined to ascertain if such experience influences the relationship of the independent variables of ESE and CSE, respectively, on SEI. As discussed previously, results indicate that both ESE (H1) and CSE (H2) have a direct effect on SEI. Analysis (Table 5.4) shows that previous social enterprise start-up moderates intentions to engage in social

Table 5.4   *Regression testing for moderation of previous SE start-up experience on relationship between ESE to SEI and CSE to SEI*

Variable	Model 1[a]		Model 2[b]		Model 3[c]	
	Unstandard B	Standardized ß	Unstandard B	Standardized ß	Unstandard B	Standardized ß
ESE	0.530	0.488**	0.741	0.682**	0.640	0.397**
Interaction previous SE start-up ESE			−0.164	−0.3.24**		
CSE					0.259	0.223**
Interaction previous SE start-up CSE					−0.160	−0.315**
R^2	0.239[a]		0.306[b]		0.348[c]	
F	62.95**		44.03**		35.33**	

Notes:
a. Predictors: (Constant), ESE.
b. Predictors: (Constant), ESE, interaction previous SE start-up EXP_ESE.
c. Predictors: (Constant), ESE, interaction previous SE start-up EXP_ESE, CSE.
** $p < 0.01$.

entrepreneurship (SEI). Having coded the moderator variable such that yes = 1 and no = 2, results suggest that those with *no* prior experience held stronger intentions to engage in social entrepreneurship than did those who had prior experience. H5a, which hypothesized that previous social enterprise start-up experience would moderate the relationship between ESE and SEI, was not supported. However, previous experience interacts with CSE to strengthen SEI, thus supporting H5b. The nature of the interaction is such that CSE was a stronger predictor of intentions to engage in social entrepreneurship for those with prior experience than for those without.

CONCLUSIONS AND IMPLICATIONS

The purpose of this research was to investigate individual-level drivers for current students and social entrepreneurs in the USA on intention to be a social entrepreneur. To accomplish this, we designed a questionnaire based on previous scales in this domain and collected data from two target populations for analysis. Through this process we can conclude that the intention to select social entrepreneurship as a career is positively influenced by higher entrepreneurial self-efficacy and collective self-efficacy. At the same time, neither empathy nor moral obligation influenced the respondents' intent to become a social entrepreneur.

These findings may be seen as both interesting and troubling for educators and future entrepreneurs. We conclude this because, as educators, we are relieved to hear that our endeavours to increase one's entrepreneurial and collective self-efficacy bear fruit in the encouragement of a career choice into an area with such potential to improve opportunities for creation of social value in our world. Previous research also supports this finding across different national contexts (for example, Ayob et al., 2013; Miller, Grimes et al., 2012; Miller, Wesley and Williams, 2012). Having this chapter parallel to Chapter 4 describing similar research in the Indian context further strengthens conclusions drawn here.

The implication of this conclusion for educators is to continue to offer courses and training that improves one's individual, task-relevant self-efficacy as entrepreneurs and one's belief that individual actions make a difference in improving complex social problems (that is, collective self-efficacy). The results may also reassure pedagogical researchers that their work in improving teaching methods is good for all – students and instructors. The conclusions offer encouragement to (continue to) invest in training in entrepreneurial tasks as these are stimuli of our intentions to select careers in which it is possible to 'do good while doing well'. The positive moderation of previous experience on the relationship between CSE and SEI is also encouraging because it suggests that providing community-based activities that give students involvement with social entrepreneurial tasks will strengthen the likelihood of pursuing social entrepreneurship as a career choice.

We submit that the conclusions are simultaneously troubling because intuition suggests and previous research has confirmed that social entrepreneurs are directed by empathy for the plight of marginalized people and compelled by social mores to act in a way that creates benefits for others – rather than focus on creating value for themselves as commercial entrepreneurs (for example, Hockerts, 2015; Mair and Noboa, 2006), yet we cannot support this conclusion based on the current study. Thus, these results prompt us to ask if this study is an anomaly that lacks generalizability, making us concerned as researchers – or if this is a continuation of mixed results as found by Mair and Noboa (2006), Bacq and Alt (2016) and others. A possible explanation for these results being contradictory to those reported among Indian respondents in Chapter 4 by Tiwari and colleagues, is the low prioritization of empathy associated with business and leadership success prevalent in the USA (for example, Holt et al., 2017; Miller, Grimes et al., 2012). While a shift may be evident towards prioritizing soft skills such as empathy, the concept is still relatively new and thus may take time to increase in importance related to organizational and management accomplishment, and subsequently social entrepreneurial intentions. Alternatively, if empathy really does not increase social entrepreneurial intentions, are the tremendous investments of educators and organizations such as Ashoka U misguided? To answer these questions additional research is clearly needed.

This study also comes with limitations and potential for deeper analysis. One of the limitations is population sample and size. Though the overall sample size is adequate for statistical conclusions, subsets of population characteristics (for example, number majoring in social entrepreneurship) limited our ability to conduct analysis and had to be removed from analysis. While we used previously reliable and valid scales to measure both independent and dependent variables and all demonstrated strong reliability in the present study, when the entrepreneurial self-efficacy (ESE) scale was used in previous studies four factors were found (that is, searching, marshalling, planning, implementing) and in this research only one factor is revealed. This suggests that the use of regression to analyse the data, while methodologically correct, may limit checks for confirmatory factor analysis and comparisons of alternative path models that could be addressed with alternate methods. For example, using path analysis (for example, partial least squares or structural equation modelling) would facilitate comparison of other relationships among the antecedents of SEI. Such methodology could help us to address propositions by previous researchers who suggest that moral obligations may be a proxy for desirability and could thus moderate or mediate the relationship between empathy and SEI (see Hockerts, 2015, p. 265). Similarly, additional research using confirmatory factor and alternative model analysis could allow for comparisons and further ascertain the effect of the high correlation among empathy, moral obligation and collective self-efficacy found in the current study (see Hockerts, 2015, p. 273).

NOTE

1. Further information on scales available from authors upon request.

REFERENCES

Ajzen, I. (1991), 'The theory of planned behavior', *Organizational Behavior and Human Decision Processes*, **50**(2), 179–211.
Ajzen, I. (2001), 'Nature and operation of attitudes', *Annual Review of Psychology*, **52**(1), 27–58.
Ashoka, U. and D.D. Brock (2011), *Social Entrepreneurship Education Resource Handbook*, accessed 15 January 2020 at https://ashokau.org/trends/2011-handbook/.
Ayob, N., C.S. Yap, D.A. Sapuan and M.Z.A. Rashid (2013), 'Social entrepreneurial intention among business undergraduates: an emerging economy perspective', *Gadjah Mada International Journal of Business*, **15**(3), 249–67.

Bacq, S. and E. Alt (2016), 'Being valued or feeling capable? Explaining why empathy inspires social entrepreneurial intentions', *Academy of Management Annual Meeting Proceedings*, **2016**(1), 11903.

Bacq, S. and F. Janssen (2011), 'The multiple faces of social entrepreneurship: a review of definitional issues based on geographical and thematic criteria', *Entrepreneurship and Regional Development*, **23**(5–6), 373–403.

Basu, A. and M. Virick (2008), 'Assessing entrepreneurial intentions amongst students: a comparative study', *VentureWell: Proceedings of Open, the Annual Conference*, pp. 79–86, accessed 15 January 2020 at http://citeseerx.ist.psu.edu/viewdoc/download?doi=10.1.1.483.7035&rep=rep1&type=pdf.

Blount, J. and P. Nunley (2014), 'What is a "social" business and why does the answer matter?', *Brooklyn Journal of Corporate, Financial & Commercial Law*, **8**(2), 278–316.

Boyd, N.G. and G.S. Vozikis (1994), 'The influence of self-efficacy on the development of entrepreneurial intentions and action', *Entrepreneurship Theory and Practice*, **18**(4), 63–77.

Conway Dato-on, M. and J. Kalakay (2016), 'The winding road of social entrepreneurship definitions: a systematic literature review', *Social Enterprise Journal*, **12**(2), 131–60.

Dees, J.G. (2001), 'The meaning of social entrepreneurship', Center for the Advancement of Social Entrepreneurship, Fuqua School of Business, Duke University, accessed 15 January 2020 at https://entrepreneurship.duke.edu/news-item/the-meaning-of-social-entrepreneurship/.

Dees, J.G. (2012), 'A tale of two cultures: charity, problem solving, and the future of social entrepreneurship', *Journal of Business Ethics*, **111**(3), 321–34.

Fishbein, M. and I. Ajzen (1975), *Belief, Attitude, Intention, and Behavior: An Introduction to Theory and Research*, New York: Addison-Wesley.

Hockerts, K. (2015), 'The social entrepreneurial antecedents scale (SEAS): a validation study', *Social Enterprise Journal*, **11**(3), 260–80.

Holt, S., J. Marques, J. Hu and A. Wood (2017), 'Cultivating empathy: new perspectives on educating business leaders', *The Journal of Values-Based Leadership*, **10**(1), 16–43.

Koe Hwee Nga, J. and G. Shamuganathan (2010), 'The influence of personality traits and demographic factors on social entrepreneurship start up intentions', *Journal of Business Ethics*, **95**(2), 259–82.

Kolvereid, L. (1996), 'Prediction of employment status choice intentions', *Entrepreneurship Theory and Practice*, **21**(1), 47–57.

Krueger, N.F. and D.V. Brazeal (1994), 'Entrepreneurial potential and potential entrepreneurs', *Entrepreneurship Theory & Practice*, **18**(3), 91–104.

Lepoutre, J., R. Justo, S. Terjesen and N. Bosma (2013), 'Designing a global standardized methodology for measuring social entrepreneurship activity: the Global Entrepreneurship Monitor social entrepreneurship study', *Small Business Economics*, **40**(3), 693–714.

Liñán, F. and Y.W. Chen (2009), 'Development and cross-cultural application of a specific instrument to measure entrepreneurial intentions', *Entrepreneurship Theory and Practice*, **33**(3), 593–617.

Mair, J. and I. Martí (2006), 'Social entrepreneurship research: a source of explanation prediction, and delight', *Journal of World Business*, **41**(1), 36–44.

Mair, J. and E. Noboa (2006), 'Social entrepreneurship: how intentions to create a social venture are formed', in J. Mair, J. Robinson and K. Hockerts (eds), *Social Entrepreneurship*, New York: Palgrave Macmillan, pp. 121–36.

Miller, T.L., M.G. Grimes, J.S. McMullen and T.J. Vogus (2012), 'Venturing for others with heart and head: how compassion encourages social entrepreneurship', *Academy of Management Review*, **37**(4), 616–40.

Miller, T.L., C.L. Wesley and D.E. Williams (2012), 'Educating the minds of caring hearts: comparing the views of practitioners and educators on the importance of social entrepreneurship competencies', *Academy of Management Learning & Education*, **11**(3), 349–70.

Mueller, S. and M. Conway Dato-on (2011), 'A cross-cultural study of gender-role orientation and entrepreneurial self-efficacy', *International Entrepreneurship and Management Journal*, **9**, 1–20.

Mueller, S., T. Brahm and H. Neck (2015), 'Service learning in social entrepreneurship education: why students want to become social entrepreneurs and how to address their motives', *Journal of Enterprising Culture*, **23**(3), 357–80.

Mueller, S., L. Chambers and H. Neck (2013), 'The distinctive skills of social entrepreneurs', *Journal of Enterprising Culture*, **21**(3), 301–34.

Neck, H., C. Brush and E. Allen (2009), 'The landscape of social entrepreneurship', *Business Horizons*, **52**(1), 13–19.

Pache, A. and I. Chowdhury (2012), 'Social entrepreneurs as institutionally embedded entrepreneurs: toward a new model of social entrepreneurship education', *Academy of Management Learning & Education*, **11**(3), 494–510.

Prabhu, G.N. (1999), 'Social entrepreneurial leadership', *Career Development International*, **4**(3), 140–45.

Sequeira, J.M., J.E. McGee and S.L. Mueller (2005), 'An empirical study of the effect of network ties and self-efficacy on entrepreneurial intentions and nascent behaviour', *Proceedings of the Southern Management Association 2005 Meeting*, Charleston, South Carolina, USA.

Smith, I.H. and W.P. Woodworth (2012), 'Developing social entrepreneurs and social innovators: a social identity and self-efficacy approach', *Academy of Management Learning & Education*, **11**(3), 390–407.

Sullivan Mort, G., J. Weerawardena and K. Carnegie (2003), 'Social entrepreneurship: towards conceptualisation', *International Journal of Nonprofit and Voluntary Sector Marketing*, **8**(1), 76–88.

Tan, W.-L., J. Williams and T.-M. Tan (2005), 'Defining the "social" in "social entrepreneurship": altruism and entrepreneurship', *The International Entrepreneurship and Management Journal*, **1**(3), 353–65.

Terjesen S., J. Lepoutre, R. Justo and N. Bosma (2009), *GEM 2009 Report on Social Entrepreneurship*, GEM Consortium.

Zahra, S.A., E. Gedajlovic, D.O. Neubaum and J.M. Shulman (2009), 'A typology of social entrepreneurs: motives, search processes and ethical challenges', *Journal of Business Venturing*, **24**(5), 519–32.

PART III

Stepping off the career ladder

Both chapters on this topic focus on the question of why women fail to make progress in or pause their management career, in India and the UK respectively.

Sumita Datta and Snehal Shah write on 'Satisficing career choices of Indian women managers'. They analyse career decision-making of women managers in India in a context of economic and cultural change. The migration from rural communities to metropolitan areas goes hand in hand with changes in the structure of family relationships. This shift from the traditional joint family to the nuclear family changes the role of women and opens up possibilities for women to develop a career. Yet, the authors' study among 31 women managers illustrates how the career aspirations of these women still conflict with family role expectations that remain rooted in the patriarchal culture of India. This dilemma leads in many cases to 'satisficing' or suboptimal career choices of women who adjust their career downwards to adapt to family responsibilities.

Angela Stephanie Mazzetti's chapter is about 'Stepping off the career ladder: exploring the impact of career shocks on women's career decisions in the UK'. Her chapter is in a sense a subset of the canvas painted in Datta and Shah's chapter. The study shows how career shocks can make women managers give up on satisficing choices and make a more drastic decision to quit. Applying the lens of conservation of resources theory, she looks at how eight UK women dealt with the resource loss caused by career shocks and the lack of support from their organization. Her analysis illustrates how positive shocks, such as a promotion, can turn into negative ones or vice versa. She also illustrates how a career shock can start a resource spiral, in which resource loss leads to more resource loss. She concludes that career shocks can be dysfunctional for both the individual and the organization and proposes the development of 'resource-enhancing environments' to mitigate those shocks.

Taken separately, both chapters provide particular lessons for the countries – India and the UK – in which the separate studies were conducted. Taken together, the chapters show you how women's career situations may not be that much different across Indian and Western cultures. Culturally established norms about gender and family roles may differ between India and the UK, yet both studies invite you to see that women are still the primary caregivers, and how the prevalence of male-defined perceptions of performance in organizations cause women managers to step off the career ladder.

6. Satisficing career choices of Indian women managers

Sumita Datta and Snehal Shah

INTRODUCTION

In the context of an emergent economy like India, discussions on gender equality have assumed increasing importance in the national landscape (Donnelly, 2015; Rath, Mohanty and Pradhan, 2015). In the last decade or more, urban India has witnessed more women entering the organized labour market (Das, 2005; Haq and Chand, 2012; Jhabvala and Sinha, 2002). However, the increasing rate of women's participation in higher education and professional careers in India has not resulted in similar progress to the upper echelons of organizations where they continue to face barriers (Budhwar and Varma, 2010; Gupta, Koshal and Koshal, 1998; Khandelwal, 2002). Mid-career workers are facing more demanding situations in the workplace, especially due to extended work hours and, at the same time, being straddled with family-related responsibilities (Datta and Aggarwal, 2017). The proportion of women leaving their job between junior to middle level is high in India as compared to other major Asian countries (McKinsey & Company, 2012). This evidence calls for a deeper level of understanding about the factors that have an effect on continuity and career advancement of women in corporate India.

The purpose of this chapter is to examine the underlying processes of career choices made by Indian women managers in order to explicate the ways in which social construction of gender and societal culture are intertwined in rational choice-making. Such an approach has rarely been adopted in extant studies of women's careers especially in the Indian context and this chapter will contribute to the emerging understanding of women's careers during a period of economic and social change in the country.

THEORETICAL OVERVIEW

Many factors are reported to influence career development of women across the echelons of management hierarchy. For the purpose of this chapter, we explore national culture and gender identity of women as macro-level ante-cedents that influence the individual and organizational factors, which in turn contribute to their career choices.

National Culture: The Leaky Pipeline of Women Managers in India

India is an extremely heterogeneous, multicultural society marked by diversity in ethnicity, religion, language and social status (Budhwar, 2009; Som, 2007). In Hofstede's (2001) cultural value framework, India leans towards collec-tivism (as opposed to individualism), greater power distance, and cultural tightness (Gelfand, Nishii and Raver, 2006). Collectivists identify strongly with their in-group and are heavily influenced by social norms. Greater power distance is associated with obedience and dependence on authority figures, as well as greater acceptance of unequal distribution of power (Hofstede, 2001). Last, tight cultures have strong social norms and severe sanctions for their violation (Gelfand et al., 2006). Consequently, family plays a vital role in life decisions for most Indians (Mandelbaum, 1970) and the role of patriarch is crucial in Indian society.

In the last two decades, increased competition and economic opportunities have resulted in migration of individuals from rural communities to metropol-itan areas. Although urbanization has begun to erode the joint family system, replacing them with nuclear family systems, strong social norms and sense of interdependence still represent a significant aspect of Indian society (Gore, 1990). With many middle-class families beginning to link their aspirations to a higher standard of living, more women are acquiring education and enter-ing the job market, thereby contributing significantly to the family income (Budhwar, Saini and Bharnagar, 2005). The changing paradigm is causing many a dilemma at different life stages of a woman, requiring her to choose between career development and family responsibilities. Such dilemmas experienced by women represent the internal conflict related to gender identity that is still deeply entrenched in the patriarchal culture of India (Blake-Beard, 2015).

Gender Identity

According to social role theory (Eagly, 1987), cultures convey shared expec-tations for the appropriate conduct of males and females, which foster gender differences in social behaviour. A meta-analytical study concluded that these gender differences are perpetuated in the early years of development by parents themselves, and the pattern of reinforcement males and females receive con-ditions gender-appropriate behaviour (Aycock, 2011). As a result of gender role socialization processes, men aspire to enter male-dominated occupations seen as calling for 'masculine', that is, agentic personal qualities, whereas women aspire to enter feminine occupations seen as calling for 'feminine', that is, communal personal qualities (Wigfield and Eccles, 2000). In India where patriarchal society with low egalitarian culture continues to prevail, one can expect Indian women to be more entrenched in 'caregiver' roles that constitute an integral part of their gender identity. In situations when career choices may be in apparent conflict with their social role expectations, gender identity is likely to play a role in influencing such decisions.

Evidence from extant literature spanning various fields in social sciences explains lower representation of women in management from both supply- and demand-side perspectives (Blau, Ferber and Winkler, 2014; Orser and Leck, 2010). Supply-side explanations cite gender differences in job preferences and psychosocial factors that constrain the 'pipeline' of women into managerial ranks (Datta and Aggarwal, 2017), whereas demand-side factors include labour market and organizational factors (O'Neil, Hopkins and Bilimoria, 2008).

Supply-side Barriers

The last three decades have seen considerable gender-related social changes that may have influenced gender identity among women. Studies have found that women's occupational aspirations have become more similar to those of men over a period of time (Farmer and Chung, 1995). Financial independence emerged as a significant motivator for pursuing a corporate career for the new-generation women managers. Earning money and being able to pay for the good things in life is an important factor in the upwardly mobile society in India (Datta and Aggarwal, 2017). However, although the entry of women into managerial occupations has increased considerably over time, evidence is mounting that men's and women's career paths begin to divide soon after.

Career aspirations
There is research at the individual level that has identified gender differences in career attitudes and behaviours as one of the most influential factors accounting for career success (Abele and Spurk, 2009). Occupational aspirations at an earlier age predict occupational attainment at a later age (Schoon, 2001). However, a study conducted on college students found that female students had more career aspirations than their male counterparts, but at the same time they perceived more career barriers (Watts et al., 2015). Perhaps there are various social and organizational factors that play a role in the dwindling career aspirations of women in organizations. As a result of gender-related social changes, gender differences in aspirations to top management are likely

to exist and the importance of gender identity is not expected to decrease over time.

Self-efficacy

According to Bandura (1997), gender is one of the most important factors affecting self-efficacy because of social expectations and social roles. Increasing self-efficacy has sustained effects on beliefs and behaviour that are reinforced in a supportive environment (Huszczo and Endres, 2013). Researchers agree that men and women perceive their achievements and abilities differently, and this affects formation of self-concept (Judge et al., 1995; Orser and Leck, 2010). While men attribute their successes to internal causes such as ability and traits, women attribute their successes to external causes such as opportunity or support. Thus, self-efficacy to pursue actions required for career advancement is likely to be different between men and women in a less egalitarian patriarchal society like India where women are expected to be caregivers.

Perceived family support

Research indicates that spousal support plays a very important role in women's career advancement (Aycan, 2004). It is also suggested that socio-cultural context determines work- and family-related values and societal norms regarding gender roles and attitudes towards women in management (Riger and Galligan, 1980). In other words, the gender role expectations in Indian society are likely to influence the perceived family support by working women. In India, spousal and family support from parents is critical for working women with children when it comes to making career choices (Datta and Agarwal, 2017). In the absence of government-aided childcare facilities, women with small children have no choice but to rely on family support for making career development choices.

Cultural value orientation

Time and again, culture theorists have highlighted the importance of cultural values, particularly social relationship values in the context of the career development process (Brown, 2002). Drawing from Kluckhohn and Strodtbeck's (1961) model, such value orientation is explained in the literature as a fundamental concept that consists of cognitive, directional and affective elements that are essentially products of one's socio-cultural environment. When a collective social relationship is a highly prioritized value for both the decision-maker and the decision-maker's family, the values of the family, depending on the family structure (for example, patriarchal), are likely to be primary determinants of career choices (Brown, 2002; Sue and Sue, 1990).

Traditionally, men have been considered as the breadwinners and women to be the caregivers, but the changing socio-economic fabric of Indian society has led to value paradoxes in life goals and individual aspirations of qualified women (Blake-Beard, 2015). These paradoxes become salient at certain life stages when individual career aspirations are at loggerheads with the cultural value orientation of the Indian woman manager.

Demand-side Barriers

Most research efforts have primarily focused on the challenges of managing diversity and inclusion in the workforce (Buddhapriya, 2013; Donnelly, 2015), the glass ceiling (Sahoo and Lenka, 2016), or factors affecting the re-entry of women into the workforce (Ravindran and Baral, 2014). Creating a gender-sensitive workplace requires more than only policy changes. Gendered roles, gendered organizational structures, discriminatory attitudes of supervisors and biased organizational culture at large often put women employees at a disadvantage. Supervisory support and HR practices (Datta and Agarwal, 2017) continue to play an important role in influencing career choices made by women professionals in India.

Supervisory support

Organizations in India still see feminine identity as detrimental to the job and women still suffer due to the boy's club phenomenon, which restricts their informal networking (Agarwal et al., 2016). In other words, despite achieving their senior managerial position through promotions and upward mobility in the organizational hierarchy, Indian women managers must work harder than their male counterparts and constantly prove themselves and their capabilities, reflecting low gender egalitarianism (Datta and Aggarwal, 2017). In such contexts, the importance of perceived support of supervisors arises as a critical element when studying Indian female employees, especially when the supervisor is also a mentor (Blake-Beard, 2015). This is in line with the cultural dimension of high power distance in India where people look up to those in authority and expect nurturance and guidance. Thus, female employees are likely to look for interpersonal support from their immediate supervisors in navigating their career development (Jung and Takeuchi, 2016).

HR practices

The work–life literature, especially that written from a feminist perspective, has focused on gender equity, promoting mothers' right to remain in the labour market following childbirth and arguing that domestic and childcare labour should be shared more equally between mothers and fathers (Maushart, 2002). Research findings showing how mothers are consistently disadvantaged within labour markets due to their actual or potential childcare responsibilities (Blair-Loy, 2003) have thus encouraged organizations to develop enhanced work–life balance policies and flexible working options (Gatrell and Cooper, 2016; Lewis and Cooper, 2005).

As women managers continue to explore the demand and supply sides of their contexts, they tend to apply a cognitive lens to evaluate their decisions. Most often than not, as described in the following section, these are 'satisficing' choices made under certain boundary conditions that women impose on themselves.

The Lens of Bounded Rationality and Satisficing Career Choices

More than half a century ago, Herbert Simon proposed a theory of individuals' decision-making as boundedly rational (Simon, 1955, 1956, 1957). Under this premise, humans do not look for optimizing solutions but they settle for what he referred to as 'satisficing' choices. These are 'good enough' choices that satisfy the individual based on some levels of acceptability. Over time, it is possible that while an individual moves towards an optimizing 'best fit' solution, in reality, she or he accepts a 'satisficing' alternative.

As the search for alternatives is undertaken, individuals need to know when to stop searching. In Simon's (1955) 'satisficing' model, the search is ended when the first alternative meets or exceeds the acceptable levels, or when the first cue that favours the alternative is found (Gigerenzer and Goldstein, 1996). Such rules presuppose cognitive mechanisms at play. However, non-cognitive cues such as emotions of love or anger can serve as simple, fast and fairly accurate rules that guide us when to stop searching. Such cues are relevant to the discussion in this chapter of how women make their career choice decisions. The seemingly self-imposed glass ceiling as reflected in her career choices limits her own career success, which has been explained 'as the accomplishment of desirable work-related outcomes at any point in a person's work experiences over time' (Arthur, Khapova and Wilderom, 2005, p. 179). Two meanings of career success have been discussed in the literature: the first is 'subjective', which suggests a form of success that is personally desirable; the second is 'objective', that is, success that is likely to rely on social comparisons. The subjective–objective career duality has been a concern for those who have studied the trade-offs between work and family or work and leisure activities. It has been further suggested in the literature that both subjective and objective aspects of career success are interdependent (Arthur et al., 2005). An interdependent perspective sees individuals as continually interpreting and reinterpreting the work experiences and career success they have had (Dai and Song, 2016). Such iterative evaluation of career success is likely to form the basis for satisficing choices taken by women managers and impact their perceived well-being.

Well-being

Well-being has been a longstanding topic of research interest amongst scholars across multiple areas of academic concentration and has been extensively studied in career development literature (Sampson et al., 2014). Many theorists have suggested that well-being has multiple dimensions and is thus a multifaceted construct (Forgeard et al., 2011). Ryan and Deci (2001) concluded that there are two major philosophical perspectives concerning well-being: one is subjective well-being (SWB), which is happiness oriented (that is, hedonism); the other is psychological well-being (PWB), which involves realizing human potential power (that is, eudemonism). Although SWB and PWB differ from each other, studies have found that these two concepts share some level of relatedness (Keyes and Lopez, 2002) and they gradually merge together in the process of personal growth as individuals gain more life experience (Zheng et al., 2015).

The literature overview of multiple streams that may have a bearing on career choices of women managers provided us with a compelling motivation to take up an exploratory study to uncover the underlying mechanisms at play.

AN EXPLORATORY STUDY: QUALITATIVE EVIDENCE FOR CAREER CHOICE MODEL

Methodology

Following a research method of discovery, we adopted a grounded theory approach (Strauss and Corbin, 1998) to understand the complicated and multifaceted career choices of Indian women managers involving their lived experiences. As we aimed to investigate the personal sensemaking that impacts career decisions of Indian women managers, the processes that we sought to study were unknown at the start of the research.

Study sample

We used a sample of 31 salaried women managers based in Mumbai, drawn from senior, middle and junior management levels. The respondents had at least a bachelor's degree with about 61 per cent of them having postgraduate qualifications. The majority were middle managers (20/31; ~65 per cent), and almost two-thirds of them were married (24/31; ~77 per cent), with children. The participants of the study worked in service-oriented (19/31; ~61 per cent) sectors, manufacturing (8/31; ~26 per cent) and educational institutions (4/31;

~13 per cent). The mean age of the entire sample was 35.5 years, with the majority of the interviewees (22/31; ~71 per cent) between 33 and 41 years of age.

Analyses

Through an iterative process we compared the similarities and differences from the raw data to identify the concepts and subsequently grouped them under similar labels. In the events of disagreement between the coders about labelling, we went back to either the research questions or the transcripts to tease out the nuances of the underlying structure. We had several discussions during the course of the research and captured the insights in messages and emails so that a great deal of conceptual detail is not lost or left undeveloped.

Results: Emergent Conceptual Model of Career Choices by Women Managers

The data revealed an interesting pattern that we had not anticipated earlier. This related to ambivalence towards career aspirations that the respondents were reporting. We discovered that this ambivalence was more about the nature of career outcomes with regard to their social context and not about their own competence or potential to achieve greater career success. There seemed to be a kind of a moderating mechanism at play that we thought needed further inquiry. Throughout the research, we remained alert to repetition of information/observation for it to be considered an emergent concept by repeatedly being present in interviews, documents and observations in one form or another or by being significantly absent.

Drawing on a data structure model proposed by Gioia, Corley and Hamilton (2013), the summary of results has been presented in Figure 6.1.

The aggregate dimensions that emerged from the study, as highlighted in the summary of results (Figure 6.1) point towards socio-cognitive mechanisms at play that can explain career choices of women managers. We posit that the view others hold about the specific role of women in society may influence the thinking of Indian women to the extent that she starts believing it is true. This social conditioning drives her behaviour in a way that is in congruence with what others expect of her. Over time, she develops her own gender identity that conforms to such a worldview. These underlying mechanisms most typically impact her career aspirations, adversely putting limits on what she can and cannot do. As she gets habituated to see her reality through these limiting filters, she may start doubting her own ability to succeed in certain careers, thus undermining her self-efficacy for career advancement. While this type of internal dialogue goes through her mind, other critical factors such as her own perception of the support received from her family members and supervisors

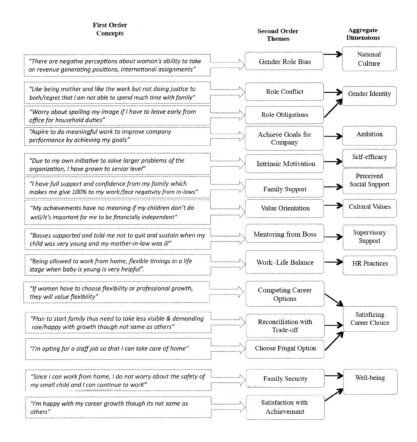

Figure 6.1   Summary of results

to enable her to balance work and family life play a crucial role in determining her career choice decisions. Beyond these factors that are more intra-personal in nature, organizational factors such as HR practices and behaviours that represent unique aspects of company culture hugely impact her career decisions. Substantial literature on gender diversity and inclusion suggests that women are more likely to thrive and move up the career ladder when HR practices and cultural ethos are women friendly, reflect gender parity and are less gender discriminatory. The proposed model thus articulates a narrative that it is the interplay of aspects of national culture, gender identity and internal as well as external aspects of her circumstances that leads her to make choices that may not be rationally optimizing in terms of career success but satisficing – within

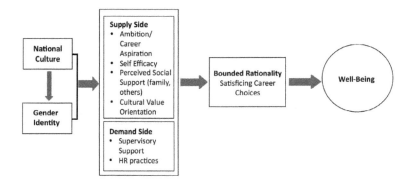

Figure 6.2   Conceptual model: satisficing career choices by women managers

the constraints of her circumstances. The emergent model of satisficing career choices by women managers as described above is presented in Figure 6.2.

CONCLUSION AND IMPLICATIONS

This chapter contributes to the emerging understanding of women's careers in India in a period of economic and social change and holds several implications for business leaders, HR practitioners and policy-makers interested in fostering career advancement of women professionals.

Traditional role expectations conflict with the individual aspirations leading to paradoxical situations wherein managerial career development falls through the cracks. To facilitate career advancement of women, policy-makers must take cognizance of the cognitive-affective strategies women apply at different life stages. Having recognized that one size does not fit all, customized organization support may be required to create an eco-system that will support women to move up the career trajectory. Additionally, meaningful purpose-oriented roles should be created that can tap into the potential of women professionals while providing them with work–family balance as critical support required in certain life stages.

It can be argued here that business leaders and policy-makers need to recognize the co-existing, equally salient identity attributes of career aspirations as well as caregiving in women professionals that are apparently at loggerheads due to the social construction of gender identity. In other words, career and familial identities need not be either/or and should rather be mutually enriching that can lead to more objectively optimal decisions. Mentoring practices must take these factors into account to be more impactful and facilitate the mentee's passage through the life and career stage transitions more smoothly.

Analysing the well-being components of the responses, the model indicates a heavy reliance on the satisfaction derived from the family role identity schema, compensating for the shortfall of objective satisfaction accrued in the form of promotion, titles, positions and other organizational rewards. Due to the high interdependency of subjective and objective career outcomes perceived by women (Arthur et al., 2005), evolving a hybrid choice set becomes critical for their overall well-being. So, from an organization's perspective, the decision-makers should consciously steer away from gender-based biases that may deprive women from being considered for opportunities such as advanced training, higher education, international assignments and visible, high-profile projects associated with gender-agnostic career advancement.

LIMITATIONS OF THE STUDY

The review of literature focused only on theories of career development, gender identity, bounded rationality and culture to explain the context of career choices made by women managers. Notwithstanding the importance and the originality of the findings reported in this study, it would be interesting to see future studies. Despite its patriarchal and collectivist culture, India is often described as a confluence of subcultures, an attribute that might question the generalizability across the different parts of the country. Another limitation is certainly the small sample size and the qualitative nature of this study. Future studies might consider using a larger sample size and a triangulation of methods between qualitative and quantitative techniques that will allow for some confirmatory research through the use of propositions and hypotheses. Finally, comparative studies looking at the nuances of culture and gender identity that influence career choices of women managers across different cultures would be very informative.

REFERENCES

Abele, A.E. and D. Spurk (2009), 'How do objective and subjective career success interrelate over time?', *Journal of Occupational and Organizational Psychology*, **82**, 803–24.
Agarwal, S., W. Qian, D.M. Reeb and T.F. Sing (2016), 'Playing the boys game: golf buddies and board diversity', *American Economic Review*, **106**(5), 272–6.
Arthur, M.B., S. Khapova and C.P.M. Wilderom (2005), 'Career success in a boundaryless career world', *Journal of Organizational Behavior*, **26**, 177–202.
Aycan, Z. (2004), 'Key success factors for women in management in Turkey', *Applied Psychology*, **53**, 453–77.

Aycock, K.J. (2011), 'Coping resources, coping styles, mastery, social support, and depression in male and female college students', dissertation, Georgia State University.

Bandura, A. (1997), *Self-Efficacy: The Exercise of Control*, New York: Freeman.

Blair-Loy, M. (2003), *Competing Devotions: Career and Family among Executive Women*, Cambridge, MA: Harvard University Press.

Blake-Beard, S.D. (2015), 'Confronting paradox: exploring mentoring relationships as a catalyst for understating the strengths and resilience of Indian professional women', in P. Kumar (ed.), *Unveiling Women's Leadership: Identity and Meaning of Leadership in India*, London: Palgrave Macmillan, pp. 25–43.

Blau, F.D., M.A. Ferber and A.W. Winkler (2014), *The Economics of Women, Men, and Work* (7th edition), Upper Saddle River, NJ: Prentice Hall/Pearson.

Brown, D. (ed.) (2002), *Career Choice and Development* (4th edition), San Francisco, CA: Jossey-Bass.

Buddhapriya, S. (2013), 'Diversity management practices in select firms in India: a critical analysis', *The Indian Journal of Industrial Relations*, **48**(4), 597–610.

Budhwar, P. (2009), 'Managing human resources in India', in J. Storey, P. Wright and D. Ulrich (eds), *The Routledge Companion to Strategic Human Resource Management*, London: Routledge, pp. 435–46.

Budhwar, P.S., D.S. Saini and J. Bhatnagar (2005), 'Women in management in the new economic environment: the case of India', *Asia Pacific Business Review*, **11**(2), 179–93.

Budhwar, P. and A. Varma (2010), 'Emerging patterns of HRM in the new Indian economic environment', *Human Resource Management*, **49**, 345–51.

Dai, L.T. and F.H. Song (2016), 'Subjective career success: a literature review and prospect', *Journal of Human Resource and Sustainability Studies*, **4**(3), 238–42.

Das, M. (2005), 'Muslim women's low labour force participation in India: some structural explanations', in Z. Hasan and R. Menon (eds), *In a Minority: Essays on Muslim Women in India*, Oxford: Oxford University Press, pp. 189–221.

Datta, S. and U. Agarwal (2017), 'Factors effecting career advancement of Indian women managers', *South Asian Journal of Business Studies*, **6**, 314–36.

Donnelly, R. (2015), 'Tensions and challenges in the management of diversity and inclusion in IT services multinationals in India', *Human Resource Management*, **54**(2), 199–215.

Eagly, A.H. (1987), *Sex Differences in Social Behavior: A Social-Role Interpretation*, Hillsdale, NJ: Laurence Erlbaum Associates.

Farmer, H.S. and Y.B. Chung (1995), 'Variables related to career commitment, mastery motivation, and level of career aspiration among college students', *Journal of Career Development*, **21**(4), 265–78.

Forgeard, M., J. Eranda, M.E.P. Kern and M. Seligman (2011), 'Doing the right thing: measuring well-being for public policy', *International Journal of Wellbeing*, **1**(1), 79–106.

Gatrell, C. and L. Cooper (2016), 'A sense of entitlement? Fathers, mothers and organizational support for family and career', *Community, Work & Family*, **19**(2), 134–47.

Gelfand, M., L. Nishii and J. Raver (2006), 'On the nature and importance of cultural tightness-looseness', *The Journal of Applied Psychology*, **91**(6), 1225–44.

Gigerenzer, G. and D.G. Goldstein (1996), 'Reasoning the fast and frugal way: models of bounded rationality', *Psychological Review*, **104**, 650–69.

Gioia, D., K. Corley and A. Hamilton (2013), 'Seeking qualitative rigor in inductive research', *Organizational Research Methods*, **16**, 15–31.

Gore, J.M. (1990), 'What can we do for you! What can "we" do for "you"?: struggling over empowerment in critical and feminist pedagogy', *Educational Foundations*, **4**(3), 5–26.

Gupta, A., M. Koshal and R.K. Koshal (1998), 'Women managers in India: challenges and opportunities', *Equal Opportunities International*, **17**(8), 14–26.

Haq, A. and S. Chand (2012), 'Pattern and impact of Facebook usage on the academic performance of students in higher education: a gender-based comparison', *Bulletin of Education and Research*, **34**(2), 19–28.

Hofstede, G.H. (2001), *Culture's Consequences: International Differences in Work-Related Values*, Thousand Oaks, CA: Sage.

Huszczo, G. and M. Endres (2013), 'Joint effects of gender and personality on choice of happiness strategies', *Europe's Journal of Psychology*, **9**, 136–49.

Jhabvala, R. and S. Sinha (2002), 'Liberalisation and the woman worker', *Economic & Political Weekly*, **37**(21), 2037–44.

Judge, T.A., D.M. Cable, J.W. Boudreau and R.D. Bretz (1995), 'An empirical investigation of the predictors of executive career success', *Personnel Psychology*, **48**, 485–519.

Jung, Y. and N. Takeuchi (2016), 'Gender differences in career planning and success', *Journal of Managerial Psychology*, **31**(2), 603–23.

Keyes, C.L.M. and S.J. Lopez (2002), 'Toward a science of mental health: positive directions in diagnosis directions in diagnosis and interventions', in C.R. Snyder and S.J. Lopez (eds), *Handbook of Positive Psychology*, New York: Oxford University Press, pp. 45–62.

Khandelwal, P. (2002), 'Gender stereotypes at work: implications for organizations', *Indian Journal of Training and Development'*, **XXXII**(2), 72–83.

Kluckhohn, F.R. and F.L. Strodtbeck (1961), *Variations in Value Orientations*, Evanston, IL: Row, Peterson.

Lewis, S. and C.L. Cooper (2005), *Work–Life Integration: Case Studies of Organizational Change*, Chichester: John Wiley & Sons.

Mandelbaum, D. (1970), *Indian Society*, Berkeley, CA: University of California Press.

Maushart, S. (2002), *Wifework*, London: Bloomsbury.

McKinsey & Company (2012), *Women Matter: An Asian Perspective: Harnessing Female Talent to Raise Corporate Performance*, accessed 15 January 2020 at https://www.boardagender.org/files/2012-McKinsey-Women-Matter-An-Asian -Perspective.pdf.

O'Neil, D., M. Hopkins and D. Bilimoria (2008), 'Women's careers at the start of the 21st century: patterns and paradoxes', *Journal of Business Ethics*, **80**, 727–43.

Orser, B. and J. Leck (2010), 'Gender influences on career success outcomes', *Gender in Management: An International Journal*, **25**(5), 386–407.

Rath, T.S., M. Mohanty and B.B. Pradhan (2015), 'Career advancement of women bank managers in India: a study in state bank of India', *XIMB Journal of Management*, **12**(1), 79–96.

Ravindran, B. and R. Baral (2014), 'Factors affecting the work attitudes of Indian re-entry women in the IT sector', *Vikalpa*, **39**(2), 31–42.

Riger, S. and P. Galligan (1980), 'Women in management: an exploration of competing paradigms', *American Psychologist*, **35**, 902–10.

Ryan, R. and E. Deci (2001), 'On happiness and human potentials: a review of research on hedonic and eudaimonic well-being', *Annual Review of Psychology*, **52**, 141–66.

Sahoo, D.K. and U. Lenka (2016), 'Breaking the glass ceiling: opportunity for the organization', *Industrial and Commercial Training*, **48**(6), 311–19.

Sampson, J.P. Jr, P.C. Hou and J. Kronholz et al. (2014), 'Annual review: a content analysis of career development theory, research, and practice – 2013', *The Career Development Quarterly*, **62**, 290–326.

Schoon, I. (2001), 'Teenage job aspirations and career attainment in adulthood: a 17-year follow-up study of teenagers who aspired to become scientists, health professionals, or engineers', *International Journal of Behavioral Development*, **25**, 124–32.

Simon, H.A. (1955), 'A behavioral model of rational choice', *Quarterly Journal of Economics*, **59**, 99–118.

Simon, H.A. (1956), 'Rational choice and the structure of the environment', *Psychological Review*, **63**, 129–38.

Simon, H.A. (1957), *Models of Man, Social and Rational: Mathematical Essays on Rational Human Behavior*, New York: John Wiley & Sons.

Som, A. (2007), 'What drives adoption of innovative SHRM practices in Indian organizations?', *The International Journal of Human Resource Management*, **18**(5), 808–28.

Strauss, A. and J. Corbin (1998), *Basics of Qualitative Research: Techniques and Procedures for Developing Grounded Theory* (2nd edition), Thousand Oaks, CA: Sage.

Sue, D.W. and D. Sue (1990), *Counseling the Culturally Different: Theory and Practice* (2nd edition), New York: John Wiley & Sons.

Watts, L., M. Frame and C. Moffett et al. (2015), 'The relationship between gender, perceived career barriers and occupational aspirations', *Journal of Applied Social Psychology*, **45**(1), 10–22.

Wigfield, A. and J.S. Eccles (2000), 'Expectancy-value theory of achievement motivation', *Contemporary Educational Psychology*, **25**(1), 68–81.

Zheng, X., W. Zhu, H. Zhao and C. Zhan (2015), 'Employee well-being in organizations: theoretical model, scale development, and cross-cultural validation', *Journal of Organizational Behavior*, **36**, 621–44.

7. Stepping off the career ladder: exploring the impact of career shocks on women's career decisions in the UK

Angela Stephanie Mazzetti

INTRODUCTION

A recent review of female representation across all management levels in the UK highlighted that the attrition rate for women progressing from junior to senior management levels is high (CMI, 2013a). The report highlighted that although women make up 60 per cent of junior management positions, only 20 per cent make up senior management positions, and when considering the number of women in CEO or board positions, the percentage is in single figures. This is despite significant efforts over the past decades to tackle gender discrimination and female underrepresentation in the UK (CIPD, 2018). However, this is not just a UK phenomenon; it is much the same picture across most of Europe, the US and Australia (Davies, 2015; Johnston and Lee, 2012). The consensus is that this 'leaking pipeline' of women is partly due to the 'glass ceiling' and partly due to the 'glass obstacle course' (CMI, 2013a). The 'glass ceiling' refers to the inherent structural and discriminatory practices that prevent women progressing to more senior management levels (CIPD, 2018; Davies, 2015; Johnston and Lee, 2012). The 'glass obstacle course' refers to the unseen hurdles and barriers that stop or dissuade women from progressing their management careers (CMI, 2013a; Davies, 2015). Much research has focused on the former, discriminatory practices such as the gender pay gap that prevent women from entering higher management levels (Johnston and Lee, 2012). However, less is known about the latter, the reasons why women decide not to climb the career ladder in the first place or opt to 'step off' the career ladder (CMI, 2013a, 2013b).

There is a general consensus that the decision-making process behind women's career planning is different from that of men (Astin, 1984; Mavin et al., 2015; O'Neil and Bilimoria, 2005; Scott and Hatalla, 1990) because of the broader cultural and social contexts underpinning women's careers (Astin, 1984; Hoffarth, 1996). For example, O'Neil and Bilimoria (2005) suggest that women more generally must juggle the role of providing dependent care with their work role and that this inherent role duality pervades women's career decisions and choices. Consequently, they suggest that this combination of factors uniquely constrains women's careers.

This chapter aims to provide a better insight into the thinking behind a group of women and their decisions to 'step off' their career ladders. Drawing on the findings of a wider study exploring career transitions, this chapter presents the experiences of four women who encountered 'career shocks', conceptualized as significant events that led to the women 'taking stock' of their career options. Research has highlighted that career shocks may influence employees' intentions to voluntarily quit their jobs (Holtom, Lee and Mitchell, 2005; Lee and Mitchell, 1994). Applying the lens of conservation of resources theory, this chapter explores how a lack of access to appropriate coping resources impacted the women's decisions to 'step off' their management career ladders and seek out alternative career options. With a growing recognition of the business case for having women at senior levels in organizations (Carter, Simkins and Simpson, 2003; CIPD, 2018), this chapter provides insights into how both organizations and individuals may incorporate career shocks into their career development plans.

THEORETICAL UNDERPINNINGS

Defining Career Shocks

Despite investing time and energy in planning a career path, an individual does not always have control over how his or her career will evolve (Sullivan et al., 2003). For example, an individual may have agency to trigger transitions such as taking on a new role or applying for a promotion; however, there will be little agency involved in transitions such as being laid off or having to cope with the effects of long-term illness. In their review of the literature on trending topics in career development, Akkermans and Kubasch (2017) highlight that in contemporary career literature there has been much focus on individual agency, but there is limited reference to the impact that unexpected and externally triggered events may have on individual career paths. Akkermans, Seibert and Mol (2018) note that careers research needs to reflect on the impact of 'career shocks'; events that have a significant impact on individual career plans, which they define in the following way (Akkermans et al., 2018, p. 4):

> [A] disruptive and extraordinary event that is, at least to some degree, caused by factors outside the focal individual's control and that triggers a deliberate thought

process concerning one's career. The occurrence of a career shock can vary in terms of predictability, and can be either positively or negatively valanced.

There are a number of components to this definition that are worthy of further discussion. First, career shocks are significant events that are experienced by most individuals over their life course (Scott and Hatalla, 1990). They may occur in the personal domain (for example, an illness) or in the organizational domain (for example, a company merger) (Lee and Mitchell, 1994). Second, shocks may be experienced negatively, neutrally, or positively (Akkermans et al., 2018; Lee and Mitchell, 1994; Seibert et al., 2013). For example, taking on a promotion is likely to be a positive experience, a new line manager may be a neutral experience, and a layoff is likely to be a negative experience (Holtom et al., 2005).

Third, career shocks are generally unexpected and outside the control of the individual. As such, there is limited opportunity for pre-emptive and proactive planning (Akkermans et al., 2018; Holtom et al., 2005). Akkermans et al. (2018) distinguish between *predictability* and *controllability* and stress that the degree of predictability and controllability may have a differential impact on shock valence and career decisions. For example, having a child is a relatively predictable and controllable event and likely to be positively valanced; however, encountering postnatal health issues for either the mother or the child is less predictable or controllable and likely to be negatively valanced. Finally, career shocks initiate a deliberate thought process about careers (Akkermans et al., 2018; Holtom et al., 2005; Lee and Mitchell, 1994). Holtom et al. (2005, p. 341) define a career shock as 'a distinguishable event that jars an employee toward deliberate judgements about his or her job'. As such, fundamental to the concept of career shocks is that they trigger individuals to 'take stock' and evaluate their careers, prompting them to make specific career decisions that may substantially alter their personal career plans (Akkermans et al., 2018; Bright, Pryor and Harpham, 2005; Holtom et al., 2005; Lee and Mitchell, 1994; Seibert et al., 2013). Career shocks have the potential therefore to impact both personal and organizational career development plans (Akkermans et al., 2018; Holtom et al., 2005).

Conservation of Resources Theory

A central tenet of conservation of resources theory is that individuals strive to acquire and preserve the resources they value (Hobfoll, 1998, 2001). Hobfoll categorizes resources as object resources (such as a house), personal characteristics (such as self-efficacy), condition resources (such as status), and energies (such as hope). Stress occurs when (1) individuals are threatened with the loss of their valued resources; (2) valued resources are lost; or (3) individuals fail to gain valued resources despite significant personal investment (Hobfoll, 2001). Furthermore, Hobfoll (2001) notes that resource loss begets further resource loss (resource spirals), while resource gain begets further gain (resource caravans).

Within the workplace, resources have an intrinsic value and, as such, a motivating effect, as they not only buffer the demands of the workplace but may also form a basis for flourishing and growth (Gorgievski, Halbesleben and Bakker, 2011). Hobfoll (2011) therefore notes that organizations can either create conditions that support and foster individual resource investment or an environment that undermines investment. He posits that organizations that imbue employees with the necessary resources and provide a climate of safety and stability will benefit in terms of greater employee resilience, commitment and engagement. Alternatively, he posits that organizations that do not deliver a resource-enhancing ecology will struggle to sustain long-term employee investment.

RESEARCH DESIGN AND PARTICIPANTS

Visual research methods have been used successfully in studies that focus on transition (for example, Barner, 2008; Stiles, 2004). This study adopted a time-line structure to enable chronology and sequencing of events, retrospection and sensemaking (Chell, 2004; Cohen and Mallon, 2001). Additionally, drawing was adopted to facilitate the exploration of complex, multifaceted and emotive issues that are often difficult to articulate verbally (Bagnoli, 2009; Barner, 2008; Broussine, 2008; Meyer, 1991; Stiles, 2004; Warren, 2009). Participants were recruited using a snowball sampling strategy and were invited to participate in a one-to-one interview. At the time of the study, they had all held, or were currently employed in, a range of management positions. The women in the study were aged between 30 and 70 and were based in the UK. The women 'drew' a timeline of their careers and included emoticons (smiley faces or sad faces) to symbolize positively valanced and negatively valanced career shocks. The 'visual timelines' approach enabled a range of career shocks to be explored over the timeline of a career, facilitating an analysis of the factors informing 'positive' or 'negative' appraisal (Mazzetti, 2014; Mazzetti and Blenkinsopp, 2012).[1]

FINDINGS

While not a homogeneous group, the women shared many similar career shocks. Analysis of the data highlighted four key themes worthy of further discussion as they ultimately influenced the women's decisions to 'step off' the career ladder. For each theme, a vignette is presented to explore the themes in more detail. The names used in the vignettes are pseudonyms and some details have been omitted to protect the identity of the participants. The quotations in italics refer to the notes written on the timelines by the participants.

Inputs versus Outputs Imbalance

Vignette 1

Jessica considered that gaining a senior role with prestige and status had been a significant achievement in her career. She drew a smiling medal with the word '*1st*' on her timeline and a picture of herself celebrating on top of a high building. She described the benefits of being in this position using the words '*more money, esteem, status and recognition*' on her timeline. However, she described that over a four-year period, she had to invest significantly to stay '*on top*'. She noted on her timeline that she was working 60 hours a week to meet her '*senior management team high standards of work quality*'. She considered that her role had become a '*prison with no release*'. She noted on her chart '*fear of falling*' as she feared that the investment required to sustain the performance levels required was having an adverse impact on her health and her family. When she was diagnosed with a serious illness, Jessica considered that she had reached '*breaking point*' and needed to revaluate the investment of her time. She experienced this as being a very stressful time, during which she felt '*confused*'. After 18 months of illness and sick leave, during which time she felt let down by the '*lack of support*' from her organization, Jessica decided to resign from her position. Jessica was still considering her future career options at the time of our discussion.

Jessica's story illustrates how an initially positively valanced career shock, a promotion, can, over time, become negatively valanced. Her failing health and worries about being able to sustain the level of investment in her role ultimately led her to leave her organization. In the context of conservation of resources theory, she had invested considerable personal resources (in terms of time, commitment and personal sacrifice) and yet she perceived they had not been justly rewarded by her organization in terms of condition resources (organizational support), or energy resources (time to recover from her illness). This perceived input/output imbalance ultimately led her to leave her organization.

Unsupportive Line Managers

Vignette 2

June considered her experience of extended absence from work due to routine surgery to be a significantly stressful period in her career. At the time, June had held a senior management position and noted on her timeline that she had always had a '*bumpy*' relationship with her line manager. However, it was her line manager's handling of her absence that '*broke the relationship*'. June described her pre-operation handover meeting as '*an out of body experience*' as she '*watched as they dismantled all* [she] *had achieved*'. After the surgery, June talked about struggling with her marginalization from her work identity. She explained that she '*checked emails hourly*' as she feared she was missing out on what was happening at work. She felt '*lonely and forgotten*' as she had limited contact with her organization. On her timeline, June noted '*THAT meeting*', to describe a tense visit she had experienced with her line manager about her return to work. At the meeting her manager made it clear that she did not want June to return to her 'old' role, and instead offered her a '*sideways move*', a role that June considered was '*less prestigious*'. June considered that the move had sent her '*back to the start again*'. On her return to work, June talked about her struggle to '*reconnect*', '*rebuild identity*' and '*rebuild self*'. After a short period in her new role, June decided to leave the organization. She was still considering her future options when we met.

June's vignette highlights the issue of the controllability of career shocks and the impact that line managers have on their handling of career shock episodes. Although her routine operation was a predictable event, the process of how her absence was managed was controlled by her manager. Having limited control over the direction of her career was her catalyst to 'step off' her career ladder. Considering the lens of conservation of resources theory, poor leadership created an environment in which she experienced the loss of condition resources (a supportive work environment) and personal resources (self-esteem and confidence).

Work–Life Balance

Vignette 3
Jillian relocated with her husband to the US. Before the relocation, she had been working in a senior professional role that demanded '*significant collaboration and decision making*'. Not only did she have to leave her job and relocate, but she also had to leave her family support network who had helped her in the UK with childcare. Jillian explained that initially she had enjoyed the break from her stressful role, but she was mindful that she did not want to become '*bored*', '*lonely*' or '*deskilled*'. Jillian decided to volunteer her professional services for a number of community groups and charities in her new area. She considered that this enabled her to keep up to date with the professional world to which she belonged. After eight years, the family relocated back to the UK and Jillian took up another senior role. She had considered that her volunteering roles had enabled her not only to explain the gap in her CV but also to keep her skills current. When we met, she was still active in her local community and had

continued to voluntarily offer her professional services to a number of charity organizations.

Jillian's story highlights how a sense of agency and control in developing the 'future' self may positively influence uncontrollable career shocks. Jillian was proactive in investing her time to plan for her future career by volunteering her skills for community organizations as a means of keeping up to date with developments in her profession. In terms of conservation of resources theory, Jillian had to deal with a number of resource losses. However, she focused on investing her time into developing future personal and energy resources in terms of enhanced skills and knowledge.

A Series of Career Shocks

Vignette 4

Over a two-year period, Jane noted a series of significant events including her husband's setting up of a new business and their relocation to a new area to live and work, a difficult relationship with her new line manager, the death of a close family member and the birth of their first child. Jane discussed how this was an overwhelming time for her and she had subsequently taken a period of sickness absence due to stress and depression. On her timeline she noted '*new baby, new business, no family, no friends, no job, no confidence*'. Jane's feelings were further exacerbated by the lack of routine she was experiencing due to being away from work and the difficulties she was having in adjusting to her medication. As the time approached for her to return to work, Jane explained that she doubted her ability to return. She noted on her timeline, '*can I still do this?*' Jane discussed how her lack of confidence was a key factor in her decision to leave her job. She considered that the decline in her self-confidence was caused by her manager who '*kept questioning* [her] *judgement*' and also by her conflicting emotions during her period of absence, noting that she had difficulty trying to define and identify who she had become. However, Jane noted that her decision to leave had created further anxieties and '*feelings of failure*'. Jane highlighted that she had also been concerned about the impact that a break in her career due to stress and depression might have on her future career prospects. She noted '*I'll never get another job if they think I'm a headcase*'.[2]

The use of the timelines approach enabled the chronology and sequencing of events to be captured. A frequent observation was the number of shocks that can happen within a relatively short space of time. Jane's story highlights the intense impact of a series of career shocks on personal well-being, sense of self and self-confidence in one's abilities. Her lack of self-confidence and her concerns over how her period of absence would be perceived by others had left her doubting if she would be able to re-enter the workplace. In the context of conservation of resources theory, she experienced a resource spiral as initial resource losses begat further resource losses.

DISCUSSION

The women's stories highlight the significant impact that career shocks can have on individual well-being and commitment to engage with their organization. From an individual's perspective, career shocks create uncertainty (Akkermans et al., 2018) as they disrupt the normal way of functioning and have the potential to conflict with personal goals, values and aspirations (Lazarus, 1999). Shocks may also place too much of a demand on an individual and tax his or her available coping resources (Halbesleben et al., 2014). Furthermore, career shocks are likely to disrupt personal evaluations of career image and identity (Akkermans et al., 2018) by disrupting the coherence of personal career 'stories', forcing individuals to engage in identity work to make sense of their world (Ibarra, 2003; Ibarra and Lineback, 2005). Career shocks therefore have the potential to be salient stressors impacting individual well-being and 'sense of self' (Sveningsson and Alvesson, 2003). From an organizational perspective, career shocks may lead to individuals disengaging with their organizations (Halbesleben, 2006) or quitting their organizations in order to pursue alternative career paths (Holtom et al., 2005). In the context of 'the leaky pipeline', career shocks may force women to evaluate their careers and decide that walking away from their careers is their best option. As such, a better understanding of the impact of career shocks may help organizations address this dysfunctional labour turnover (Lee and Mitchell, 1994). Drawing on the findings from this research study, three recommendations are put forward to facilitate the incorporation of career shocks into personal career planning and organizational talent and retention planning. These will now be discussed in more detail.

Creating Resource-enhancing Work Environments

Many of the women talked about their perceived imbalance between the efforts put in to sustain their role and the output they received in terms of organizational support and acknowledgement. Elraz (2018) highlights that high-performance cultures place a high value on performance and achievements and, as such, there is a negative perception of those who are perceived as not performing to the culturally established norm (see also Chapter 6 by Datta and Shah). O'Neil and Bilimoria (2005) highlight that male-defined perceptions of performance pervade organizational work cultures and, as such, Mavin et al. (2015, p. 312) suggest that women will frequently have to confront 'masculine heroic leader expectations' of performance. Organizations therefore need to address the issue of how 'performance' is culturally defined and measured within their institutions (CMI, 2013b; Mavin et al., 2015). Women's definitions of merit might look different from men's and, therefore, organizations need to acknowledge that there is more than one predefined 'norm' (CMI, 2013a). Organizations should strive to foster a more supportive performance culture – for example, by measuring performance in terms of one's output rather than by hours spent at one's desk (CMI, 2014).

Additionally, women still tend to take on the primary caregiver roles for both children and other dependants, and their career decisions are moulded by work–family pressures (O'Neil and Bilimoria, 2005). Women therefore often make 'satisficing choices', putting their families' well-being before their career advancement (see also Chapter 6 by Datta and Shah). Recent research suggests that childcare is still one of the main barriers to women progressing in the workplace, accounting for women in their late 20s and 30s dropping out of the workforce and women in their 40s failing to return (CMI, 2013b). There is therefore a need to foster more inclusive work cultures that provide women with the condition resources (for example, in terms of flexible working patterns) to enable women to continue in their careers while continuing to maintain their family responsibilities (O'Neil and Bilimoria, 2005). Bardoel et al. (2014) suggest a range of supportive work practices such as the development of strong workplace social support networks; occupational health, safety and employee assistance programmes; and flexible work arrangements, reward and benefits systems. Furthermore, organizations need to invest in the training and development of line managers not only to enable them to implement more inclusive measures of performance (CMI, 2014) but also to address negative work relationships that lead to employee depersonalization and disengagement (Halbesleben, 2006).

Investment in Early Support Interventions

The loss of one resource begets the loss of other resources (Hobfoll, 2001). As such, it is imperative that organizations create 'resource caravans' that can ameliorate the impact of resource loss (Hobfoll, 2011). Hobfoll (2001) posits that the value ascribed to resources may be specific to the organizational context (such as prestige and status) or more universal (such as health, well-being and a positive sense of self). Five of the women in this study had experienced periods of ill health. Elraz (2018) suggests that it is difficult for someone who is ill to situate themselves within a high-performance culture as they must not only invest resources in managing their condition but also in managing the stigma associated with poor performance. She highlights that this may have a knock-on impact in terms of a worsening of their condition. Foster (2017) further suggests that this may be particularly the case for those with 'invisible' disorders such as mental health conditions. She suggests that a focus on 'ableism' may prevent disclosure of invisible conditions, which in turn leads to a worsening of health. Some of the women talked about their reluctance to disclose their conditions, and this was particularly the case for those dealing with stress, anxiety and depression. They considered their work cultures a contributing factor to the worsening of their condition. For some, this impacted their ongoing willingness to engage with their organization; and for others contributed to their resource spiral. This highlights the need for organizations to deal with the issue of stigma and to develop a climate of trust to facilitate early interventions that may ultimately provide the necessary nurturing climate for both a safe disclosure of the condition and also a successful return to work (Follmer and Jones, 2018; Leufstadiusa, Eklunda and Erlandsson, 2009). For example, Follmer and Jones (2018) suggest peer support networks, regular union and employee communications, strong employee assistance programmes, and continuous contact between the organization and employees during a period of sickness absence.

Women as Project

Mavin et al. (2015) suggest that the work–life interface should not be a barrier to women progressing in their careers, as women should take agency in both balancing their work and family commitments and investing in their long-term careers. For example, they suggest that women should be proactive in searching out organizations that have a good reputation for 'women-readiness' and that women put in place a sound infrastructure to manage their work and family commitments. Additionally, Mavin et al. (2015, p. 316) suggest that women need to 'balance exceptional credibility without working too hard to prevent exhaustion'. They highlight that in the context of high-performance work cultures, women need to see themselves as 'the project', ensuring that they invest efforts into their own personal development as well as their organization's development.

   Career shocks initiate a period of reflection and decision-making about one's future career. Beatty and McGonagle (2016) suggest that proactive career coaching may be of benefit in such circumstances, as coaching may facilitate the sensemaking process. Additionally, having access to internal and external female role models in senior positions may provide an effective support network for women struggling to come to terms with the challenges they are encountering within the workplace or their dilemmas regarding their next career steps (CMI 2013a, 2013b, 2014; Mavin et al., 2015).

CONCLUSION

Despite growing numbers of women participating in the workplace, the number of women in senior management positions is still surprising low. Applying the lens of conservation of resources theory, this chapter presents the experiences of four women who lost valued resources as a result of career shocks. Their experiences resulted in the women opting to 'step off' their career ladders rather than continuing in their management positions. This chapter puts forward three recommendations to support women incorporating career shocks into their personal career development planning and also to support organizations to incorporate career shocks into their talent retention planning.

NOTES

1. Pictures from the timelines are available from the author.
2. A colloquial term for 'being mad'.

REFERENCES

Akkermans, J. and S. Kubasch (2017), 'Trending topics in careers: a review and future research agenda', *Career Development International*, **22**(6), 586–627.

Akkermans, J., S.E. Seibert and S.T. Mol (2018), 'Tales of the unexpected: integrating career shocks in the contemporary careers literature', *SA Journal of Industrial Psychology*, **44**(0), 1–10.

Astin, H.S. (1984), 'The meaning of work in women's lives: a sociopsychological model of career choice and work behaviour', *The Counseling Psychologist*, **12**(4), 117–26.

Bagnoli, A. (2009), 'Beyond the standard interview: the use of graphic elicitation and arts-based methods', *Qualitative Research*, **9**(5), 547–70.

Bardoel, E.A., T. Pettit, H. De Cieri and L. McMillan (2014), 'Employee resilience: an emerging challenge for HRM', *Asia Pacific Journal of Human Resources*, **52**(3), 1–19.

Barner, R. (2008), 'The dark tower: using visual metaphors to facilitate emotional expression during organizational change', *Journal of Organizational Change Management*, **21**(10), 120–37.

Beatty, J.E. and A. McGonagle (2016), 'Coaching employees with chronic illness: supporting professional identities through biographical work', *International Journal of Evidence Based Coaching and Mentoring*, **14**(1), 1–15.

Bright, J.E.H., R.G.L. Pryor and L. Harpham (2005), 'The role of chance events in career decision making', *Journal of Vocational Behavior*, **66**(3), 561–76.

Broussine, M. (ed.) (2008), *Creative Methods in Organizational Research*, London: Sage.

Carter, D.A., B.J. Simkins and W.A. Simpson (2003), 'Corporate governance, board diversity and firm value', *The Financial Review*, **38**(1), 33–53.

Chartered Institute of Personnel and Development (CIPD) (2018), *Diversity and Inclusion at Work: Facing Up to the Business Case*, accessed 4 October 2019 at https://www.cipd.co.uk/Images/diversity-and-inclusion-at-work_2018-facing-up-to-the-business-case-1_tcm18-44146.pdf.

Chartered Management Institute (CMI) (2013a), *Women in Management: Tackling the Talent Pipeline* [white paper], accessed 4 October 2019 at https://www.managers.org.uk/insights/research/current-research/2013/november/women-in-management-tackling-the-talent-pipeline.

Chartered Management Institute (CMI) (2013b), *Women in Leadership* [white paper], accessed 4 October 2019 at https://www.managers.org.uk/insights/research/current-research/2013/march/women-in-leadership-white-paper?sc_trk=follow%20hit,{86CB756B-AB02-44E6-995A-305C69252B29},women+in+leadership.

Chartered Management Institute (CMI) (2014), *Women in Management: The Power of Role Models* [white paper], accessed 4 October 2019 at https://www.managers.org.uk/insights/research/current-research/2014/may/the-power-of-role-models?sc_trk=follow%20hit,{86CB756B-AB02-44E6-995A-305C69252B29},role+models.

Chell, E. (2004), 'Critical incident technique', in C. Cassell and G. Symon (eds), *Essential Guide to Qualitative Methods in Organizational Research*, London: Sage, pp. 45–60.

Cohen, L. and M. Mallon (2001), 'My brilliant career? Using stories as a methodological tool in careers research', *International Studies of Management & Organization*, **31**(3), 48–68.

Davies, M. (2015), *Improving the Gender Balance of British Boards: Women on Boards Davies Review: Five Year Summary October 2015*, accessed 4 October 2019 at https://www.gov.uk/government/publications/women-on-boards-5-year-summary-davies-review.

Elraz, H. (2018), 'Identity, mental health and work: how employees with mental health conditions recount stigma and the pejorative discourse of mental illness', *Human Relations*, **71**(5), 722–41.

Follmer, K.A. and K.S. Jones (2018), 'Mental illness in the workplace: an interdisciplinary review and organizational research agenda', *Journal of Management*, **44**(1), 325–51.

Foster, D. (2017), 'The health and well-being at work agenda: good news for (disabled) workers or just a capital idea?', *Work, Employment & Society*, **32**(1), 186–97.

Gorgievski, M.J., J.R.B. Halbesleben and A.B. Bakker (2011), 'Expanding the boundaries of psychological resource theories', *Journal of Occupational and Organizational Psychology*, **84**(1), 1–7.

Halbesleben, J.R.B. (2006), 'Sources of social support and burnout: a meta-analytic test of the conservation of resources model', *Journal of Applied Psychology*, **91**(5), 1134–45.

Halbesleben, J.R.B., J.P. Neveu, S.C. Paustian-Underdahl and M. Westman (2014), 'Getting to the "COR": understanding the role of resources in conservation of resources theory', *Journal of Management*, **40**(5), 1334–64.

Hobfoll, S.E. (ed.) (1998), *Stress, Culture, and Community: The Psychology and Philosophy of Stress*, New York: Plenum Press.

Hobfoll, S.E. (2001), 'The influence of culture, community, and the nested-self in the stress process: advancing conservation of resources theory', *Applied Psychology: An International Review*, **50**(3), 337–70.

Hobfoll, S.E. (2011), 'Conservation of resource caravans and engaged settings', *Journal of Occupational and Organizational Psychology*, **84**(1), 116–22.

Hoffarth, V.B. (1996), 'Perspectives on career development of women in management', *Equal Opportunities International*, **15**(3), 21–43.

Holtom, B.C., T. Lee and T. Mitchell (2005), 'Shocks as causes of turnover: what they are and how organizations can manage them', *Human Resource Management*, **44**(3), 337–52.

Ibarra, H. (ed.) (2003), *Working Identity: Unconventional Strategies for Reinventing Your Career*, Boston, MA: Harvard Business School Press.

Ibarra, H. and K. Lineback (2005), 'What's your story?', *Harvard Business Review*, **83**(1), 64–71.

Johnston, D.W. and W. Lee (2012), 'Climbing the job ladder: new evidence of gender inequality', *Industrial Relations*, **51**(1), 129–49.

Lazarus, R. (ed.) (1999), *Stress and Emotion*, New York: Springer Publishing Company.

Lee, T.W. and T.R. Mitchell (1994), 'An alternative approach: the unfolding model voluntary employee turnover', *Academy of Management Review*, **19**(1), 51–89.

Leufstadiusa, C., M. Eklunda and L. Erlandsson (2009), 'Meaningfulness in work – experiences among employed individuals with persistent mental illness', *Work*, **34**(1), 21–32.

Mavin, S., J. Williams, P. Bryans and N. Patterson (2015), 'Woman as project: key issues for women who want to get on', in A. Broadbridge and S. Fielden (eds), *Handbook of Gendered Careers in Management: Getting In, Getting On and Getting Out*, Cheltenham, UK and Northampton, MA, USA: Edward Elgar Publishing, pp. 305–21.

Mazzetti, A. (2014), 'Using a visual timeline method in stress research', *Sage Research Methods Cases*, accessed 4 October 2019 at https://methods.sagepub.com/case/using-a-visual-timeline-method-in-stress-research.

Mazzetti, A. and J. Blenkinsopp (2012), 'Evaluating a visual timeline methodology for appraisal and coping research', *Journal of Occupational and Organizational Psychology*, **85**(4), 649–65.

Meyer, A.D. (1991), 'Visual data in organizational research', *Organization Science*, **2**(2), 218–36.

O'Neill, D.A. and D. Bilimoria (2005), 'Women's career development phases: idealism, endurance, and reinvention', *Career Development International*, **10**(3), 168–89.

Scott, J. and J. Hatalla (1990), 'The influence of change and contingency factors on career patterns of college-educated women', *The Career Development Quarterly*, **39**(1), 18–30.

Seibert, S.E., M.L. Kraimer, B.C. Holtom and A.J. Pierotti (2013), 'Even the best laid plans sometimes go askew: career self-management processes, career shocks, and the decision to pursue graduate education', *Journal of Applied Psychology*, **98**(1), 169–82.

Stiles, D. (2004), 'Pictorial representation', in C. Cassell and G. Symon (eds), *Essential Guide to Qualitative Methods in Organizational Research*, London: Sage, pp. 127–39.

Sullivan, S., D.F. Martin, W.A. Carden and L.A. Mainiero (2003), 'The road less travelled: how to manage the recycling career stage', *Journal of Leadership and Organizational Studies*, **10**(2), 34–42.

Sveningsson, S. and M. Alvesson (2003), 'Managing managerial identities: organizational fragmentation, discourse and identity struggle', *Human Relations*, **56**(10), 1163–93.

Warren, S. (2009), 'Visual methods in organizational research', in D. Buchanan and A. Bryman (eds), *The SAGE Handbook of Organizational Research Methods*, London: Sage, pp. 566–82.

PART IV

MBA careers across the globe

Both chapters on this topic demonstrate how contextual factors influence individual career decisions and outcomes of MBA alumni. In one chapter, they study MBAs from a limited number of schools in the same country. In the other chapter, they study alumni from the same MBA degree but who studied in different countries. They both illustrate that an MBA degree is not universal; its value differs between contexts.

Vivek G. Nair and Leena Chatterjee write on 'Economic structural changes and subjective career success of MBAs in India'. They study two cohorts of Indian MBA alumni from a selected group of programmes: one cohort who got their MBA degrees before the Liberalization, Privatization and Globalization (LPG) reforms in the early 1990s and another cohort who graduated after these reforms. The LPG reforms changed India from a centralized to a liberal market economy. The qualitative study shows how perceptions of career success differ between alumni who graduated before or after the reform. Whereas the 'older' MBA alumni attach importance to 'giving back to society', the 'younger' are more concerned with their individual growth and development.

Elizabeth Houldsworth, Chris Brewster and Richard McBain's chapter titled 'How an MBA contributes to the unfolding of careers: a comparative analysis' also studies how differences in the economic structure influence career outcomes of MBA alumni. Instead of looking at changes in the economic structure of one country, they study how alumni of one and the same UK-based MBA programme develop different careers based on the economy they live in. That is, they hold the 'brand' of the programme constant and compare four groups of alumni based on their regional location. They find that the four groups of alumni differ in the career choices, career outcomes and satisfaction gained after completing their MBAs.

An MBA degree has value in a global world. Yet, this value is not universal. It remains context specific. Both chapters show that the context in which MBA holders' careers take form is highly influential in shaping the paths they develop. Moreover, a particular contextual factor is the openness of the host economy. The consistency of the interdependence between MBA graduates' careers and their surrounding context encourages deeper exploration of the nature of that interdependence for other professional groups and degrees. You may also want to consider what these two chapters suggest for any qualification you or other employees hold, and how its value depends on the particular context of the work.

8. Economic structural changes and subjective career success of MBAs in India

Vivek G. Nair and Leena Chatterjee

INTRODUCTION

A highly competitive global business environment, together with advancements in technology, diversity in family structures, and changing demography are shaping contemporary careers all over the world (Greenhaus and Kossek, 2014). Such a globalized economy can both offer opportunities (such as new growth sectors and innovative business models) and entail risks (such as job losses due to newer technology) to an individual's career. The type of career opportunities available varies depending on where one is located in the global economy. This is nicely illustrated in the paired chapter by Houldsworth et al. (Chapter 9). Their study shows that career outcomes for alumni who attended a common MBA programme are different depending on the economic structure in which they live. The location of this chapter is India, which provides a point of comparison with MBAs from the Western world.

We present an emic view from India, based on in-depth, semi-structured interviews of 38 MBA graduates. More specifically, we showcase how structural changes in the Indian economy, commonly referred to as the LPG (Liberalization, Privatization and Globalization) reforms affected perceptions of career success among Indian MBAs. The study addresses an identified research gap wherein the impact of LPG reforms on individual careers, particularly of experienced professionals, has received limited attention.

LITERATURE REVIEW

Subjective Career Success

Scholars have distinguished between objective and subjective careers (Khapova, Arthur and Wilderom, 2007). While the subjective career refers to an individual's personal interpretation of his or her career situation at any given time, the objective career refers to parallel interpretations provided by society, usually based on formal structures within organizations. With widespread changes to the global context, the traditional notion of a career within a few organizations is becoming replaced by boundaryless (Arthur and Rousseau, 1996) and protean (Hall, 2004) perspectives, where careers are increasingly self-directed. In such a context, objective measures of career success such as promotions or salary increases become less salient and subjective notions of career success gain in prominence.

Subjective career success captures 'individuals' subjective judgments about their career attainments' (Ng et al., 2005, p. 368). These individual judgments are likely to be influenced by the context in which the careers unfold. In this regard, the 5C (Cross-Cultural Collaboration on Contemporary Careers) project is a major collaborative effort by career researchers to seek a 'globally applicable view of how people understand their career, career success and career transitions' (Mayrhofer et al., 2016, p. 198). Such a view acknowledges the value of an emic perspective, that is, careers experiences reported from within the context, without an over-reliance on preformed categorizations (Tams and Arthur, 2007). As part of the 5C project, researchers conducted semi-structured interviews of participants belonging to different cultural clusters in their local languages and identified seven globally relevant meanings or dimensions of career success (Mayrhofer et al., 2016). These were financial security, financial achievement, learning and development, work–life balance, positive relationships, positive impact and entrepreneurship. Different cultures, genders and age cohorts are likely to value each of these differently. Studies have suggested that at low levels of economic development, meanings of career success are quite simple (Kaše et al., 2018; Mayrhofer et al., 2016). Only after some assurance of financial security do individuals seek or value other dimensions of career success (for instance, seeking work–life balance or entrepreneurial pursuits) (Mayrhofer et al., 2016).

Research has found that national cultural dimensions such as collectivism, power distance and uncertainty avoidance moderate the relation between proactive career behaviours and two dimensions of career success, namely, financial achievement and work–life balance (Smale et al., 2019). Another study included the impact of institutional factors such as general country development, labour market flexibility and standardization of education systems on the various subjective meanings of career success (Kaše et al., 2018). Based on a cognitive mapping of 28 participants from each country across seven occupational strata and both genders, the study found Indians to have the lowest within-country convergence. Given that the other countries included highly individualistic countries such as the US, Belgium, Italy and Norway, the data suggests that notions of career success could vary across different occupational strata within India. We therefore study the subjective notions of career success among a more focused sample of Indian MBAs.

Indian Economy

India's economy has undergone major changes over its 70 years of independent history. After independence, India initially relied largely on central planning and public sector enterprises to drive the economy. However, in the early 1990s, triggered by a foreign currency crisis, India started opening up its economy to greater private and foreign investments (Prashad, 2013). As a result, several multinational enterprises (MNEs) entered India. Domestic firms also upgraded their capabilities to cope with increased competition (Krishnan and Jha, 2011). Simultaneously, the government started a process of diluting its stake in various public sector undertakings (PSUs). The structural changes to the Indian economy are often captured under the label 'LPG reforms'.

Since the early 1990s, India's gross domestic product (GDP) has been growing at an average rate of about 7 per cent (World Bank, 2017). The economy grew to five times its size in 1993. The Indian middle-class population grew from 25 million in 1995–96 to 153 million in 2009–10 (Shukla, 2010). Much of the growth has been driven by IT, IT-enabled services and financial services owing to factors such as the availability of low-cost skilled personnel who could speak English and reliable Internet connectivity (Fernandes and Heller, 2006; Kapur and Ramamurti, 2001). The economic growth has led to improvements in living conditions in India. Between 1990 and 2017, India's Human Development Index (HDI) value increased by nearly 50 per cent, which implies longer lifespans (by 11 years) and more years of schooling (by 4.7 years) (United Nations Development Programme, 2018). In higher education (18–23 years), the gross enrolment ratio rose from 8.1 per cent in 2001–02 to 25.8 per cent in 2017–18 (Ministry of Human Resource Development, 2018).

In the context of LPG reforms, HR functions of organizations in India were more focused on organizational performance (Cooke and Budhwar, 2015). One of the key challenges identified relates to dealing with age-based diversity, as younger employees are typically more educated and have different aspirations. So far, there is limited research on the impact of LPG reforms on individual careers. Kulkarni (2006) contends that increasing demands to learn new skills and adopt new ways of work may lead to burnout. Finally, various scholars agree that these economic reforms are likely to bring about generational differences (Erickson, 2009; Ghosh and Chaudhuri, 2013; Srinivasan, 2012) and that the beneficiaries of this growth include the professional-managerial class (Fernandes and Heller, 2006). Placement records at India's top management schools have been excellent, wherein students get multiple offers and typically the entire group gets placed in three to four days. In our study, therefore, we study the impact of LPG reforms on a sample of Indian MBA graduates.

Career Studies in the Indian Context

India is often characterized as a culture with high power distance and moderate levels of collectivism (Hofstede, 1984; Hofstede Insights, 2017). Ancient India also provides the *ashrama* (life-stage) system, which takes a lifespan approach and outlines specific duties for each of the four stages of life (Arulmani and Nag-Arulmani, 2004). In the first stage called *brahmacharya ashrama*, one is expected to complete one's education. In the second stage, called *grihastha ashrama*, an individual gets married and provides for the family. One of the primary roles in this stage is that of a worker, and the production of wealth, wherein pursuit of personal prosperity is regarded as a life duty (Arulmani, 2007). In the third stage, called *vanaprastha ashrama*, the individual is expected to continue to work with vigour, but to serve society and not only to fulfil the objective for personal gain. Finally, in the *sanyasa ashrama*, the individual is to be devoted purely to spiritual service. This framework is deeply embedded in Indian culture and such cultural beliefs may be useful in career counselling (Arulmani, 2011). However, such expectations may also translate into societal pressures that specify age limits to start earning and get married.

Career research in India has largely focused on the impact of family or cultural dimensions (particularly collectivism) on career development (Agarwala, 2008; Bhatnagar and Rajadhyaksha, 2001; Thatchenkery and Koizumi, 2010). Most of the studies typically studied young employees (in their early 20s) or purely student populations and have found parents to be a significant influence on individual careers. A notable exception to the above pattern is the study of Indian managers from a ten-year longitudinal inquiry of MBA graduates of the Indian Institute of Management (IIM) Ahmedabad (Garg and Parikh, 1994). The study interviewed 125 men who graduated from 1972 to 1976, and results indicate that participants' attempts to apply management techniques that they had learned were at odds with traditional Indian management practices. Changes in spending habits, a common two-year stay away from home and new life roles due to marriage also raised significant adjustment issues in reintegrating with the family. However, with joint – that is, intergenerational – household structures weakening among the urban, educated, professional class (Shah, 1996), MBAs are likely to face different challenges today.

METHOD

Research question. The changes to the Indian economy in a distinct cultural setting are likely to have had an impact on individual careers and subjective career success. Hence, our broad research question was: how did economic structural changes impact subjective career success among Indian MBAs?

Following Rodrigues, Guest and Budjanovcanin (2013), we used qualitative methods as the research sought to understand 'how' the opportunities and challenges were perceived and 'why' individuals responded in certain ways. Therefore, semi-structured interviews were conducted with the participants.

Participants. We selected experienced MBA graduates as the sample. Participants were selected across a diverse age range (from 27 to 67 years) to capture changes in context over time. Participants were approached through personal contacts and subsequent snowballing. Thirty-eight MBA graduates were interviewed. The sample's average age was 42 years and included nine women (24 per cent).

Data collection. Questions in the interview protocol pertained to educational and family background, past career choices, career goals and significant experiences/achievements. All interviews, except one, were audio-recorded with permission and then fully transcribed. For the interview that was not recorded (at the participant's request) we took detailed notes. Interviews lasted 89 minutes on average. Most of the interviews were conducted between August 2017 and April 2018.

Data analysis. We followed a thematic analysis approach (Braun and Clarke, 2006). We grouped our sample into two roughly equal cohorts based on age. One cohort had participants aged above 40 (we refer to them as the older cohort, averaging age 50). Someone of average age would have been 25 in 1993. The rest were in the younger cohort, averaging 33 years old, with someone of average age being eight in 1993. The data was analysed by comparing and contrasting the participants' accounts from each of these cohorts, anticipating that differences between the cohorts might be observed and attributed to the LPG effect initiated in 1993.

The first author collated the excerpts from the transcripts and identified the themes. Meetings held with the second author helped to refine the themes further. For triangulation, we collected participants' résumés or LinkedIn profiles to cross-check their career paths. Their profile information and interview accounts were compared. Clarifications were obtained in cases of any discrepancy to obtain a more accurate view.

FINDINGS

We found two differences between the contexts that the two cohorts experienced in their careers. First, while the older cohort started their careers in the public or private sector, the younger cohort started their careers almost exclusively in the private sector. Second, we found that the two cohorts differed in the importance given to different dimensions of subjective career success. Excerpts from participant interviews are provided within quotation marks and marked with the participant's gender (M for Male, F for Female) and age (at the time of the interview).

All Roads Lead to Rome: The Different Paths to the Private Sector

Our participants in the older cohort joined the workforce in the 1980s and 1990s. At the time, the general perception was that one studied only till one secured a job. It was quite rare to pursue postgraduate degrees such as an MBA after one had secured a reputable well-paying job:

> Beyond BTech [undergraduate studies)] … He [my father] said, 'Now you're going to take pains because two more guys [siblings] are waiting. Up to graduation level, yes, it is my duty [to educate you]. After that, it is your own outlook'. So, I had to study and then foot the bill. (M, 55)

There were some instances of resistance from the family as this delayed marriage and the transition to the householder stage:

> My parents were absolutely upset … their ignorance level was so high … they were not willing to allow me to go. Very interestingly, they had looked for a girl, and they were very keen that marriage has to be fixed and all that stuff. In fact, they forced me to see the girl! (M, 60)

In the younger cohort, there was lesser resistance to pursuing an MBA. While 25 000 took the MBA entrance exam (CAT) in 1990, the number had risen to 241 000 in 2018 (Ministry of Human Resource Development, 2008; Saha, 2019). There is a large test preparation market that caters to these test-takers. Many participants in the younger cohort reported having studied in coaching centres for CAT.

In the 1980s and early 1990s, opportunities considered attractive were largely in the public sector. In the words of a participant from the older cohort, 'India was not awash with opportunities'. While jobs in the public sector may not have paid much, they offered stability and decent living conditions. Six of our participants in the older cohort had worked in public sector firms early in their careers. Even when participants in the older cohort joined the private sector, they had long stints in their first jobs. Participants in the older cohort-stayed with their first employer after their MBA for an average of seven years (median five years).

The older cohort seemed to transition from seeking financial security to other meanings of career success (outlined in the next section):

> Prior [to] 1991, I would say the [workplace] culture was lifelong employment. Both employers and employees used to be a little more kind and accommodative to each other. I have seen a drastic change after 1991. Neither the employer nor the employee is willing to accommodate each other. (M, 67)

With various sectors opening up in the 1990s, participants took advantage of the new employment opportunities that arose in domains such as insurance, investment banking and asset management. Gradually, the older cohort switched to the private sector. Such opportunities typically coincided with regulatory changes:

> In 1991, a company did not have the option of fixing its [stock issue] price. This was regulated by the government ... so when SEBI (Securities and Exchange Board of India) was set up around '92. They said, now, it is a free market pricing ... So, the role of merchant banker like [Company B] is to really work out a premium [for the stock]. (M, 54)

On the other hand, almost all the participants in the younger cohort had spent their entire careers in the private sector. Also, the younger cohort lasted about three years with their first employer after their MBA (though the median was close to 1.5 years). The younger cohort seemed to have started with valuing financial achievement and then moved on to other meanings of career success. '[When] I started working, all I wanted was a good job and a good salary. But now I think I seek more from my career in terms of my knowledge and personal development' (M, 32).

Over time, the gap between the two cohorts reduced, with the average duration with each employer being five years for the older cohort and three years for the younger cohort (median duration being three years for the older cohort and 2.5 years for the younger cohort). The convergence in the average duration with an employer could be due to contextual factors that affected both the cohorts in a similar manner. For instance, in the aftermath of the global financial meltdown in 2008, firms in various sectors merged or were acquired. Corporate decisions and protective measures taken in the more developed parts of the world triggered uncertainty regarding jobs in India. Since these decisions were not necessarily based on local realities, employees in India were sometimes caught unaware. As one participant recounted:

> Towards the end of 2011, the company in the US changed hands ... and they said we are no longer thinking of expanding beyond the US. So, they decided to shut down India, Latin America, so on and so forth. So that was that. (F, 47)

Thus, individuals had to find ways to cope with the possibility that such events could affect their careers without much notice: 'You have to be always prepared and always have your plan B ready if you are planning to be in business or in corporate' (M, 39).

In a competitive market, organizational fortunes could also fluctuate. For instance, 22 out of 50 index stocks (44 per cent) in the largest national stock exchange index could not retain their top spots in ten years (NSE Indices Limited, 2018). Participants reported having to deal with tremendous stress, particularly when companies resorted to playing 'the volume game' or pushing for sales targets. 'One of the key things [that made me quit] was the stress factor. I really understood that if I keep continuing to go there, I will also end up like my boss' (M, 36). The participant refers to his boss, who had a severe heart attack in his early 40s, as a victim of the pressures of work. Several participants reported health problems such as high blood pressure and gaining or losing weight, which they attributed to their long working hours or work-related stress.

Participants looked to maintain their employability by acquiring new skills or moving to fast-growing sectors. Participants reported updating their résumés and profiles regularly on job portals and professional networking websites to remain updated with the latest job opportunities. Participants also reported negotiating with multiple recruiters simultaneously to get better employment terms during a job search.

In sum, the path to the private sector was very different for the two cohorts. While the older cohort began their careers seeking stability, the younger cohort sought opportunities for financial achievement. Over time, circumstances such as the global recession affected both cohorts, leading to greater stress and uncertainty.

Meanings of Career Success: Difference Between Cohorts

In their interviews, our participants reflected on their career paths so far and outlook for the future. The two cohorts differed in terms of the importance attached to the various meanings of success in their current careers.

Positive impact for the older cohort

Participants in the older cohort felt a need to give back to the nation and society. However, they were quite disillusioned by profit-seeking corporations and did not expect any opportunity for positive impact there. A participant opined, 'At some fundamental level, the corporate system was flawed' (M, 52). Another referred to early influences: 'The economy was liberalized only after I passed the MBA, which was in 1988. Opportunities were limited, and thinking was different because you are used to a socialist kind of thinking' (M, 56). Participants reported meeting people from different walks of life, reading books and interactions with non-profits, which prompted them to measure success very differently. Participants felt they were not in control and their work was often not very meaningful: 'I had just lost sight of what difference was I making to anybody or anything' (F, 47). Or as another respondent (M, 52) said: 'In a corporate setting, the targets are half given to you. You may set the targets as a leader of the business, but it is still within a corporate set-up'. Participants coped with these feelings by opting for early retirement, focusing more on corporate social responsibility initiatives, moving to the non-profit sector or joining professions such as academia that are culturally perceived as nobler. Participants reported instances where they took a heavy pay cut (as high as 90 per cent) to join work environments where they could make a positive impact.

Participants noted that much of their education was subsidized. Some of them felt grateful for the government scholarships that they had received:

> I felt very uncomfortable [by] the fact that I have done OK in life and it was totally subsidized by the government. So, to that extent, I have assuaged whatever guilt I felt during that reunion. Whatever had to be done, I did. (M, 56)

Thus, alumni reunions and alumni associations were a mechanism through which participants tried to give back. Some participants took to teaching or mentoring youngsters in their spare time.

Growth or balance for the younger cohort

Participants in the younger cohort often had one out of the two career goals: opportunities for learning and development or work–life balance. A participant noted: 'The role was good, a lot of running around, a lot of work is happening but as per personal growth, there was a limitation' (M, 33). Another participant explained her motivators:

> Now because I'm financially secure, I can support my family fully. Obviously, that continues to be a motivator. But I think the larger motivator is … how can I really challenge myself and keep learning. (F, 31)

Other participants showed excitement towards emerging sectors such as the solar power and edu-tech industry.

Some of the participants in the younger cohort reported life roles related to family (being a parent, child, or spouse) as being salient; 'My daughter is the most important person in my life right now' (F, 34). The desire for work–life balance manifested mostly in terms of maintaining work hours or preferring to stay in one city, often with their parents: 'My son can grow up with my parents, which is something I value a lot' (M, 33). Another participant opined: 'As of now, I have been able to convince them [my company] that I want to be in Kolkata and no promotion is okay with me' (M, 33). Some participants in their early 40s, though technically in the older cohort, also sought balance. However, overall, these meanings of career success reduced in importance for older participants. In sum, the younger cohort focused on learning and development or work–life balance, while older participants were interested in exploring non-corporate avenues for creating a positive impact.

DISCUSSION

The above themes illustrate how individual careers are being dynamically shaped by economic structural changes. In spite of the global forces operating, career behaviours are largely in line with local cultural values.

Drawing parallels from Chapter 9 by Houldsworth et al., changes to the Indian economy can perhaps be best characterized as a shift from a social democratic economy (SDE) to a liberal market economy (LME). Our findings showcase MBAs' perceptions of objective changes to the broader structure of opportunities available to Indian MBA graduates. These changes led MBAs to adapt to the newer conditions. However, certain aspects of the economic and cultural context endured and exerted a major influence on the subjective notions of career success.

The dimensions of career success deemed meaningful by the two age cohorts were different. These were in line with cultural values. The differential salience led to different career behaviour. The older cohort moved to non-corporate organizations in a bid to give back to society. While some in the younger cohort searched for opportunities for learning and growth, others were more concerned about work–life balance to manage other life roles better.

CONCLUSIONS

While, of late, some attention is being given to research on career development in the Asian context, particularly China, collectivism is the primary variable that is used to explain differences in context (Sheu and Bordon, 2017). While collectivism is definitely relevant, other aspects of the context also merit attention. Our study illustrates the impact of structural economic changes on notions of career success among Indian MBA graduates. On a similar note, differences in cultural context are usually understood in terms of Hofstede's cultural dimensions or GLOBE's cultural clusters (Kaše et al., 2018; Smale et al., 2019). We showcase a cultural framework that prescribes duties across the lifespan, which shapes the salience of the different dimensions of subjective career success. We call for further research in non-US and non-European contexts that explore a more diverse range of variables with an emic approach.

Our study has implications for organizations. Human resource management (HRM) systems for MNEs typically tend to support diffusion of global practices to the subsidiaries in emerging markets (Brewster, Mayrhofer and Cooke, 2015). Our findings suggest that MNEs might need to be flexible and willing to customize their HRM practices to incorporate cultural differences. We also found evidence to suggest that the older, experienced MBAs were looking for opportunities to give back to society. But they also perceived that a corporate set-up was unlikely to provide them those opportunities. Given that older employees have been found to be more engaged, loyal, and willing to work hard and less likely to quit or be absent voluntarily, compared with younger colleagues, organizations can benefit by making their job content more meaningful (Newman, 2011). Organizations could enable individuals to engage in job crafting, which leads to greater person–job fit and meaningful work (Tims, Derks and Bakker, 2016). Organizations could motivate their younger employees by offering them job rotation or training through distance-learning or web-based programmes.

Our study has its limitations. First, most of our MBAs were from the Indian Institutes of Management (IIMs) and other top-tier management schools. MBAs from lower-tier management schools might not always have as much human or social capital to handle the challenges of the changing economic conditions. Within the Indian sample, career success schemas (cognitive structures) were different for people from different occupations (Kaše et al., 2018). Scholars have now begun to study the changing nature of work due to economic structural changes on diverse occupations ranging from academics to domestic workers (Vijay, 2019). Further research is needed to get a more holistic picture of the phenomenon.

In conclusion, we presented a view of how the socio-economic context provided Indian MBAs with a distinctive set of opportunities and challenges. We hope that this leads to similar studies in newer contexts and populations that help in designing contextually appropriate interventions.

REFERENCES

Agarwala, T. (2008), 'Factors influencing career choice of management students in India', *Career Development International*, **13**(4), 362–76.

Arthur, M.B. and D.M. Rousseau (1996), 'Introduction: the boundaryless career as a new employment principle', in M.B. Arthur and D.M. Rousseau (eds), *The Boundaryless Career: A New Employment Principle for a New Organizational Era*, New York: Oxford University Press, pp. 3–20.

Arulmani, G. (2007), 'Counselling psychology in India: at the confluence of two traditions', *Applied Psychology*, **56**(1), 69–82.

Arulmani, G. (2011), 'Striking the right note: the cultural preparedness approach to developing resonant career guidance programmes', *International Journal for Educational and Vocational Guidance*, **11**(2), 79–93.

Arulmani, G. and S. Nag-Arulmani (2004), *Career Counselling – A Handbook*, New Delhi: Tata McGraw-Hill.

Bhatnagar, D. and U. Rajadhyaksha (2001), 'Attitudes towards work and family roles and their implications for career growth of women: a report from India', *Sex Roles*, **45**(7–8), 549–65.

Braun, V. and V. Clarke (2006), 'Using thematic analysis in psychology', *Qualitative Research in Psychology*, **3**, 77–101.

Brewster, C., W. Mayrhofer and F.L. Cooke (2015), 'Convergence, divergence and diffusion of HRM in emerging markets', in F. Horwitz and P.S. Budhwar (eds), *Handbook of Human Resource Management in Emerging Markets*, Cheltenham, UK and Northampton, MA, USA: Edward Elgar Publishing, pp. 451–69.

Cooke, F.L. and P.S. Budhwar (2015), 'Human resource management in China and India', in F. Horwitz and P.S. Budhwar (eds), *Handbook of Human Resource Management in Emerging Markets*, Cheltenham, UK and Northampton, MA, USA: Edward Elgar Publishing, pp. 337–56.

Erickson, T.J. (2009), 'Generational differences between India and the U.S.', *Harvard Business Review*, 1 March 2009, accessed 5 April 2009 at https://hbr.org/2009/02/global-generations-focus-on-in.

Fernandes, L. and P. Heller (2006), 'Hegemonic aspirations: new middle class politics and India's democracy in comparative perspective', *Critical Asian Studies*, **38**(4), 495–522.

Garg, P. and I. Parikh (1994), *Young Managers at the Crossroads: The Trishanku Complex*, New Delhi: Sage.

Ghosh, R. and S. Chaudhuri (2013), 'Inter-generational differences in individualism/collectivism orientations: implications for outlook towards HRD/HRM practices in India and the United States', *New Horizons in Adult Education and Human Resource Development*, **23**(4), 5–21.

Greenhaus, J.H. and E.E. Kossek (2014), 'The contemporary career: a work–home perspective', *Annual Review of Organizational Psychology and Organizational Behavior*, **1**(1), 361–88.

Hall, D.T. (2004), 'The protean career: a quarter-century journey', *Journal of Vocational Behavior*, **65**(1), 1–13.

Hofstede, G. (1984), 'Cultural dimensions in management and planning', *Asia Pacific Journal of Management*, **1**(2), 81–99.

Hofstede Insights (2017), 'Country comparison: what about India?', accessed 26 September 2018 at https://www.hofstede-insights.com/country-comparison/india/.

Kapur, D. and R. Ramamurti (2001), 'India's emerging competitive advantage in services', *Academy of Management Executive*, **15**(2), 20–32.

Kaše, R., N. Dries and J.P. Briscoe et al. (2018), 'Career success schemas and their
contextual embeddedness: a comparative configurational perspective', *Human
Resource Management Journal*, Special Issue, 1–19, accessed 17 January 2020 at
https://onlinelibrary.wiley.com/doi/10.1111/1748-8583.12218.

Khapova, S.J.N., M.B. Arthur and C.P.M. Wilderom (2007), 'The subjective career in
the knowledge economy', in H.P. Gunz and M. Peiperl (eds), *Handbook of Career
Studies*, Thousand Oaks, CA: Sage, pp. 114–30.

Krishnan, R.T. and S.K. Jha (2011), 'Innovation strategies in emerging markets: what
can we learn from Indian market leaders', *ASCI Journal of Management*, **41**(1),
21–45.

Kulkarni, G. (2006), 'Burnout', *Journal of Occupational and Environmental Medicine*,
10(1), 3–4.

Mayrhofer, W., J.P. Briscoe and D.T. Hall et al. (2016), 'Career success across the
globe: insights from the 5C project', *Organizational Dynamics*, **45**(3), 197–205.

Ministry of Human Resource Development (2008), *Report of IIM Review Committee*,
New Delhi: Government of India.

Ministry of Human Resource Development (2018), *Educational Statistics at a Glance
2018*, accessed 17 January 2020 at https://mhrd.gov.in/sites/upload_files/mhrd/files/
statistics-new/ESAG-2018.pdf.

Newman, K.L. (2011), 'Sustainable careers: lifecycle engagement in work',
Organizational Dynamics, **40**(2), 136–43.

Ng, T.W.H., L.T. Eby, K.L. Sorensen and D.C. Feldman (2005), 'Predictors of objective and subjective career success: a meta-analysis', *Personnel Psychology*, **58**(2),
367–408.

NSE Indices Limited (2018), 'Historical data reports', accessed 17 October 2018 at
http://www.niftyindices.com/reports/historical-data.

Prashad, V. (2013), *The Poorer Nations: A Possible History of the Global South*, New
York: Verso Books.

Rodrigues, R., D. Guest and A. Budjanovcanin (2013), 'From anchors to orientations:
towards a contemporary theory of career preferences', *Journal of Vocational
Behavior*, **83**, 142–52.

Saha, P.K. (2019), 'Jobs over careers: India's premier B-schools keep making the
wrong choice', *The Ken*, 20 March 2019, accessed at https://the-ken.com/story/jobs
-over-careers-indias-premier-b-schools-keep-making-the-wrong-choice/.

Shah, A.M. (1996), 'Is the joint household disintegrating?', *Economic and Political
Weekly*, **31**(9), 537–42.

Sheu, H.B. and J.J. Bordon (2017), 'SCCT research in the international context:
empirical evidence, future directions, and practical implications', *Journal of Career
Assessment*, **25**(1), 58–74.

Shukla, R. (2010), *How India Earns, Spends and Saves – Unmasking the Real India*,
New Delhi: Sage and NCAER-CMCR.

Smale, A., S. Bagdadli and R. Cotton et al. (2019), 'Proactive career behaviors and
subjective career success: the moderating role of national culture', *Journal of
Organizational Behavior*, **40**(1), 105–22.

Srinivasan, V. (2012), 'Multi generations in the workforce: building collaboration',
IIMB Management Review, **24**(1), 48–66.

Tams, S. and M.B. Arthur (2007), 'Studying careers across cultures: distinguishing international, cross-cultural, and globalization perspectives', *Career Development International*, **12**(1), 86–98.

Thatchenkery, S. and N. Koizumi (2010), 'Lab coats versus business suits: a study of career preferences among Indian adolescents', *Career Development International*, **15**(6), 524–43.

Tims, M., D. Derks and A.B. Bakker (2016), 'Job crafting and its relationships with person–job fit and meaningfulness: a three-wave study', *Journal of Vocational Behavior*, **92**, 44–53.

United Nations Development Programme (2018), 'India ranks 130 on 2018 Human Development Index', 14 September 2018, accessed 27 August 2019 at http://www .in.undp.org/content/india/en/home/sustainable-development/successstories/india -ranks-130-on-2018-human-development-index.html.

Vijay, D. (2019), 'Introduction to the special issue: changing nature of work and organizations in India', *Decision*, **46**(2), 93–7.

World Bank (2017), 'World development indicators – GDP growth rate', accessed 17 January 2020 at https://data.worldbank.org/country/india.

9. How an MBA contributes to the unfolding of careers: a comparative analysis

Elizabeth Houldsworth, Chris Brewster and Richard McBain

INTRODUCTION

MBAs are viewed by many as a licence to practice as a manager regardless of context. But is an MBA 'universal' or do regional differences still prevail? Using a survey of over 700 alumni from a prestigious UK programme, we test the power of MBAs in globalizing career outcomes and find that regional characteristics still endure.

Historically, the purpose of the MBA degree was to train (or re-train) individuals who were technically skilled to provide them with the functional knowledge and skills necessary to manage people and operations (Rubin and Dierdorff, 2013). From its origins in the USA, the MBA concept has grown into a single, globally recognized brand name in management education (Juusola, Kettunen and Alajoutsijarvi, 2015; Mellahi, 2000) and some argue that it has become a prerequisite for senior posts (Baruch and Peiperl, 2000). If this universalistic approach to management is accepted and universal prescriptions around how to manage apply in all contexts, then the 'best practice/ one best way' taught on most MBA courses is appropriate. However, MBAs have been criticized for not reflecting the complexity and socially and eco-logically fraught nature of the world (Waddock and Lozano, 2013). 'Good' practice in one situation may not work in another. Using data from a UK MBA programme and theories of comparative capitalisms (Amable, 2003; Jackson and Deeg, 2008) we examine whether reported career choices, outcomes and satisfaction post-MBA are differentiated by regional location. We conclude that context matters (Egri, 2013) and successful and legitimate management processes, and management careers, are likely to vary with type of market economy.

IS THE MBA A HOMOGENIZING FORCE?

MBAs are popular: more programmes reported growing application volumes for the 2016–17 class year than reported declining volumes (GMAC, 2016). Thus, the MBA continues to be a professional qualification associated with prestige, reputation, personal authority and distinction (Doherty and Dickmann, 2009; Mayrhofer et al., 2004). Most applicants hope for increased job opportunities and increased salary potential (GMAC, 2016) and that does seem to be the effect (Zhao et al., 2006) irrespective of gender, MBA grade-point average, pre-MBA work experience, or ethnic background (Zhao et al., 2006). Completing an MBA requires a considerable investment and companies may fund this education, either partially or in full, as a means of investing in their human resources. Alternatively, individuals may self-finance, which may be interpreted as an example of 'individuals taking ownership of their own career' (Arthur, Khapova and Richardson, 2017; Crowley-Henry, 2006), or 'boundaryless careers' (Arthur and Rousseau, 1996; Guan et al., 2019).

There are alternative approaches to whether the MBA is a 'globalizing' force. First, it is argued that the MBA is an example of the development of 'global mindsets' (Mellahi et al., 2013) by which home and host country identities are superseded. Acquisition of such academic credentials can facilitate greater transnational mobility for individuals (Waters, 2007). According to this approach, we might expect MBA alumni to have similar career experiences and behave in similar ways post-qualification. An alternative standpoint is presented by the growing literature on comparative human resource management (Brewster and Mayrhofer, 2012), which by its nature is more pluralistic. The comparative human resource management literature uses cultural and institutional theories to emphasize the differences between nation states and types of market. The comparative capitalisms literature (Amable, 2003; Jackson and Deeg, 2008; Hall and Soskice, 2001; Whitley, 1999), on which much of this approach is based, implies that the management process – what would be seen as good management – and managerial careers will vary from context to context, reflecting the territorial embeddedness described by Hall and Appleyard (2009).

The outcomes of management training and development may therefore differ depending on location and context, and this is likely to have a knock-on effect on the expectations of career development among the managers themselves. Ramirez and Mabey (2005) and Mabey and Ramirez (2011) have highlighted nationally distinctive approaches to management development, reflecting markedly different conceptions of what management means. As part of this argument, and given the dominance of Western and particularly US schools, the MBA credential has been criticized as 'ethnocentric' and 'neo-colonial'

(Mellahi, 2000; Usdiken, Kieser and Kjaer, 2004). These arguments are particularly relevant to our study, which revolves around a UK-based MBA programme being delivered (via blended learning) in a number of locations, including some 'developing states' (Nkomo, 2015).

Career success has been defined as 'the real or perceived achievement individuals have accumulated as a result of their work experiences' (Judge et al., 1999, p. 622) and has been divided into objective and subjective success (Ng et al., 2005). Objective career success includes elements visible to everyone, such as promotions and job moves. Subjective career success relates to the individual's own judgments about job attainment and satisfaction (Judge et al., 1999). Both may be impacted by perceived organizational support (POS), including funding. For this study we were also interested in former students' attribution for their career success: who/what did they think was responsible for it? Thus, there are parallels between this chapter and the one that is paired with it in this volume by Nair and Chatterjee (Chapter 8). In the current study, our focus, too, is on subjective career satisfaction. Both chapters also note the role of agency in shaping career outcomes.

DIFFERENT TYPES OF ECONOMY AND THEIR IMPACT ON MANAGEMENT EDUCATION AND DEVELOPMENT

We defined regional location according to the comparative capitalisms literature and used the three established groupings of coordinated market economies (CMEs), social democratic market economies (SDEs) and liberal market economies (LMEs), confirmed as relevant to personal development by Goergen et al. (2012). For countries included in each category see Table 9.1. From the comparative capitalisms literature, we know that LMEs are based on competition between and within firms, and on a focus on short-term results for the owners of businesses. In the CMEs, firms collaborate much more with each other and with government and are focused on survival and the long-term interests of a wider group of stakeholders. Firms are more supported, or restricted, by legislation. The Nordic SDE countries have fewer legal restrictions than CMEs but a more normative acceptance of a stakeholder approach to business, high trade union membership, high taxes and high welfare provision (Amable, 2003). In terms of management education, one effect is that in the CMEs, employees tend to stay with one employer for longer and transfers between firms are less common: so, for both employer and employee, investing in education and development becomes a more cost-effective decision than it is in LMEs (Goergen et al., 2012). We might expect that within CMEs, qualifications are highly valued; being sent on an MBA programme is a mark of selection as a 'high-potential' and graduates are expected by their employer

Table 9.1   Country groupings used in this study

Type of Capitalism	Number of Respondents
Coordinated market economy countries: Belgium, France, Germany and the Netherlands	88
Social democratic economy countries: Denmark, Finland, Norway and Sweden	117
Liberal market economy countries: UK, Ireland, Australia and New Zealand	411
Southern African countries: Botswana, Lesotho, Malawi, Mozambique, South Africa, Tanzania and Zimbabwe	50
Caribbean countries: Barbados, Guyana, St Lucia and Trinidad and Tobago	36

and themselves to remain in the organization. As a corollary, we might expect CME graduates to be rewarded with promotions. In the LMEs, graduates may find their qualifications are given less credit and that they must change employer to make progress in their careers. Having changed employer, there may then be a wait before getting promoted. SDE graduates may be in a similar position to those from the CMEs.

Given the diversity of our sample we were able to compare these established varieties of capitalism with two other regional groupings: Southern Africa and the Caribbean (Table 9.1).

There is little evidence in the literature about the kinds of market economy in the Southern African and Caribbean regions, though the Southern African model has been dubbed a segmented business system (Bischoff and Wood, 2012; Wood and Frynas, 2006), with employee–employer interdependence in large organizations and subsidiaries of multinational corporations (MNCs) but clear employee subordination in the extensive, informal, small firms' sector. It is likely that all MBA students will come from large firms and the MNC subsidiaries sector, so that interdependence will be high. There is no literature to guide us as to the situation in the Caribbean.

DO MBA CAREER OUTCOMES VARY BY CONTEXT?

What about career outcomes? Objective success might be measured by post-MBA career mobility in terms of number of promotions and changes to level of work. Contextual factors may be likely to influence the extent to which an individual will pursue advancement within their current organization or by moving to another. From Whitley's (1999) interdependence theory, we expect that it is more normal for individuals from an LME context to move between organizations in pursuit of career advancement, thus, to use the MBA for personal marketability. Randlesome (2000) suggests that in Germany employees enjoy career development and career enhancement without needing to move organization, whilst noting that despite German companies' preference for technical qualifications, the addition of an MBA is likely to increase an applicant's prospects (Randlesome, 2000).

Other researchers have argued that the Nordic countries constitute a separate SDE group (Amable, 2003), with fewer legal restrictions than CMEs but a more normative acceptance of a stakeholder approach to business, high trade union membership, high taxes and high welfare provision. La Porta et al. (1999) also note the distinctiveness of Nordic countries as something of a 'hybrid', typically displaying weaker vocational education and training than would be expected in a CME, and different labour market norms. These norms have been labelled 'flexicurity': focused on lifetime employment possibilities rather than the same employer (Goergen et al., 2012; Origo and Pagani, 2009). In the light of these labour market norms, we might expect to see a higher level of training investment in SDEs than in CMEs.

Broadly similar arguments might apply to subjective career success (how the individual perceives their career situation). Randlesome (2000) described Germany, the leading CME, as an economy in which the MBA was gaining increased credence, with much of this pressure coming from potential applicants. Securing company support for such endeavours is likely therefore to be highly valued by the recipient. Qualifications in CMEs and SDEs tend to be given more value (House et al., 2004), so the kind of employees who undertake an MBA are likely to be in a close and continuing relationship with their employer. As Goergen et al. (2012) point out, graduates in the CMEs and SDEs will have high job security, meaning there are fewer pressures for them to job hop or constantly monitor the external labour market. This may translate into further promotions and a feeling of satisfaction with their investment in the MBA if promotions are perceived by the individual as a desired career outcome. Graduates in the LMEs will be in a less certain position, perhaps feeling that they may have to change employer to get ahead, and they may question the value of their qualification. Louw, Bosch and Venter (2001) report from a study in South Africa that no support could be found for the assertion that the MBA was a waste of time and money and that the value of the MBA qualification was overemphasized, whereas for the Caribbean it is difficult to assess beforehand what the situation will be.

In the CMEs and SDEs, investments in development and, in particular, management development, can take place over an extended time period, since the employer has more certainty that the employee will stay with the organization after completing such programmes, and they are therefore more likely to get a return on their investment. Higher levels of training investment in SDEs than in CMEs (Goergen et al., 2012) might translate into higher perceived POS. Although there are no prior studies, we might expect something similar from the graduates in Southern Africa and the Caribbean, but for a different reason. This is because they are operating in a smaller employment market with the MBA having a high premium. Such graduates will not want to go into the small firm and/or informal sectors of the economy, and employment in the public sector, large firms and MNC subsidiaries is limited. Employers will want to show faith in such employees in order to retain valuable staff. In the LMEs, firms are not heavily involved in skill formation and workers have an incentive to acquire general skills that are broadly portable across the various industries and firms in which they might seek employment (Thelen, 2007). In consequence, employers try to limit their investment, knowing that many employees will be moving (probably to a competitor, since they tend to stay in the same industry) within a few years, in order to secure their career progression.

A final issue we examined in our research was who it is that graduates see as responsible for their career success. A prior study by Ozbilgin, Kuska and Erdogmus (2005) found similar results across MBA students from Britain, Israel and Turkey with individuals feeling personally responsible for their success. We anticipate similar responses across the three established market economies of CMEs, SDEs and LMEs, but that this may be different for the alumni from the Caribbean and Southern Africa, given that the MBA market is newer, and recipients may therefore feel like members of an elite group. Given that the cultures in the latter two regional groups are likely to be more hierarchical, and perhaps more religious, we anticipate that there may be less of a belief in the individual as the driver of career success, with more recognition of the role of others (such as sponsoring employer or even business school).

METHODS

In 2014, we conducted an online survey of the MBA alumni of a leading international business school headquartered in the UK, whose students have an average age of 37 and around ten years' managerial experience. We received 816 responses and we grouped the corresponding countries where respondents were based (not necessarily nationality) into regions, removing groups with less than ten members. This resulted in a total of five groups and 702 respondents, with year of graduation ranging from 1999–2013 as more recent graduates were not surveyed. Since the group composed of alumni from LME countries was considerably larger than the others, we selected a random sample of 110 members from this group and compared the results of the full sample with those using this subsample to check that the results of the full data set were consistent. They were, and we use the results from the full sample, only reporting statistically significant results.

Measures

MBA alumni were asked to indicate job changes, employer changes and country changes since completion of the MBA. For objective career outcomes, MBA alumni were asked about the number of promotions they had received post-MBA, and their hierarchical level. For subjective career satisfaction we used a seven-item Likert scale to measure career satisfaction (based on an earlier study by Jokinen et al., 2008). We found the coefficient alphas to be 0.92 for satisfaction related to extrinsic factors and 0.77 for intrinsic factors.

For perceived organizational support, respondents were asked to report their perception both pre- and post-MBA. Since these were measured at the same time, we recognize that there may be the possibility of self-report and retrospective memory bias. These measures were previously used by Jokinen, Brewster and Suutari (2008). The reliability of the scale for pre- and post-MBA POS in this study was 0.89. For attribution for career success, we asked respondents to reflect on their career development since their MBA and suggest whether any success they had enjoyed had been mostly due to themselves or others, and to identify the other if this was cited.

We included measures of respondent age, years since graduation and gender (a dummy variable with female = 0 and male = 1) as control variables and no specific hypotheses were developed concerning their effects. We created grouping variables comprising three broadly equal-sized groups from the numeric variables of age and years since graduation for the chi-square analysis in connection with objective career success.

FINDINGS

Alumni working in CMEs are least likely to remain in the same job post-MBA (9.1 per cent), followed by those from SDEs (12.8 per cent) and LMEs (14.0 per cent), while graduates from the Caribbean (22.0 per cent) and Southern Africa (18.0 per cent) are the most likely to remain in the same job. However, in terms of employer, as expected, CMEs report the highest frequency (36.4 per cent) of remaining, with the LME alumni reporting a lower likelihood (32.1 per cent). Alumni from SDEs are least likely (28.8 per cent) to have remained with their employer post-MBA. Alumni from CMEs are most likely to have changed country (33.0 per cent), followed by alumni from Southern Africa (22.0 per cent) and LMEs (19.5 per cent). These findings varied, as might be expected, with age and years since graduation. Multinomial logistic regression analyses indicate that region is not a statistically significant predictor when controlling for age, years since graduation and gender.

In terms of objective career success, we examined promotions and hierarchical position using chi-square for the variables level of work and region while controlling for age and years since graduation (both of which were divided into three broadly equal groups) and gender. We find a significant association for senior management roles both pre- and post-MBA. Although CME alumni enjoy the greatest levels of objective career success post-MBA, with the highest average number of promotions and greater propensity to change job role and country, it is LME alumni who report the largest average increase in hierarchical position pre- and post-MBA.

Pre-MBA there is a significant difference in the reported hierarchical position, with students beginning the MBA from CMEs being less likely to report being in a senior management position than students from LME and SDE regions. Post-MBA, despite the considerable seniority gains achieved by CME graduates, it is alumni from LMEs and Southern Africa who are more likely to report being in senior management roles compared with those from CMEs, the SDEs and the Caribbean. It seems that the likelihood of being in a senior role is highest amongst LME alumni.

In terms of the subjective career, we expected satisfaction with career outcomes post-MBA to be highest in the CMEs and lowest in the LMEs. Controlling for age, years since graduation and gender, we found region was non-significant in terms of predicting satisfaction with objective career factors (salary and progress), though those from LMEs were least satisfied. Although region was not statistically significant, alumni from SDEs and CMEs were more satisfied in terms of subjective career success than those from LMEs. Of the control variables, only years since graduation was a significant predictor. Region did emerge as a significant predictor of pre-MBA POS and is also significantly related to post-MBA POS. Alumni from SDEs have significantly higher levels of post-MBA POS than those from CMEs, although they have significantly lower levels than alumni from Southern Africa, who reported the highest POS. The lowest levels of post-MBA POS were reported by graduates from CMEs and the Caribbean. So, region does emerge as a significant predictor of POS post-MBA, but, surprisingly, alumni from CMEs report less POS than those from other regions and reported being less likely to have been fully funded than those from SDEs and LMEs. This may be because the MBA is seen as a way of easing movement between employers, and in contexts where that is not the norm employers may be less enthusiastic. The higher POS within the SDE group may be because training is more highly valued there, so they are more likely to have received full funding for their studies than CME students. Indeed, around 50 per cent of alumni from both SDE and Southern African regions report full funding for their MBA studies.

Finally, we considered attribution for success across the five regional groups. Controlling for age, years since graduation and gender, respondents from CMEs, SDEs, LMEs and Southern Africa all report similarly high levels of belief in their individual agency as the foundation of their career success, thus echoing the findings of Chapter 8 by Nair and Chatterjee. However, in the Caribbean region there is a greater tendency to attribute personal success to another in the form of the employer, the business school, or God.

DISCUSSION

A key theme emerging from this study is the limits of homogenization, with differences being reported in terms of MBA career trajectories by region. Whitley (1999) previously described CME employees as being more closely connected to their employer and less likely to change employer than those in LMEs, and our study suggests that this also holds true for MBA graduates. Thus, despite the global recognition of the MBA qualification it does not overcome local labour market conditions emerging from variation in form of capitalism. This is reflected in the fact that one of the differences emerging from this study is that LME alumni report the greatest frequency of changing country and transitioning from technical roles to senior management positions, thus reflecting Whitley (1999). Interestingly, despite it being more 'normal' for MBA graduates from LMEs to move employers in pursuit of career gain, this mobility does not necessarily translate into career satisfaction, with LMEs appearing the least satisfied of all the groups.

If we turn our attention to the most satisfied students, these were from the SDEs and Southern Africa. In the case of the SDEs, we expected to see greater investment in training and development (Goergen et al., 2012; Origo and Pagani, 2009). Although less has been previously written about the emerging cadre of MBA graduates in Southern Africa, our findings do resonate with the earlier research by Louw et al. (2001).

Region also emerged as a significant predictor in terms of POS, with alumni from SDEs reporting higher levels of post-MBA POS than is reported in LMEs, but not significantly so, and at a lower level than that perceived by alumni from Southern Africa. Alumni from CMEs felt they had the lowest support across all five regions post-MBA. Thus, it would appear that despite career stability, CME alumni may not feel supported in a market where external hiring is less common (Hamori and Kakarika, 2009). Once again, the emerging economies perform well, with Southern Africa reporting the highest levels of POS, reflecting the career benefits that learners attribute to their MBA qualification.

In terms of possible future work, it would appear that satisfaction for MBA graduates is supported by employment security and perceived organizational support (including financial support for their studies). This is highlighted by the fact that the most satisfied grouping of Southern Africa and SDE also has the highest incidence of full funding (around 50 per cent). Recent developments in the UK to provide an apprenticeship levy supported MBA process may provide an opportunity to explore this link more fully.

CONCLUSION

The findings from this study support the application of the comparative capitalisms literature to career development. As anticipated, alumni from CMEs, despite having an MBA, do not mimic the behaviours of alumni from LMEs: they remain less likely to move employer. To a lesser degree, the same is true of alumni in the less established economies of Southern Africa and the Caribbean, where there may be fewer opportunities. Given that in our study the respondents had all studied the same MBA programme, delivered via a UK-based institution using common materials and teaching methods, we can suppose that differences must relate to the environmental context of work and careers. This is a key finding from this study, as it reinforces the notion that, despite the much-heralded move towards globalization, context matters, and that this is reflected in management education and development. Thus, despite the global currency of the MBA as a qualification, the characteristics of local labour markets, as described in the comparative capitalism literature, endure. We do find some evidence for homogeneity. This is manifested in the mind set of MBA graduates around their personal attribution for career success as, with the exception of the alumni from the Caribbean, views were relatively uniform, reflecting what Ozbilgin et al. (2005) describe as a belief in individual agency in terms of career choice.

In summary, we conclude that, despite the claim that globalization is creating homogeneity, a comparative analysis of MBA careers provides useful insights into the importance of context in management education. Thus, an understanding of labour market norms is helpful for ongoing analysis of the career outcomes of MBA-level education.

REFERENCES

Amable, B. (2003), *The Diversity of Modern Capitalism*, Oxford: Oxford University Press.

Arthur, M.B. and D.M. Rousseau (1996), *The Boundaryless Career*, New York: Oxford University Press.

Arthur, M.B., S.N. Khapova and J. Richardson (2017), *An Intelligent Career: Taking Ownership of Your Own Career*, Oxford: Oxford University Press.

Baruch, Y. and M. Peiperl (2000), 'The impact of an MBA on graduate careers', *Human Resource Management Journal*, **10**(2), 69–90.

Bischoff, C. and G.T. Wood (2012), 'The practice of HRM in Africa in comparative perspective', in C. Brewster and W. Mayrhofer (eds), *Handbook of Research on Comparative Human Resource Management*, Cheltenham, UK and Northampton, MA, USA: Edward Elgar Publishing, pp. 494–511.

Brewster, C. and W. Mayrhofer (eds) (2012), *Handbook of Research on Comparative Human Resource Management*, Cheltenham, UK and Northampton, MA, USA: Edward Elgar Publishing.

Crowley-Henry, M. (2006), 'The protean career', *International Studies of Management & Organization*, **37**(3), 44–64.

Doherty, N. and M. Dickmann (2009), 'Exposing the symbolic capital of international assignments', *The International Journal of Human Resource Management*, **20**(2), 301–20.

Egri, C. (2013), 'From the editors: context matters in management education scholarship', *Academy of Management Learning & Education*, **12**(2), 155–7.

GMAC (2016), *2016 Application Trends Survey Report*, Reston, VA: Graduate Management Admission Council.

Goergen, M., C. Brewster, B. Wood and G. Wilkinson (2012), 'Varieties of capitalism and investments in human capital', *Industrial Relations*, **51**(1), 501–27.

Guan, Y., M.B. Arthur, S.N. Khapova, R.J. Hall and R.G. Lord (2019), 'Career boundarylessness and career success: a review, integration and guide to future research', *Journal of Vocational Behavior*, **110**, 390–402.

Hall, P.A. and D. Soskice (2001), *Varieties of Capitalism: The Institutional Foundations of Comparative Advantage*, Oxford: Oxford University Press.

Hall, S. and L. Appleyard (2009), '"City of London, city of learning?" Placing business education within the geographies of finance', *Journal of Economic Geography*, **9**(5), 597–617.

Hamori, M. and M. Kakarika (2009), 'External labor market strategy and career success: CEO careers in Europe and the United States', *Human Resource Management*, **48**(3), 355–78.

House, R.J., P.J. Hanges, M. Javidan, P.W. Dorfman and V. Gupta (eds) (2004), *Culture, Leadership and Organizations: The GLOBE Study of 62 Societies*, London: Sage.

Jackson, G. and R. Deeg (2008), 'Comparing capitalisms: understanding institutional diversity and its implications for international business', *Journal of International Business Studies*, **39**, 540–61.

Jokinen, T., C. Brewster and V. Suutari (2008), 'Career capital during international work experiences: contrasting self-initiated expatriate experiences and assigned expatriation', *The International Journal of Human Resource Management*, **19**(6), 979–98.

Judge, T.A, C.A. Higgins, C.J. Thoresen and M.R. Barrick (1999), 'The big five personality traits, general mental ability, career success across the life span', *Personnel Psychology*, **52**, 621–52.

Juusola, K., K. Kettunen and K. Alajoutsijarvi (2015), 'Accelerating the Americanization of management education: five responses from business schools', *Journal of Management Inquiry*, **24**(4), 347–89.

La Porta, R., F. Lopez-de-Silanes, A. Shleifer and R. Vishny (1999), 'Corporate ownership around the world', *Journal of Finance*, **54**(2), 471–517.

Louw, L., J. Bosch and D. Venter (2001), 'Graduates' perceptions of the quality of MBA programmes', *Quality Assurance in Education*, **9**(1), 40–44.

Mabey, C. and M. Ramirez (2011), 'Comparing national approaches to management development', in C. Brewster and W. Mayrhofer (eds), *Handbook of Research on Comparative Human Resource Management*, Cheltenham, UK and Northampton, MA: Edward Elgar Publishing, pp. 185–210.

Mayrhofer, W., A. Iellatchitch, M. Meyer, M. Steyrer, J. Schiffinger and G. Strunk (2004), 'Going beyond the individual: some potential contributions from the career field and habitus perspective for global career research and practice', *The Journal of Management Development*, **23**(9), 870–84.

Mellahi, K. (2000), 'The teaching of leadership on UK MBA programmes: a critical analysis from an international perspective', *Journal of Management Development*, **19**(4), 297–308.

Mellahi, K., D. Mehmet, D.G. Collings, E. Tatoglu and M. Hughes (2013), 'Similarly different: a comparison of HRM practices in MNE subsidiaries and local firms in Turkey', *The International Journal of Human Resource Management*, **24**(12), 2339–68.

Ng, T.W.H., L.T. Eby, K.L. Sorensen and D.C. Feldman (2005), 'Predictors of objective and subjective career success: a meta-analysis', *Personnel Psychology*, **58**, 367–408.

Nkomo, S.M. (2015), 'Challenges for management and business education in a "developmental" state: the case of South Africa', *Academy of Management Learning & Education*, **14**(2), 242–58.

Origo, R. and L. Pagani (2009), 'Flexicurity and job satisfaction in Europe: the importance of perceived and actual job stability for well-being at work', *Labour Economics* **16**, 547–55.

Ozbilgin, M., F. Kuska and N. Erdogmus (2005), 'Explaining influences on career "choice": the case of MBA students in comparative perspective', *The International Journal of Human Resource Management*, **16**(11), 2000–2028.

Ramirez, M. and C. Mabey (2005), 'A labour market perspective on management training and development in Europe', *The International Journal of Human Resource Management*, **16**(3), 291–310.

Randlesome, C. (2000), 'Development changes in management culture and competencies: the German experience', *Journal of Management*, **19**(7), 629–42.

Rubin, R.S. and E.C. Dierdorff (2013), 'Building a better MBA: from a decade of critique toward a decennium of creation', *Academy of Management & Education*, **12**(1), 125–41.

Thelen, K. (2007), 'Contemporary challenges to the German vocational training system', *Regulation and Governance*, **1**, 247–60.

Usdiken, B., A. Kieser and P. Kjaer (2004), 'Academy, economy and polity: Betriebswirtschaftslehre in Germany, Denmark and Turkey before 1945', *Business History*, **46**(3), 381–406.

Waddock, S. and J.M. Lozano (2013), 'Developing more holistic management education: lessons learned from two programs', *Academy of Management Learning & Education*, **12**(2), 265–84.

Waters, J.L. (2007), 'Roundabout routes and sanctuary schools: the role of situated education practices and habitus in the creation of transnational professionals', *Global Networks*, **7**, 477–97.

Whitley, R. (1999), *Divergent Capitalisms: The Social Structuring and Change of Business Systems*, Oxford: Oxford University Press.

Wood, G. and G. Frynas (2006), 'The institutional basis of economic failure: anatomy of the segmented business system', *Socio-Economic Review*, **4**(2), 239–77.

Zhao, J.J., A.D. Truell, M.W. Alexander and I.B. Hill (2006), 'Less success than meets the eye? The impact of Master of Business Administration education on graduates' careers', *Journal of Education for Business*, **81**(5), 261–8.

PART V

Breaking and re-entry

The chapters on this topic look at re-entry of women after a child-related career break.

In their chapter 'Women's careers: starting a new chapter post career break', Pavni Kaushiva and Chetan Joshi focus on an Indian employer's decision to hire or not to hire a woman after she has taken a career break. They conduct an experimental study to look at the effect of neosexism on the decision whether to hire a woman applicant returning to work. The results show that support programmes may suppress employers' neosexist attitudes towards women. Support programmes offer an internship to women who want to return to work. They allow employers to get to know the qualities of the woman and this may suppress neosexist attitudes. While deeply entrenched stereotypes may contribute to a downward spiral in the representation of women in the Indian workforce, the study shows that certain organizational practices may help to turn the tide.

Anna Katharina Bader and John Blenkinsopp focus in their chapter, titled 'Can we release the brake on the career re-entry of mothers? A UK perspective', on challenges and determinants of mothers' return to work after a child-related career break. They focus on legal, infrastructural and cultural specificities and compare the context of the UK and India. Their analyses clearly show that women in the UK also face barriers when wanting to return to work after a career break, despite the existence of a robust legal framework intended to support their careers. In a final section, they turn to the roles that organizations can play as implementers of policy and legislation, and as the providers of the direct, career-shaping experiences that returning mothers face.

The combination of both chapters reveals that even though the contexts between India and the UK differ considerably, where the UK context is more egalitarian than the Indian one, social norms about motherhood and traditional gender roles still prevail and impact careers of women. This leads to a question of what can be learned from the similarities between these outcomes, and a further question of to what extent would proposed solutions in one setting work in the other setting? What social norms do you see around you, and how can you apply what you have read to your own situation?

10. Women's careers: starting a new chapter post career break

Pavni Kaushiva and Chetan Joshi

INTRODUCTION

There is a recent organizational focus on increasing and managing gender diversity, stressing the rehiring of women who seek a new chapter of professional work after a career break. One such company-initiated programme involves a six-month internship opportunity offered to women trying to return to the workforce by multinational companies such as IBM, Microsoft, and many more. These are referred to in this study as 'support programmes'. Most such programmes have a certain period of mentorship offered to the applicant, after which they form part of a common talent pool in the organization for allocation to different projects (SHEROES, 2018). These programmes are a part of a broader effort towards increasing gender diversity in organizations.

While women may now have an equivalent likelihood of getting hired for entry-level jobs, situational voluntary turnover is high among women in India due to greater prescriptive norms of family roles. For example, over 80 per cent of Indians believe that 'changing diapers, giving kids a bath, and feeding kids are the mother's responsibility' (Sabnavis, 2015, para. 6). According to a report by the World Economic Forum (2014), India is a poor performer among the five major emerging national economies (Brazil, Russia, India, China and South Africa – BRICS countries) in handling gender diversity. It ranks 3.9 on the ability of women to rise to enterprise leadership positions on a scale of 1 to 7, supported by a statistic of women forming only 7 per cent of the members of the boards of listed companies (Singh, 2015).

Recent initiatives at increasing the number of women employed at various levels of an organization are a step towards plugging the leaky pipeline (Cabrera, 2009). However, studies show discrimination against an individual with a career break during hiring, with females facing additional penalization for a family-related career break (Andersson, 2015). India offers an opportunity for studying the efficacy of recent initiatives such as the above-described support programme, within a national culture defining traditional family-oriented roles for women.

The effect of initiatives such as support programmes that offer an internship but no guarantee of a job after the internship has not been studied. Women seeking to re-enter after a career break can either apply directly to the organization or may apply to be selected for a support programmes for re-entry. The effect of the use of these programmes on the subsequent careers of women contributes to studies aimed at understanding the efficacy of diversity initiatives and policies. We are interested in understanding how the use of support programmes affects returning women's opportunities at work as compared to women applicants who do not complete such a programme.

This study focuses on examining an employer's attitude towards women applicants who have completed such support programmes. Specifically, the study is designed to understand the expression of neosexism by employers towards women and the differential effect of target programmes on the evaluation of such applicants when being considered for hiring.

LITERATURE REVIEW

Women's Non-linear Careers: A New Chapter Post Career Break

Women's careers have gathered significant academic interest in the past several years due to the recognition of different career trajectories for men and women. Moving beyond the traditional idea of linear careers, complexities arising out of work and non-work lives of women have been recognized and analysed (Rawat et al., 2019). Studies report a career shift after a career break, with women leaning towards organizations that offer flexible work schedules and other supportive policies (Lovejoy and Stone, 2012). Women rarely return to the same job following a career break, and more commonly opt for a career change with respect to the industry or job type. Zimmerman and Clark (2016) call for further research on individual and organizational strategies that can assist women in their attempts to return to industry. In this chapter, we focus on a group of women who wish to start a new chapter post career break by seeking re-entry into the same industry as their previous job before they quit.

While many scholars recommend organizational initiatives for successful re-entry of women, few have actually tested the effectiveness of such strategies. This chapter aims at examining the effectiveness of one organizational measure, namely, an internship programme aimed at hiring women seeking re-employment after a career break. Women primarily face barriers due to stereotypical perceptions of mothers as less committed or competent at re-entry. Career breaks heighten these perceptions. The completion of an internship after a career break may highlight information regarding the woman's skill over the information regarding the career break. Various explanations and examination of instances of such discrimination against women are described in the next section of the literature review.

Sexism in Organizational Re-entry

Being female, married and having a lower level of education reduces employability (Andersson, 2015). Koeber and Wright (2006) showed that women faced the bias of employers as well as a lower net human capital due to prevalent stereotypes about women workers, resulting in significantly less likelihood to be re-employed than men. Such studies report the expression of 'hostile sexism'.

There is also evidence of discrimination against pregnant women (Hebl et al., 2007) and mothers during both hiring and job evaluations (Morgan et al., 2013). Correll, Benard and Paik (2007) investigated the 'motherhood penalty' by asking participants to evaluate a pair of job applicants who differed only on parental status. Mothers were rated as less competent and were deemed not worthy of salaries and other rewards. The researchers sent out the same applications to real-life job vacancies. Mothers received half the number of call-backs as non-mothers. Other researchers found various instances of different forms of expression of prejudice and stereotyping toward specific subtypes of women, which result in the same overall negative effect on the women's evaluations (Stamarski and Son Hing, 2015).

The majority of studies on discrimination during hiring present a male versus female design (Andersson, 2015; Koeber and Wright, 2006; Zikic, Burke and Fiksenbaum, 2008). Some studies report discrimination against pregnant women (Hebl et al., 2007) and mothers during hiring as well as job evaluations (Morgan et al., 2013). While the expression of blatant sexism has declined due to increasing stress on egalitarian behaviour in organizations, subtle expressions of sexism still exist. The various discriminatory attitudes towards women include hostile sexism, benevolent sexism and neosexism. Hostile sexism is based on the belief of lower skills and lower status of women as compared to men, while benevolent sexism explains protective, paternal behaviour towards women where women are stereotyped as weak and needing protection. Both these forms of sexism lead to fewer opportunities for challenge, limiting women's growth (Glick and Fiske, 2001). Neosexism is defined as the 'manifestation of a conflict between egalitarian values and residual negative feelings toward women' (Tougas et al., 1995, p. 843). We propose that neosexism may better explain attitudes towards internship programmes and their effect on the hiring of re-entering women.

Expression of Neosexism

Despite a decline in blatant sexism, subtle sexism is still prevalent, though not openly expressed by individuals. Neosexists are likely to show less support for social policies as a means to acceptably oppose women aspiring to pursue their growth at work (Tougas et al., 1995). Neosexists see themselves as not discriminatory and argue against stereotypes. However, their prejudice can be suppressed when they are presented with certain justifications, such as proof of skill for the applied position. Stamarski and Son Hing (2015) highlight the effects of organizational structures and processes on decision-makers' sexism. Due to the openness of personnel-related decisions to individual biases, the resulting promotions, training opportunities and other such evaluations may reflect discrimination against women.

The justification-suppression model (JSM) by Crandall and Eshleman (2003) is useful in explaining the processes that lead to the expression of prejudice. JSM describes an individual's acquired, firm prejudice towards out-groups as 'genuine' prejudices that are not directly expressed but restrained by beliefs, values and norms that suppress them. These prejudices are then expressed under situations that offer even subtler justifications. As cultural norms increasingly denounce blatant sexism and other prejudices, individuals become skilled at suppressing them but remain motivated to look for justifications that allow them to manifest their prejudice without being questioned or experiencing any guilt (Crandall and Eshleman, 2003).

Previous studies on discrimination have shown the suppressive effect of individuating information provided by the stigmatized individual on the level of interpersonal discrimination experienced (Singletary and Hebl, 2009). This compensatory strategy enables others to see them as individuals rather than as representatives of a stigma. When perceivers lack information about an individual, they tend to rely on stereotypes. For example, when asked to select a leader, both men and women are more likely to select a man than a woman because they rely upon gender stereotypes, but once perceivers have additional information about targets, they are much less likely to use gender as the deciding factor in choosing a leader (Eagly and Karau, 1991). We use JSM here to analyse the impact of return programmes on the expression of discriminatory behaviour due to neosexism towards women workers. Studies have focused on sexism between genders, showing the higher likelihood of discrimination against women than against men. Our study proposes a differential expression of discrimination between two cases of women applicants for the role of a senior systems engineer in an IT firm, with similar credentials and an equivalent period of break in their work experience. The only difference introduced is in the manner of application for a job during re-entry – either 'direct' or through the use of support programmes.

Based on previous literature of discrimination against women due to the presence of a career break, we hypothesize that in the absence of information regarding work ability shown by the completion of the support program, women applying directly after a career break will be evaluated lower than women who applied after the completion of a support programme. Therefore, we hypothesize the following:

H1: Participants will be less likely to invite a woman applicant who had taken a career break but not completed a support programmes for an interview than a woman applicant who had taken an equivalent career break and completed a support programmes for re-entry.

No main effect of neosexism is predicted. We expect individuals with higher levels of neosexism to be less likely to hire women trying to re-enter after a career break. However, in the presence of information regarding an organizational initiative indicating support and inclusion for women trying to re-enter, the expression of prejudice is suppressed. Information regarding training during the programmes and validation of the skill of the woman suppress the expression of prejudice by providing individuating information about the woman (Morgan et al., 2013). The use of targeted programmes to seek re-entry after a career break is expected to act as an acceptable suppression factor to disallow the expression of opposition to women-centric policy. However, neosexism is expected to have an effect on the evaluation of women who did not use a support programme. Thus, we hypothesize the following:

H2: Participants' neosexist attitude affects the invitation for a hiring interview of the woman applicant in the absence of a support programmes after a career break such that participants with higher scores on neosexism will be less likely to invite the woman applicant without a support programme than participants who scored lower on neosexism. Participants' neosexist attitude will have no effect on the invitation for a hiring interview of the woman applicant who has completed a support programme after a career break for an interview.

METHOD

Participants

Fifty-eight respondents filled out a large questionnaire as part of an executive education course in a well-known institute of management in Eastern India. All respondents were senior managers with an average age of 38.6 years (*SD* = 5.016) and average work experience of 15.6 years (*SD* = 4.095). Of the participants, 52 were male and six were female. Participation was voluntary and participants were recruited for two supposedly independent studies: a questionnaire study and an in-basket exercise. In-basket exercises are realistic simulations of the decision-making environments faced by organizational members.

Procedure

The experiment consisted of two separate questionnaire studies. Participants were first asked to complete a questionnaire intended to measure their attitudes. We then requested the participants to fill an in-basket of managerial decisions they had to take, assuming the given managerial role in an IT firm, which included the evaluation of a résumé of a woman for a given position in the firm. Participants were randomly assigned to one of two versions of the résumé: support programme condition and no support programme condition. They were instructed to read silently and respond individually to each memorandum in the in-basket. Once the questionnaires were completed and returned, we debriefed the participants.

Materials

In the in-basket exercise, participants play the role of Mr Suraj Sethi, a manager in an information technology (IT) services firm called CreateIT, who was asked to screen an application for the position of a senior systems engineer for a new project. The recruited person should have a minimum experience of four years in the software development area within the IT industry. The descriptions of both applicants followed the memorandum on screening applicants. Applicants' gender and marital status were clearly mentioned along with their education and employment experience. Each participant evaluated only one applicant. Both applicants had experience of close to five years in the IT industry with at least five months in the position of a senior systems engineer before the break in career. Both résumés met the professional requirements stated by the HR department of the company and had a break of 20 months before applying for the position of senior systems engineer in the firm described in the in-basket. One applicant had completed a support programme called 'My Return', described to the candidate in the previous memorandum. The manipulation was embedded in the résumés of the applicants. Participants in the 'support programme' condition read the following in the résumé they evaluated: 'Professional experience: completed 6 months internship on a live project through "My Return" programmes at CreateIT from Apr 2018 to Sept 2018'. Participants in the 'no support programme' condition did not receive this manipulation.

Measures

The evaluation memorandum was used to capture participants' reactions to the support programme in the résumé. The support programme condition and neo-sexism scores were used as independent variables. Participants had answered items from a neosexism scale (Tougas et al., 1995) amongst other scales in the first part of the study. The mean score of 11 items on neosexism was 3.26 (*SD* = 0.79) with a Cronbach's alpha of 64. The item 'Discrimination against women in the labour force is no longer a problem in India' was removed from the neosexism scale to gain internal reliability.

For the regression analyses, a dummy variable was created for the two levels of the experimental condition of career break, namely, support programme condition and no support programme condition. The dummy variable was labelled B_Ret such that direct application after a career break was coded 0 and the completion of support programme after a career break was coded 1.

In both experimental conditions, participants were asked to indicate the likelihood of inviting this applicant for an interview on a seven-point scale from 1 ('Definitely NOT Invite') to 7 ('Definitely Invite') as well as a six-digit salary figure they would like to offer the applicant if selected.

To check that the participants recognized the qualifications of the applicant, participants were asked to evaluate the quality of the applicants' education and work experience on a scale of 1 (Extremely Poor) to 7 (Extremely Good).

RESULTS

A *t*-test revealed no difference in the evaluation of the applicants' education of the résumé in the condition of career break without support programme (*M* = 5.15, *SD* = 0.86) as compared to the résumé in the condition of career break with support programme (*M* = 5.29, *SD* = 0.78, *t* (58) = 0.66, *ns*). In addition, there was no difference in the evaluation of the applicants' work experience of the résumé in the condition of career break without support programme (*M* = 4.74, *SD* = 1.13) as compared to the résumé in the condition of career break with support programme (*M* = 5.16, *SD* = 1.07, *t* (58) =1.45, *ns*). Hence, the applicants' qualifications did not affect the participants' response to invite for an interview.

The correlations, means, standard deviations and internal consistency reliabilities for all the variables are reported in Table 10.1. We did not find a significant correlation of the résumé version with the evaluation of the woman applicant. Thus, hypothesis H1 was not supported.

Consistent with hypothesis H2, for a woman applicant who did not use the support programme after a career break, the higher the neosexism score of the respondents, the more negative was the response to 'Invite for interview'

Table 10.1   *Descriptive statistics, means and correlations*

	Mean	SD	1	2	3	4	5
1. Gender	0.90	0.31	1				
2. Age	38.59	5.02	0.14	1			
3. Neosexism	3.26	0.79	0.25	−0.14	1		
4. Manner of re-entry	0.53	0.50	−0.09	0.02	0.09	1	
5. Invite for interview	5.57	1.08	0.13	0.06	−0.21	0.01	1

$(r(27) = -0.52, p < 0.01)$. Neosexism did not show a significant correlation with 'Invite for interview' for the woman applicant who had completed the six-month support programme.

A step-wise regression with 'Invite for interview' as the dependent variable was performed to test hypothesis H2. Gender and age, entered as variables in Step 1, did not create a significant change in R^2. In Step 2, neosexism scores and the dummy variable, B_Ret, were entered as independent variables and produced no significant change in R^2. In Step 3, the interaction term was entered, resulting in a change in R^2 of 0.06, tending to significance at $p = 0.06$ $(B = 0.72, p = 0.06)$. To understand the nature of the interaction, we did simple slope analysis for the neosexism score on the mean response on 'Invite for interview' criteria for each applicant condition. Figure 10.1 depicts the interaction, which is consistent with H2. As neosexism increases, the likelihood to invite a woman applicant with no support programme decreases significantly $(B = -0.62, p < 0.01)$. Conversely, for a woman applicant who had used a support programme, neosexism did not relate to likelihood to invite for interview $(B = 0.10, ns)$.

Thus, participants with higher neosexism scores were less likely to invite a woman who did not have the support programme in her résumé for an interview than a woman who had the support programme in her résumé.

DISCUSSION AND WAY FORWARD

The results show that the presence of a support programme in the résumé of a woman applicant acts as a suppression factor for neosexist attitudes towards women. Neosexism contrasts with traditional sexism, which is an overt expression of prejudicial attitude towards women as a group. The principal hypothesis of neosexism is that while it may be correlated to traditional sexism, it is a better predictor of opposition to measures whose objectives are to reduce gender inequalities, resulting in a negative impact on the evaluation of women's potential. However, information about the completion of support programmes that do not guarantee a job post internship period reduces the

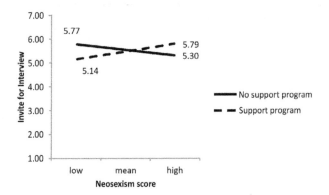

*Figure 10.1   Participants' invited for interview as a function of neosexism
and manner of re-entry of applicant (directly after career
break/after completion of support programme post career
break)*

ambiguity regarding women's professional capabilities after a career break. It
is possible that the lack of a guarantee of a job distinguishes such programmes
from affirmative action programmes, which may have led to a reverse result.

The support programmes analysed in this study and similar diversity
initiatives are being developed and implemented by various multinational
companies across their global offices. These locations also include offices in
nations that provide similar or more egalitarian maternity benefits as compared
to India. Women can avail themselves of maternity leave benefits in over 150
nations, with the United States being the only developed nation not to provide
paid maternity leave to women (Catalyst, 2018). Indian law mandates paid
maternity leave of 26 weeks to women workers (Ministry of Law and Justice,
2017). As such, the possible interpretation of such programmes as unfair and
unnecessary by neosexist individuals would be similar in any nation sharing
the above two commonalities. The results of this study could thus be generalizable to other national contexts where such misperceptions due to individual
attitudes could occur.

However, we do not refute existence of contextual differences (Ridgeway
and Correll, 2004) that may affect individual attitudes. While males and
females are situated differently in Indian society, and workplaces reflect
this societal structure (Datta and Bhardwaj, 2015), current global business
initiatives for women in leadership positions have led to the creation of
women-centric policies and budgets in India as well (Sharma, 2019). As
a majority of our respondents were employed in multinational companies, such

industrial-level transition into diversity might have suppressed the expression of overt neosexist attitudes, which is captured in our study.

Direction by authority is another factor that may cause suppression of overt discriminatory behaviour. As the programme was described as an organizational initiative communicated by the HR department to be noted while sharing the résumé of the applicant, an additional study on the effect of authority on the relationship of the respondents' neosexism scores and the evaluation of women applicants is proposed. Brief and colleagues' (2000) study on the expression of racism in hiring decisions found that the average rating of black applicants was lower in a climate of racial bias. Justification to act on the bias was derived from the norm that seemed to portray racial discrimination as acceptable. With the introduction of several targeted programmes inviting women who had taken a break from their career to re-join the industry, we propose that the prevalence of a norm of support for such women applicants will impact evaluation of applicants even in the condition of no support programme in the résumé. With many multinational companies in India seeking to improve gender friendliness in their workplaces (Rajesh, 2013; SHEROES, 2018), a future study could compare the evaluation of women who complete the support programme from a different company than from the same company.

CONCLUSION

Our study provides information on the effect of neosexism on the evaluation of woman returning to work after a career break, and the suppression effect of the completion of a support programme. We have discussed scope for further research that would provide a deeper understanding of factors affecting the efficacy of support programmes. Such information would be useful for organizations looking to begin new initiatives, as well as examining the effect of current practices.

REFERENCES

Andersson, K. (2015), 'Predictors of re-employment: a question of attitude, behavior, or gender?', *Scandinavian Journal of Psychology*, **56**(4), 438–46.

Brief, A.P., J. Dietz, R.R. Cohen, S.D. Pugh and J.B. Vaslow (2000), 'Just doing business: modern racism and obedience to authority as explanations for employment discrimination', *Organizational Behavior and Human Decision Processes*, **81**(1), 72–97.

Cabrera, E.F. (2009), 'Fixing the leaky pipeline: five ways to retain female talent', *People and Strategy*, **32**(1), 40–45.

Catalyst (2018), 'Women in the workforce – global: quick take', 31 October 2018, accessed 20 January 2020 at https://www.catalyst.org/research/women-in-the -workforce-global/.

Correll, S.J., S. Benard and I. Paik (2007), 'Getting a job: is there a motherhood penalty?', *American Journal of Sociology*, **112**(5), 1297–338.

Crandall, C. and A. Eshleman (2003), 'A justification-suppression model of the expression and experience of prejudice', *Psychological Bulletin*, **129**(3), 414–46.

Datta, S. and G. Bhardwaj (2015), 'Exploring the impact of gender, proportional numerical strength at workplace and gender typing of jobs on the experienced work alienation', *Indian Journal of Health and Wellbeing*, **6**(5), 453–60.

Eagly, A.H. and S.J. Karau (1991), 'Gender and the emergence of leaders: a meta-analysis', *Journal of Personality and Social Psychology*, **60**(5), 685–710.

Glick, P. and S.T. Fiske (2001), 'An ambivalent alliance: hostile and benevolent sexism as complementary justifications for gender inequality', *American Psychologist*, **56**(2), 109–18.

Hebl, M.R., E.B. King, P. Glick, S.L. Singletary and S. Kazama (2007), 'Hostile and benevolent reactions toward pregnant women: complementary interpersonal punishments and rewards that maintain traditional roles', *Journal of Applied Psychology*, **92**(6), 1499–511.

Koeber, C. and D.W. Wright (2006), 'Gender differences in the reemployment status of displaced workers human capital as signals that mitigate effects of bias', *The Journal of Socio-Economics*, **35**(5), 780–96.

Lovejoy, M. and P. Stone (2012), 'Opting back in: the influence of time at home on professional women's career redirection after opting out', *Gender, Work & Organization*, **19**(6), 631–53.

Ministry of Law and Justice (2017), 'The Maternity Benefit (Amendment) Act, 2017 No. 6 of 2017 (India)', accessed 13 July 2017 at https://labour.gov.in/sites/default/files/Maternity%20Benefit(Amendment)%20Act,2017.pdf.

Morgan, W.B., S.S. Walker, M.R. Hebl and E.B. King (2013), 'A field experiment: reducing interpersonal discrimination toward pregnant job applicants', *Journal of Applied Psychology*, **98**(5), 799–809.

Rajesh, S. (2013), 'Second career of women professionals in India: a corporate perspective', *Asian Journal of Management Research*, **4**, 27–47.

Rawat, P.S., S.K. Rawat, A. Sheikh and A. Kotwal (2019), 'Women organization commitment: role of the second career & their leadership styles', *Indian Journal of Industrial Relations*, **54**(3), 458–70.

Ridgeway, C. and S. Correll (2004), 'Motherhood as a status characteristic', *Journal of Social Issues*, **60**(4), 683–700.

Sabnavis, C. (2015), 'What holds back women?', *Livemint*, 30 August 2015, accessed 22 September 2015 at http://www.livemint.com/Leisure/zEm2eraMvVDGfOhwBvYXpI/What-holds-back-women.html.

Sharma, Y. (2019), 'Government at work to give women a bigger role', *The Economic Times*, 5 June 2019, accessed 6 June 2019 at https://economictimes.indiatimes.com/news/economy/policy/government-at-work-to-give-women-a-bigger-role/articleshow/69657834.cms?from=mdr.

SHEROES (2018), '25 returnee program for women in India' (2020), accessed 2 January 2018 at https://sheroes.com/articles/25-returnee-programs-for-women-in-india/Njg0NQ.

Singh S. (2015), 'The diversity dialogue', *Livemint*, 17 August 2015, accessed 10 January 2016 at http://www.livemint.com/Leisure/9bbWZQoWcnvJGJmHNya5CJ/The-diversity-dialogue.html.

Singletary, S. and M. Hebl (2009), 'Compensatory strategies for reducing interpersonal discrimination: the effectiveness of acknowledgments, increased positivity, and individuating information', *Journal of Applied Psychology*, **94**(3), 797–805.

Stamarski, C.S. and L.S. Son Hing (2015), 'Gender inequalities in the workplace: the effects of organizational structures, processes, practices, and decision makers' sexism', *Frontiers in Psychology*, 6, article 1400.

Tougas, F., R. Brown, A.M. Beaton and S. Joly (1995), 'Neosexism: plus ça change, plus c'est pareil', *Personality and Social Psychology Bulletin*, **21**(8), 842–9.

World Economic Forum (2014), *The Global Gender Gap Report*, Geneva: World Economic Forum.

Zikic, J., R.J. Burke and L. Fiksenbaum (2008), 'Gender differences in involuntary job loss and the reemployment experience: less there than meets the eye', *Gender in Management: An International Journal*, **23**(4), 247–61.

Zimmerman, L.M. and M.A. Clark (2016), 'Opting-out and opting-in: a review and agenda for future research', *Career Development International*, **21**(6), 603–33.

11. Can we release the brake on the career re-entry of mothers? A UK perspective

Anna Katharina Bader and John Blenkinsopp

INTRODUCTION

Despite increases in workforce participation of mothers in the UK, only 65 per cent of mothers, whose youngest child is a toddler, work (Office for National Statistics [ONS], 2017) and many decide to leave (or feel forced to leave) after they return from a child-related career break (Department for Business Innovation and Skills [BIS] and Equality and Human Rights Commission [EHRC], 2016). Furthermore, 93 per cent of women think it is difficult to combine a successful career and a family, and therefore 61 per cent of women returning from a career break come back on a part-time basis (PricewaterhouseCoopers [PwC], 2016). The picture is even more dramatic in India, which has only a 27 per cent participation rate; among G-20 countries this is only better than Saudi Arabia (Saha, 2017). While there are many reasons for dropout and career disruptions experienced by women (for a review, see Kossek, Su and Wu, 2017), there are specific factors that affect the return of mothers to the workplace and their later career after taking a break to give birth to and raise a child. The term 'motherhood penalty' has been coined to describe the disadvantages women face in earnings and career when deciding to become a mother (England et al., 2016; Petersen, Penner and Høgsnes, 2014), even though pregnancy and maternity are protected characteristics under the UK Equality Act 2010. Furthermore, taking demographic changes and the resulting reduction in available talent into account, retaining mothers in the workforce is of utmost importance, as a high dropout of mothers also means a great loss of skills and labour force potential.

In our chapter, we first review the main challenges mothers face when they want to return to work after a child-related break. We focus specifically on periods of pregnancy, maternity leave and immediate return and do not include challenges that may arise in the longer term. We then present research findings on factors on the individual, organizational and country level that influence whether, how and when mothers return, and develop a conceptual model that highlights the relevance of contextual, country-level factors. As a response to Chapter 10 by Kaushiva and Joshi, who used India as their research context, we will then look at the specific situation of returning mothers in the context of the UK (with reference to available information and data in India). Specifically, we present the legal and infrastructural situation (that is, the state of childcare) as well as cultural specificities in the UK in order to understand the challenges mothers face when returning to work there. Building on this, we then aim to identify mechanisms to reduce barriers to re-entry and provide recommendations on how to support the transition of mothers back to work.

RETURNING TO WORK AFTER A CHILD-RELATED CAREER BREAK

Challenges of Return

The challenges of being a working mother start long before the actual return, when women become pregnant. Research shows that while pregnant women receive much support in non-work roles, they are often penalized and discriminated against in work situations (BIS and EHRC, 2016; Hebl et al., 2007; Morgan et al., 2013) and many career-oriented women try to hide or downplay their pregnancy (Little et al., 2015). The journey continues when mothers come to make decisions about their return, as they are still expected to take the main responsibility for the upbringing of children. For instance, in the UK, the proportion of the population who believe that children will suffer if mothers are working outside home for pay is still 31 per cent (OECD, 2019a); in India it is even higher, at 76 per cent (OECD, 2019b). In consequence, mothers are likely to consider either staying at home or at least accepting career drawbacks upon return as a price for their motherhood.

When returning to work, mothers face stereotyping and suffer from distinct discrimination. Chapter 10 by Kaushiva and Joshi points towards mothers being associated with less knowledge, lower productivity and lower commitment to the job. Generally, mothers are considered less significant and competent in the workplace (Ridgeway and Correll, 2004b). Furthermore, they are typically associated with higher work–life balance struggles than fathers, as they are still expected to take the main responsibility for family care (Kossek and Ozeki, 1998; Van der Lippe, Van Breeschoten and Van Hek, 2019). Kaushiva and Joshi take an interesting approach to explain the persistence of such stereotypes and the lack of support mothers receive by using neosexism as their theoretical lens. Neosexism relates to a more subtle form of sexism based on a negative view of women hidden in cultural norms and the belief that women have achieved gender equality and only claim unfair advantages (Swim and Cohen, 1997). Kaushiva and Joshi argue that while blatant and open sexism and discrimination toward mothers have declined over the years, neosexism is on the rise. This creates a context that decreases the likelihood of managers and organizations appreciating the challenges of being a working mother and that makes them less likely to offer support to mothers. Consequently, returning mothers often suffer from indirect and more subtle forms of discrimination.

Factors Influencing Return-to-Work Decisions

Prior research highlights that various factors on different levels influence mothers' decisions about their return to work after a child-related career break (see Figure 11.1). First, on the individual level, personal characteristics such as high socio-economic status, income and education, full-time work and a lower number of children (Wallace, Saurel-Cubizolles and EDEN, 2012) as well as readiness to return, high work orientation and confidence of the mother (Desai and Waite, 1991; Hock, Christman and Hock, 1980; Ladge, Humberd and Eddleston, 2018; Vujinović, 2014) increase the likelihood of an early return. Additionally, family variables such as gender-role attitudes of the couple, gender egalitarianism and occupational level of the father (Katz-Wise, Priess and Hyde, 2010; Sterz et al., 2017; Wallace et al., 2012) have an effect on whether, when and how mothers return. Second, on the organizational level, organizational policies and practices such as offers of financial support during maternity leave, flexible work options and other return-to-work support (Bright Horizons, 2019) are supposed to help women find the best way of returning. Furthermore, in terms of organizational culture, hostility or support in the workplace affect mothers' decision-making (Ladge et al., 2018; Little et al., 2018). Third, on the country level, national influence can also be observed, and research reveals differences in return decisions of mothers according to country context. Macro variables such as maternity legislation (Gangl and Ziefle, 2015; Lalive et al., 2014) or care infrastructure and costs (Barrow, 1999) seem to greatly shape how return to work is planned within a society. Furthermore, cultural assumptions about the value and status of motherhood frame and shape decisions to return (Ridgeway and Correll, 2004a).

According to institutional theory, such country-level variables are of crucial importance as they strongly influence behaviour of organizations. For instance, formal institutions such as governments (North, 1990), provide a legal framework for women returning to work that organizations must adhere to and that they must implement and complement (Javornik and Oliver, 2019). Informal institutions such as shared cultural norms further affect organizational values that shape the behaviour in the organization. Adding to

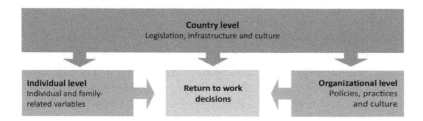

Figure 11.1   The meaning of country-level influences for return-to-work decisions

this, they entail guidance on how much deviation from legal frameworks is tolerated in a society (Meyer and Rowan, 1977; Oliver, 1991) – for example, in terms of discrimination. It is also well established that institutions on the country level shape behaviour of individuals (North, 1990) as, for example, societal values influence individual preferences toward gender roles (House et al., 2004). Therefore, acknowledging the importance of country-level, contextual variables for individuals and organizations, we turn now to a specific examination of the UK context with a focus on legislation, infrastructure and culture affecting returning mothers. To provide comprehensive insights, we compare the features in the UK with the Indian context and other contexts where appropriate.

THE UK CONTEXT

Rights During Pregnancy

The legal rights of mothers in the UK are very established and various regulations exist that protect (soon to be) mothers at work and influence their return. During pregnancy, women have special rights in terms of health and safety as well as receive sick pay in case of any pregnancy-related issues and paid leave for medical appointments (UK Government, 2019c). More importantly in terms of returning to work, the Equality Act 2010 protects pregnant women from unfair treatment and pregnancy-related dismissal. Therefore, dismissing women because they are pregnant is penalized by law, which ensures the probability of having a job upon return. In India, similar rules apply (Civilsdaily, 2016). However, looking at the lived experience of becoming mothers in the UK, a recent study (BIS and EHRC, 2016) reveals that they face significant discrimination at work. For instance, despite legal rights, it is estimated that 10 per cent of pregnant women are discouraged from attending medical appointments during work and 20 per cent experience negative comments and harassment at the job. Such experiences are likely to reduce the probability of return.

Maternity Leave

In the UK, maternity leave is more generous compared to India. Mothers have the right to up to 39 weeks of Statutory Maternity Pay, which they are entitled to if they have been in constant employment with the same company or organization for 26 weeks prior to the 15th week of their pregnancy and earn on average at least £118 per week (UK Government, 2019b), whereas, in India, mothers are only entitled to 26 weeks of paid maternity leave (Ministry of Law and Justice, 2017). Statutory Maternity Pay in the UK comprises 90 per cent of the average weekly earnings before tax for the first six weeks and is continued at £148.68 or 90 per cent of the average weekly earnings (whichever is lower) for the subsequent 33 weeks. Compared to other countries, mothers therefore often feel pressured to return to work early in the UK. For example, in Germany, parents are entitled to €300 to €1800 per month depending on their prior income (which is 65 per cent of the prior income or more, if prior income was very low) for 12 (if only one parent takes parental leave) or up to 14 months (if both partners take parental leave and both take at least two months) (Federal Ministry for Family Affairs, Senior Citizens, Women and Youth, 2019). Generally, mothers in the UK are entitled to 26 weeks of Ordinary Maternity Leave and 26 weeks of Additional Maternity Leave, which can partly be taken as Shared Parental Leave. Compared to Finland, where parents are given 161 weeks, this is rather restrictive; compared to the US, as the only developed country without statutory paid leave, in turn, the UK is quite supportive (Misra, 2018).

When analysing mothers' decisions on whether, when and how to return, the length of maternity leave policies is a critical and balancing act. On the one hand, time with small children is particularly valuable for mothers and they need a certain time to spend with their children before they are ready to return (Vujinović, 2014). Consequently, if mothers are pressured to return earlier than they feel happy with, this is likely to cause regret and resulting work–life conflicts decrease mental health in the long run (Carlson et al., 2011). On the other hand, extended leave policies have been shown to reduce mothers' overall labour force commitment (Gangl and Ziefle, 2015).

Rights Upon Return

Having made up their mind to return to their workplace, mothers have several rights that aim to support them in balancing their work and family needs. First, if they decide to extend time at home, they are allowed to do so but must give at least eight weeks' notice (UK Government, 2019b). If more care is required, parents are furthermore entitled to take up further unpaid parental leave later on. To ensure women can return to their career, women have the right to return to the same job and workplace after their maternity leave. However, many mothers experience job derailment or unwanted job changes and report worse treatment than before their pregnancy at the workplace (BIS and EHRC, 2016; PwC, 2016), even though this is explicitly outlawed.

In order to enable returning mothers to continue breastfeeding, employers must conduct a specific job assessment and provide suitable facilities (National Health Service, 2019). However, the UK has one of the lowest breastfeeding rates in the industrialized world and often women prefer to stop before they return to work (Boyer, 2012). To accommodate their preferences, returning mothers – as with every other employee – also have the right to claim flexible or reduced working time in order to balance their work and family responsibilities (UK Government, 2019a). Requiring returning mothers to work full-time is indirect discrimination as, despite progress towards equality, it remains the case that more women than men have childcare responsibilities. Yet, 38 per cent do not request flexible working, as they anticipate it will not be approved and many others experience disadvantages because of their part-time status (BIS and EHRC, 2016).

Childcare in the UK

Availability of childcare is one of the most important factors for working mothers. In the UK, the policy narrative has supported the return to work of mothers by increasing the amount and quality of childcare places available (May, 2011; Truss, 2013). In that regard, the government has intensified and expanded childcare policy – for example, by providing the right to free childcare for 30 hours a week. This has led to an almost 10 per cent increase in return to full-time work by mothers with young children (ONS, 2017). However, this policy only applies to children above the age of three; childcare for younger children is only supported via tax reductions (Department for Education, 2018). In India there is no system of public-funded early years education, yet family and social ties are quite strong, and families privately organize childcare. However, organizations with 50 or more employees are required to provide daycare facilities and permit mothers to visit those four times a day (Ministry of Law and Justice, 2017). In contrast, there is no such regulation in the UK. Furthermore, for example in Germany, every child over 12 months has the legal right to a childcare place (Heine, 2013); in the UK, children only have the right (and obligation) to attend education from school age on.

The UK childcare infrastructure is well established. The Department for Education (2018) estimated in spring 2018 that there were more than 80 000 providers offering more than 2.8 million childcare places. Most providers had spare capacity, indicating that most parents who need to arrange childcare would be able to find a place. However, childcare is quite expensive and the government has to support low-income families for them to be able to afford it. The policy context seems to send mixed signals. While there is a strong push for mothers to return there is neither a right to nor full financial support for childcare and 'the rhetoric of parental choice is linked to social class, access and affordability' (Page, 2013, p. 550). Furthermore, mothers often challenge the suitability of the childcare approach in such facilities and struggle with the guilt of not being there for their children (Page, 2013). Thus, despite genuine progress, the availability, cost and quality of childcare in the UK is still an important factor affecting decisions to stay at home.

Value of Motherhood in the UK

Generally, the UK has a more egalitarian approach to gender than India. The GLOBE study indicates that gender egalitarianism, that is, the degree to which societies try to minimize gender differences, is higher in the UK than in India (House et al., 2004). Similarly, the Social Institutions and Gender Equality Index indicates that gender inequalities are very low in the UK, compared to medium in India (OECD, 2019b, 2019a). With specific reference to being a mother in the UK, there seems, however, to be a paradoxical tension between a political push for women to work and the negative image of working mothers. Being a working mother is often linked to being a 'bad' mother and a risk for the children by more than 30 per cent of the UK population (OECD, 2019a). It is regularly perceived as indicating an egoistic 'wanting to have it all' mentality (Page, 2013), whereas staying at home has become a valued, personal choice of middle-class women (even) in the post-feminist era (Orgad and De Benedictis, 2015).

Fathers are still expected to take the breadwinner role and to work long hours in the UK. In consequence, their use of parental leave is still quite low (Kaufman, 2018), which reproduces traditional gender roles. Yet, contemporary research also shows that those traditional images are being challenged. A study analysing social media entries on definitions of 'good' motherhood shows that many entries highlight that 'good' mothers need interests outside their care responsibility and become role models for their kids. Yet, nurturing and 'being always there' for children is still seen as an important determinant of being a 'good' mother (Pedersen, 2016). Confronting these ambivalent messages might be one explanation why many women do not return to work, or return only part-time in order to comply with such requirements.

SUMMARY AND IMPLICATIONS FOR ORGANIZATIONAL RETURN TO WORK SUPPORT

In the UK, there has been much discussion on the policy level about how women can be supported in their journey back to work. Our chapter has highlighted the meaning of anti-discrimination laws as well as maternity leave, return, breastfeeding and flexible-working regulations and showed that in the UK the legal setting supports an early return. However, low maternity pay and the lack of free childcare for early years care often puts conflicting pressures on mothers as they are pushed to return early, but do not receive sufficient financial support for childcare. Furthermore, many mothers experience discrimination at work, report worse treatment than before their pregnancy, and encounter social tensions between their will or need to work and the role a good mother is expected to take.

To improve the experience of working mothers, legislation and also organizations are of particular importance. This is for two reasons. On the one hand, they are among the main actors responsible for implementing policy and legislation and must ensure that, for example, anti-discrimination and health legislation are respected. On the other hand, they are of high relevance as they strongly shape the experience of mothers through their policies, practices and culture before and after return. Interestingly, about 30 per cent of employers still do not offer any further support to returning mothers beyond financial support of maternity leave and the offer of flexible work and phased return (Bright Horizons, 2019). Offering flexible work and part-time working options are thus among the most frequently implemented practices. Other forms of support include return support programmes, as suggested in Chapter 10 by Kaushiva and Joshi, support for finding childcare or individual keep-in-touch and coaching offers (Bright Horizons, 2019; PwC, 2016). Furthermore, destigmatizing part-time (leadership) roles and reducing bias within organizations is of importance (PwC, 2016). Unfortunately, there is a lack of academic research identifying and assessing the effectiveness of return-to-work support policies and practices on actual return rates. Therefore, we conclude that more research is necessary such as Chapter 10 by Kaushiva and Joshi that identifies avenues to better understand the needs of returning mothers and offering effective support.

CONCLUSION

Mothers face distinct challenges when returning to work after a career break. In the UK context, mothers face ambivalent pressures as, on the one hand, policies support early return, while the general public still seem to support traditional mothering roles. Furthermore, discrimination and job derailments are a common experience of returning mothers. In consequence, beyond improving regulations at the policy level, organizations have a great responsibility to create environments that enable mothers continue their careers, as smoothing the return to work is a crucial first step to reducing the 'motherhood penalty'.

REFERENCES

Barrow, L. (1999), 'Childcare costs and the return-to-work decisions of new mothers', *Economic Perspectives*, **23**(4), 42–55.

Boyer, K. (2012), 'Affect, corporeality and the limits of belonging: breastfeeding in public in the contemporary UK', *Health and Place*, **18**(3), 552–60.

Bright Horizons (2019), *Parental Leave Policy & Reward Benchmark 2019*, accessed 1 October 2019 at https://www.myfamilycare.co.uk/resources/white-papers/parental -leave-policy-and-reward-benchmark-2019/.

Carlson, D.S., J.G. Grzywacz, M. Ferguson, E.M. Hunter, C.R. Clinch and T.A. Arcury (2011), 'Health and turnover of working mothers after childbirth via the work–family interface: an analysis across time', *Journal of Applied Psychology*, **95**(5), 1045–54.

Civilsdaily (2016), 'BLOG: 7 rights every pregnant woman in India should know about', 4 February 2016, accessed 1 October 2019 at https://www.thebetterindia .com/44843/rights-pregnant-women-india-janani-shishu-suraksha-karyakram/.

Department for Business Innovation and Skills (BIS) and Equality and Human Rights Commission (EHRC) (2016), *Pregnancy and Maternity-Related Discrimination and Disadvantage: Experiences of Mothers*, accessed 1 October 2019 at https:// www.equalityhumanrights.com/sites/default/files/mothers_report_-_bis-16-146 -pregnancy-and-maternity-related-discrimination-and-disadvantage-experiences-of -mothers_1.pdf.

Department for Education (2018), *Survey of Childcare and Early Years Providers: Main Summary, England*, accessed 1 October 2019 at https://assets.publishing .service.gov.uk/government/uploads/system/uploads/attachment_data/file/788753/ Survey_of_Childcare_and_Early_Years_Providers_2018_Main_Summary.pdf.

Desai, S. and L.J. Waite (1991), 'Women's employment during pregnancy and after the first birth: occupational characteristics and work commitment', *American Sociological Review*, **56**(4), 551–66.

England, P., J. Bearak, M.J. Budig and M.J. Hodges (2016), 'Do highly paid, highly skilled women experience the largest motherhood penalty?', *American Sociological Review*, **81**(6), 1161–89.

Federal Ministry for Family Affairs, Senior Citizens, Women and Youth (2019), 'Elterngeld' [Parental allowance], accessed 1 October 2019 at https://familienportal .de/familienportal/familienleistungen/elterngeld.

Gangl, M. and A. Ziefle (2015), 'The making of a good woman: extended parental leave entitlements and mothers' work commitment in Germany', *American Journal of Sociology*, **121**(2), 511–63.

Hebl, M.R., E.B. King, P. Glick, S.L. Singletary and S. Kazama (2007), 'Hostile and benevolent reactions toward pregnant women: complementary interpersonal punishments and rewards that maintain traditional roles', *Journal of Applied Psychology*, **92**(6), 1499–511.

Heine, F. (2013), 'Germany promises daycare for all', *Spiegel International*, accessed 1 October 2019 at https://www.spiegel.de/international/germany/law-goes-into-effect -requiring-child-care-for-most-german-children-a-914320.html.

Hock, E., K. Christman and M. Hock (1980), 'Factors associated with decisions about return to work in mothers of infants', *Developmental Psychology*, **16**(5), 535–6.

House, R.J.J., P.J. Hanges, M. Javidan, P.W. Dorfman and V. Gupta (2004), *Culture, Leadership, and Organizations – The GLOBE Study of 62 Societies*, Thousand Oaks, CA: Sage.

Javornik, J. and L. Oliver (2019), 'Converting shared parental leave into shared parenting: the role of employers and use of litigation by employees in the UK', in M.A. Yerkes, J. Javornik and A. Kurowska (eds), *Social Policy and the Capability Approach*, Bristol: Policy Press, pp. 61–82.

Katz-Wise, S.L., H.A. Priess and J.S. Hyde (2010), 'Gender-role attitudes and behavior across the transition to parenthood', *Developmental Psychology*, **46**(1), 18–28.

Kaufman, G. (2018), 'Barriers to equality: why British fathers do not use parental leave', *Community, Work and Family*, **21**(3), 310–25.

Kossek, E.E. and C. Ozeki (1998), 'Work–family conflict, policies, and the job–life satisfaction relationship: a review and directions for organizational behavior–human resources research', *Journal of Applied Psychology*, **83**(2), 139–49.

Kossek, E.E., R. Su and L. Wu (2017), '"Opting out" or "pushed out"? Integrating perspectives on women's career equality for gender inclusion and interventions', *Journal of Management*, **43**(1), 228–54.

Ladge, J.J., B.K. Humberd and K.A. Eddleston (2018), 'Retaining professionally employed new mothers: the importance of maternal confidence and workplace support to their intent to stay', *Human Resource Management*, **57**(4), 883–900.

Lalive, R., A. Schlosser, A. Steinhauer and J. Zweimüller (2014), 'Parental leave and mothers' careers: the relative importance of job protection and cash benefits', *Review of Economic Studies*, **81**(1), 219–65.

Little, L.M., S. Paustian-Underdahl, A.S. Hinojosa and K.P. Zipay (2018), 'Managing the harmful effects of unsupportive organizations during pregnancy', *Journal of Applied Psychology*, **103**(6), 631–43.

Little, L.M., V. Smith Major, A.S. Hinojosa and D.L. Nelson (2015), 'Professional image maintenance: how women navigate pregnancy in the workplace', *Academy of Management Journal*, **58**(1), 8–37.

May, T. (2011), 'The Home Secretary's speech on women and the economy', *Gov.uk*, accessed 1 October 2019 at http://www.homeoffice.gov.uk/media-centre/speeches/ home-sec-equality-speech.

Meyer, J.W. and B. Rowan (1977), 'Institutionalized organizations: formal structure as myth and ceremony', *American Journal of Sociology*, **83**(2), 340–53.

Ministry of Law and Justice (2017), *Maternity Benefit (Amendment) Act, 2017*, accessed 1 October 2019 at https://labour.gov.in/sites/default/files/Maternity%20Benefit %20Amendment%20Act%2C2017%20.pdf.

Misra, J. (2018), 'The US is stingier with childcare and maternity leave than the rest of the world', *The Conversation*, 19 April 2018, accessed 1 October 2019 at http:// theconversation.com/the-us-is-stingier-with-child-care-and-maternity-leave-than -the-rest-of-the-world-94770.

Morgan, W.B., S.S. Walker, M.R. Hebl and E.B. King (2013), 'A field experiment: reducing interpersonal discrimination toward pregnant job applicants', *Journal of Applied Psychology*, **98**(5), 799–809.

National Health Service (2019), 'Breastfeeding and going back to work', accessed 1 October 2019 at https://www.nhs.uk/conditions/pregnancy-and-baby/breastfeeding -back-to-work/.

North, D.C. (1990), 'An introduction to institutions and institutional change', in D.C. North (ed.), *Institutions, Institutional Change and Economic Performance*, Cambridge, UK: Cambridge University Press, pp. 3–10.

OECD (2019a), 'Discrimination in the family', *Social Institutions & Gender Index: United Kingdom*, accessed 1 October 2019 at https://www.genderindex.org/wp -content/uploads/files/datasheets/2019/GB.pdf.

OECD (2019b), 'Discrimination in the family', *Social Institutions and Gender Index: India*, accessed 1 October 2019 at https://www.genderindex.org/wp-content/ uploads/files/datasheets/2019/IN.pdf.

Office for National Statistics (ONS) (2017), 'More mothers with young children working full-time', 26 September 2017, accessed 1 October 2019 at https://www.ons.gov .uk/employmentandlabourmarket/peopleinwork/employmentandemployeetypes/ articles/moremotherswithyoungchildrenworkingfulltime/2017-09-26.

Oliver, C. (1991), 'Strategic responses to institutional processes', *Academy of Management Review*, **16**(1), 145–79.

Orgad, S. and S. De Benedictis (2015), 'The "stay-at-home" mother, postfeminism and neoliberalism: content analysis of UK news coverage', *European Journal of Communication*, **30**(4), 418–38.

Page, J. (2013), 'Will the "good" [working] mother please stand up? Professional and maternal concerns about education, care and love', *Gender and Education*, **25**(5), 548–63.

Pedersen, S. (2016), 'The good, the bad and the "good enough" mother on the UK parenting forum Mumsnet', *Women's Studies International Forum*, **59**, 32–8.

Petersen, T., A.M. Penner and G. Høgsnes (2014), 'From motherhood penalties to husband premia: the new challenge for gender equality and family policy, lessons from Norway', *American Journal of Sociology*, **119**(5), 1434–72.

PricewaterhouseCoopers (PwC) (2016), *Women Returners: The £1 Billion Career Break Penalty for Professional Women*, accessed 1 October 2019 at https://www .pwc.co.uk/economic-services/women-returners/pwc-research-women-returners -nov-2016.pdf.

Ridgeway, C.L. and S.J. Correll (2004a), 'Motherhood as a status characteristic', *Journal of Social Issues*, **60**(4), 683–700.

Ridgeway, C.L. and S.J. Correll (2004b), 'Unpacking the gender system: a theoretical perspective on gender beliefs and social relations', *Gender & Society*, **18**(4), 510–31.

Saha, D. (2017), 'Only 27% Indian women are in labour force – the lowest among BRICS countries', *Business Standard*, 4 May 2017, accessed 1 October 2019 at https://www.business-standard.com/article/current-affairs/rising-income-stability -linked-to-declining-working-females-in-india-117050400150_1.html.

Sterz, A.M., T. Grether and B.S. Wiese (2017), 'Gender-role attitudes and parental work decisions after childbirth: a longitudinal dyadic perspective with dual-earner couples', *Journal of Vocational Behavior*, **101**, 104–18.

Swim, J.K. and L.L. Cohen (1997), 'Overt, covert, and subtle sexism: a comparison between the attitudes toward women and modern sexism scales', *Psychology of Women Quarterly*, **21**(1), 103–18.

Truss, E. (2013), *More Great Childcare: Raising Quality and Giving Parents More Choice*, London: Department for Education.

UK Government (2019a), 'Flexible working', accessed 1 October 2019 at https://www .gov.uk/flexible-working.

UK Government (2019b), 'Maternity pay and leave', accessed 1 October 2019 at https://www.gov.uk/maternity-pay-leave.

UK Government (2019c), 'Pregnant employees' rights', accessed 1 October 2019 at https://www.gov.uk/working-when-pregnant-your-rights.

Van der Lippe, T., L. van Breeschoten and M. van Hek (2019), 'Organizational work–life policies and the gender wage gap in European workplaces', *Work & Occupations*, **46**(2), 111–48.

Vujinović, N. (2014), '"… There's no substituting actual time with your child": understanding first-time mothers' readiness to return to work', *Journal of Industrial Relations*, **56**(4), 488–507.

Wallace, M., M. Saurel-Cubizolles and EDEN mother–child cohort study (2012), 'Returning to work one year after childbirth: data from the mother–child cohort EDEN', *Maternal Child Health Journal*, **17**(8), 1432–40.

PART VI

Academic careers

The chapters under this topic discuss academic careers. They both point to the convergence towards the Anglo-Saxon model but also highlight that this model is adapted to the local context.

Ravishankar Venkata Kommu and Amit Dhiman write about the 'The changing nature of academic careers in management education in India'. They take the French sociologist Pierre Bourdieu's widely used Western theory of practice and apply it to a particular 'career field' of Indian career owners, namely, academics in management education. Like other authors, they highlight the 'winds of change' that passed through the Indian economy in the early 1990s. They point out that those winds of globalization, neoliberalism and managerialism led to a change in the particular career field. Careers in the field of management education in India are now more expected to develop according to the standards of the Anglo-Saxon model. The chapter sharply illustrates the tension between Western thinking and indigenization in Indian business schools.

Yehuda Baruch discusses 'The changing nature of academic careers in management education in Western societies'. He also uses the lens of Bourdieu's theory of practice to analyse how the academic career identity of scholars in management education has changed in the West. Next, he takes a broader ecological view of these scholars' career patterns. He describes a business ecosystem made up of interconnected individuals, institutions and social entities, and also identifies a dominant Anglo-Saxon model across the global management education arena. In this, supply and demand factors of participating universities shape and are shaped by academic career paths.

In comparing the two chapters, you can see two separate perspectives on management academics' careers shaped by overlapping economic forces and stemming from distinctive Eastern and Western contexts. Both chapters show how academic careers in management education are evolving in the same direction. Yet, they also clearly point out how contextual differences still matter. Your opportunity is to compare the two perspectives, as well as to appreciate wider differences in what they contribute to the examination of a particular profession in both Indian and Western contexts. You may also see a further opportunity to consider similar contrasts between other professions with which you are familiar.

12. The changing nature of academic careers in management education in India

Ravishankar Venkata Kommu and Amit Dhiman

INTRODUCTION

Arthur and Rousseau have cited academic careers in the American context as an ideal example of boundaryless careers because of frequent migration of academics across universities, well-defined criteria for upward mobility, strong career autonomy and because academic careers draw validity and marketability from outside their organizations. Baruch and Hall (2004) argued that given its characteristics, the academic career could act as a model for future careers. The autonomy and perceived self-management of careers by academics emphasize the role played by agency in their careers with minimal structural interventions. Academics seek validation from their peers outside of academia via contributions to peer-reviewed journals and participation in conferences, even though universities do impose criteria for promotion, funding and so on. Furthermore, academics are also known to have their own values that they adhere to, which significantly shape their careers. In other words, academic careers are also protean.

This is not to say that there are no structural constraints. In labour economics, Ehrenberg (2003) showed that faculty at public universities were progressively paid less than at private universities because of a reluctance to increase student tuition fees. He also reported that there was a growing dispersion of academic salaries across all academic institutions and that funding for research was higher in private institutions. In other words, similar to much of the career research in the past, with a few exceptions (for example, Dany, Louvel and Valette, 2011; Duberley, Cohen and Mallon, 2006) studies on academic careers have been dominated by either the agency or the structure point of view.

Much research on higher education research has been conducted on issues pertaining to the governance of academics and rising managerialism. Klikauer (2015, p. 1105) defined managerialism as an ideology 'that justifies the application of its one-dimensional managerial techniques to all areas of work, society, and capitalism on the grounds of superior ideology, expert training, and the exclusiveness of managerial knowledge necessary to run public institutions and society as corporations'. The key project of managerialism is a perpetuation of the idea that managerial techniques transcend not only industries but also institutions such as universities and every other public or private organization/activity in society. The roots of managerialism are in ideas such as the 'profit motive' and in management philosophies such as Taylorism and Fordism. Managerialism co-evolved with neoliberalism, and throughout the world managerialism has followed neoliberalization, therefore the two ideologies can sometimes be conflated. Neoliberalism is an ideology that advocates free markets, deregulation and privatization. Neoliberalization has led to the shifting of political priorities from welfare to deregulation and individuals becoming more aspirational and expecting a lot less from the state in the form of welfare schemes. Managerialism advocates the conduct of all institutions to imitate corporations through managerial techniques. The introduction of performance appraisal systems in various public sector enterprises that are supposed to deliver essential services to the public is a case in point.

Scholars in teaching evaluation research have for long maintained that the increasing use of student evaluations of teaching in performance appraisals of faculty members is a result of the increasing neoliberalism and managerialism in university administrations (Valsan and Sproule, 2008). Vannini (2004) studied the authenticity and inauthenticity felt by academics in America and showed that freedom and passion were critical for them to feel authentic. Further studies by the same author showed that the push towards 'publish or perish' and forced grade distributions were causes of inauthenticity among faculty members (Vannini and Williams, 2009). More recently, Cannizzo (2018) showed that motivations of academic workers are influenced by the ideal of an authentic self, realized through engaging in values and norms of the profession. In the higher education research tradition, focus has been around rising managerialism, neoliberalism and performativity (Kolsaker, 2008).

In this chapter, we attempt to trace the 'career field', as defined by Chudzikowski and Mayrhofer (2011), of academics in management education in India and the impact of structural changes such as neoliberalization and globalization on the career field. Very little work has focused on careers in India, and even less on academic work and academic careers. Unlike in Western countries with home-grown traditions of management and social science research in general, management as a discipline was largely adopted in India.

These educational dependencies coupled with sweeping economic changes make India a context where academic career scripts have evolved dramatically.

CAREER FIELDS AND CAREER HABITUS

In this section, we attempt to briefly introduce Bourdieu's theory, followed by an argument for employing Bourdieu's theory in career studies as suggested by Iellatchitch, Mayrhofer and Meyer (2003). Bourdieu (1977) uses the metaphor of a game to explain the concept of a social field, and the various capitals that help in acquiring a status within that field. Every game has its own rules. These rules are known to all the players participating in it. Bourdieu calls these rules *doxa*. These rules are nothing but legitimized popular opinion. Every individual is endowed with certain economic as well as cultural and social capital. Cultural capital in the form of tastes in clothing, music, cuisine, mannerisms, accent and diction, and social capital in the form of the right networks, help them substantially in furthering their interests. This cultural capital is further classified into three forms called embodied, objectified and institutionalized. Embodied cultural capital is everything that is inherited and non-genetic, that is, part of one's persona due to socialization of cultures and traditions through family. Objectified cultural capital is tangible objects such as works of art or scientific instruments. Institutional cultural capital represents institutional recognition such as academic degrees or professional memberships that help an individual gain an advantage in life. In every game, only a certain kind of endowment is useful. This subset of the overall endowment that is relevant to a particular field or game is called symbolic capital.

In every game, the player develops a certain feel and style over a period of time, which he or she uses almost unconsciously while playing the game. These tendencies, style and 'feel' that the player has developed over time that keep changing with further engagement in the game (field) are called *habitus*. The dominant players in any field have the right symbolic capital and the necessary habitus to be successful. In other words, habitus is the socialized norms and tendencies that guide behaviour and thinking. Formally, habitus is 'the way society becomes deposited in persons in the form of lasting dispositions, or trained capacities and structured propensities to think, feel and act in determinant ways, which then guide them' (Wacquant, 2005, p. 316).

Bourdieu argues that power is socially, culturally and symbolically constructed and relegitimized with the interplay of agency and structure. Bourdieu draws heavily from scholars in linguistics such as Lacan and Saussure to show how the process of legitimization of power plays in the case of language. The 'standard language' at any given point of time is a 'normalization' of the language spoken by the dominant class. This 'standard language', however, is subject to change, with competing classes indulging in symbolic violence.

The emergent victor claims the right to 'standard language' (Bourdieu, 1991). Bourdieu also empirically showed through meticulous studies that 'taste' was an important signifier of class, a construct deeply internalized by individuals right from childhood, and was an important tool in the hands of the bourgeoisie and the petite bourgeoisie that helped them in both social and cultural reproduction of class and to also subjugate the lower classes as well as impede their upward social mobility (Bourdieu, 1984).

The groundwork for applying Bourdieu's theory to career studies was done by Iellatchitch et al. (2003), who extended the concept of habitus to career habitus and fields to career fields. They defined career habitus as:

> [...] a *habitus* that fits a particular career field and may be defined by the dispositions which tend to be actualized automatically within a career field. A particular career *habitus* ensures that an agent acts, perceives and thinks according to the rules of the field, and his movements within the field of career appear as the natural way. He/she acts intentionally without intention. Agents that have dominant positions within a field are prototypic carriers of career *habitus* specific for this field. (Iellatchitch et al., 2003, p. 738)

Iellatchitch et al. (2003), Chudzikowski and Mayrhofer (2011) and Inkson et al. (2012) draw attention to another aspect of careers that came back into focus thanks to the boundaryless careers literature, which is boundaries themselves. From a Bourdieusian perspective, boundaries are nothing but career fields to which individuals belong. It is now understood that boundaries are socially constructed and also personally constructed in the sense that an individual's approach towards their career is best understood when we know which career they think they are in. For example, academics may see themselves as intellectuals, or teachers, or researchers and in some cases consultants. Inkson et al. (2012) call for further empirical work that reports how individuals construct boundaries, defend their boundaries and how they cope with changing boundaries or cross boundaries.

In a study of partners in Big 4 professional service firms across five nations, Spence et al. (2015) unravel the habitus using qualitative interviews and find that partner habitus in Bangladesh is very different from other countries in terms of entrepreneurial and public service dispositions. They point out that understanding the habitus helps us map the dynamics of transnational careers. Fernando and Cohen (2016) use accounts of 32 Indian immigrant academics in a research-intensive university in UK to understand their habitus and show that, contrary to popular perception, the Indian academics are much better placed to outperform their British counterparts, due to the transferability of various capitals and their motivations for work that are a result of the competitive atmosphere in their home country from which they have arrived.

THE FIELD OF ACADEMIC CAREERS IN MANAGEMENT EDUCATION IN INDIA

The task of viewing academia as a 'field' was performed by Bourdieu himself in his analysis of the events surrounding the 1968 student unrest in France: that academics recognized a shared disposition (habitus), that they in turn perpetuated by way of 'indoctrination' and training of new entrants. The '*doxa*' or the rules of the game that all participants recognized included acts like completion and publication of a thesis or seeking the right supervisor (Bourdieu, 1988). In this section, we attempt to delineate the 'field' of academic careers in management education in India. The choice of the discipline of management is a matter of convenience and location as the author is affiliated to the Indian Institute of Management Calcutta, a premier business school in India. The experience of an individual in a business school is not necessarily shared by an individual pursuing a career in a traditional university, and the story of the Indian Institutes of Management (IIM) (as we will see later) is certainly distinct from the other academic institutions in India. However, an analysis of academic careers in management education in India is bound to also inform us, at least partially, of the practice of academic careers in disciplines other than management and in institutions other than IIMs in India. It is also important to note that this chapter keeps in mind work life of academics in IIMs at Ahmedabad, Bangalore, Calcutta and Lucknow. While institutional environments are similar in other IIMs, they are also different in many ways. Apart from the IIMs, the majority of management institutions in the country are governed by somewhat different guidelines, and therefore their evolution in a fast neoliberalizing socio-economic set-up may have followed a different trajectory. However, it is safe to say that the four IIMs, as the highest-ranked business schools in India, have had considerable influence on how other business schools conducted their affairs.

The IIMs are a group of 20 academic institutions of management education and research in India. The IIMs at Ahmedabad (A) and Calcutta (C) were the earliest to be set up in 1961, followed by Bangalore (B) in 1973, Lucknow (L) in 1984, Kozhikode (K) and Indore (I) in 1996 and Shillong (S) in 2007. A group of six IIMs were set up in 2010 at various locations, followed by another seven in 2015–16. Each new IIM was 'mentored' by one of the older IIMs. All IIMs have more or less identical processes of administration. All the IIMs primarily run the flagship postgraduate programme (Postgraduate Diploma in Management, equivalent to an MBA) along with the Fellow Programme in Management (FPM, equivalent to a PhD). Since the inception of the first IIMs, these institutions have garnered significant media attention for their ability to assure jobs and flourishing careers for their alumni. IIMs together with IITs have been symbols of social mobility and merit.

Unlike in the US, academic careers in India are largely (usually) restricted to one single institution. In the IIMs there are typically two kinds of faculty members: those with somewhat long careers in the industry or government, after which they acquire a PhD degree and then take up an academic job; and those who have remained in academia throughout life. A PhD (or an equivalent) degree was not mandatory for a permanent job as a faculty member at an IIM up to 2010.

The IIMs were at the forefront of the development of management education in India. The institutional practices adopted at IIMs have influenced management institutes across the country. A further investigation into the origin of these institutions was conducted by Sancheti (1986), who through detailed historiographical accounts traced the lobbying efforts made by American educationists such as Dr Douglas Ensminger in favour of investing in an 'American model of management education'. Dr Douglas Ensminger was the head of the Ford Foundation in early independent India, and the foundation subsequently funded and oversaw the establishment of both IIM Ahmedabad and IIM Calcutta. The exercise of soft power by an American philanthropic institution such as the Ford Foundation played on the need felt by the planners of early independent India to 'modernize' and to catch up with the scientific progress made by the rest of the world (Sancheti, 1988). Jammulamadaka (2017) argues that the years following the establishment of IIMs as evangelical schools of American managerial thought, prompted attempts at nativist theorizations of management practice, particularly in the domains of people management and organizational behaviour. This 'indigenization' was done through reading management theories from an Indian perspective or strategies such as including the economic, political and historical context of India in the curriculum of MBA students and in research agendas. Several scholars pursued this indigenization of management as a discipline – however, with a stated acceptance of the dominance of management and managerialism as conceived in the West.

Scholars such as Thakur and Babu (2017), themselves faculty members at IIM Calcutta, continue to call for incorporating the perspectives of the Global South to move beyond the prevailing Western ethnocentrism in the praxis of management. The quasi-socialist outlook of the planners of the economy of newly independent India also viewed these institutions primarily as suppliers of the much needed managerial workforce, and hence the primary function of the faculty member at these institutions was to deliver an understanding of management as understood in the West to the future manager in India. Each faculty member at these institutions was teacher first, and research, administration and training/consulting to clients in the industry were the other components of work that were treated as secondary.

The stated policy prescriptions by the Ford Foundation for various aspects of administration were implemented, the most significant of which was the emphasis on training of faculty in the American system, either in the form of PhD degrees obtained in American institutions or in the form of hiring American scholars for short durations of one or two years for the purpose of instilling the right 'culture' in the IIMs. Therefore, the very origin of these institutions, while international in nature, was imitative and dependent on resources from their American counterparts/'mentor' institutions. Over the years, while the financial dependence on the Ford Foundation was done away with, the influence of pedagogies, knowledge systems and administrative patterns adopted from the American mentors, persisted.

In Bourdieusian terms, in the 'career field' of an academic in the management education scene in India, the institutional capital obtained by association with American educational institutions was rewarded. Training as academics in the IIMs themselves was treated as next best, and training in the existing universities in India was deemed undesirable, although many with PhDs from Indian university set-ups eventually did populate the ranks of the IIMs. More specifically, the career field of academics in management in India was defined by their dependence on their Western counterparts for core constructs in management, pedagogies and administrative patterns. However, there were active attempts to resist these dependencies and IIMs carved their own identity by indigenizing the knowledge they were transmitting. Second, as institutions that captured public imagination as arbiters of social mobility, the IIMs were regarded as a success story primarily as teaching institutions. Therefore, as institutions that were strongly autonomous and faculty administered, the dominant components of a faculty member's job description were teaching and providing consulting and training services to industry executives. Research was driven more by personal motivation and peer pressure to publish rather than any institutional requirements (Kumar and Israel, 2013). It is important to remember that these institutional requirements were to a large extent instituted after seeking inputs from faculty members themselves. The relatively small size of each institute (older IIMs averaging 100 and younger IIMs averaging less than 50) and the autonomy given to faculty members meant that voices of faculty members were heard through various committees and by the directors of their respective institutes.

In terms discussed in Arthur and Rousseau (1996), Baruch (2013) and Baruch and Hall (2004), in spite of many efforts to Americanize, the academic career in management education in India was restricted largely to only one institution. The perceived peers of the practitioners of this academic career were largely restricted to India, predominantly employed in IIMs, although sometimes also in management or social science departments at traditional universities. The aspect of the career most pertinent to the conception in Arthur and Rousseau (1996) was the strong autonomy of the faculty members, the freedom accorded to them to pursue their own interests, but most importantly giving them the freedom to contribute to institute-level policy-making that had bearing on their careers as well. Therefore, while they were not boundaryless in most senses, they were boundaryless in the sense that they had the agency to conduct their careers as they pleased.

WINDS OF CHANGE

In the year 1991, in exchange for being bailed out of a balance of payments crisis, India accepted a set of fundamental changes to its economy as prescribed by the International Monetary Fund. Called the Liberalization Reforms, these reforms were along three lines: liberalization, globalization and privatization. Liberalization meant a relaxation or in many cases discontinuation of controls on production of goods and services. Globalization meant a relaxation of tariffs and a journey towards integration with the global economy and discarding protectionism. As a part of quasi-socialist economic regime, the Indian government had since independence established various public sector enterprises that were in many cases virtual monopolies in their respective industries. The government committed to gradually exit from these companies; this process of privatization is still underway.

These reforms had significant consequences for the economy. Several new industries such as the information technology sector flourished under the new regime. The most important change, however, came in the form of the neoliberalization of everyday discourse. Principles of free market economics became a part of common sense logic and the expectations of citizens from the government and institutions began to change drastically, and continue to change (Sinha, 2017). Even private corporations began to function differently, with the very nature of management as a profession changing. as documented by Pratap and Saha (2018). Earlier, Varman, Saha and Skålén (2011) had through interviews of MBA students in IIM Calcutta shown how students were getting indoctrinated into a neoliberal governmentality and market subjectivity as a part of the exercises in job search and preparations for post-MBA career.

The neoliberalization of everyday discourse led subsequent governments to withdraw financial support to older IIMs and expect them to be autonomous by raising their own funds through fees and revenue from consulting and training programmes. Also, the proliferation of ranking exercises in various national and international magazines that have their own criteria for evaluating a business school led to the older IIMs participating in a few influential ones. By participating in these rankings, IIMs were for the first time evaluating themselves against a global set of benchmarks, however arbitrary they may be, and for the first time began to be affected by how other academic institutions around the world competed among themselves. This meant that the career scripts of academics in Western context began to influence the expectations from their 'peers' in India, most significantly in the form of research output. With increasing participation in global ranking lists and with increasing pressure from the government to perform on par with elite global institutions, IIMs began directing more attention and resources towards research (Umarji, 2016).

This emphasis on research was also aided by changes in management as a discipline itself, as argued by Ojha (2017). The scientificof management, with increasing emphasis on generalizable knowledge to obtain the legitimacy of natural sciences followed by a marketization of business schools, led to accreditation agencies such as the Association to Advance Collegiate Schools of Business (AACSB) adapting their expectations from business schools seeking accreditations. Business schools in India, much like business schools in Europe and Asia, almost naturally had to seek this accreditation to establish their credibility as schools as good as their American counterparts. The requirements of accreditation agencies have many documented undesirable impacts on research output, such as an increase in the number of co-authors. The biggest impact of the accreditation agencies was the curtailing of institutional identity and conforming to a global standard, disallowing institutions from responding to their specific context.

A combination of these factors led to rapidly increasing demand for research, with quality research output becoming mandatory to get a job or promoted in the academic career. Studies such as the one conducted by Sahoo et al. (2017) became more prevalent as research output has now become the most important quantifier of faculty 'output'. While Sahoo et al. (2017) performed various analyses to evaluate the research output of each and every faculty member of close to 25 management institutes or departments in India, the data as represented in Figure 12.1 is most telling.

The collective research output began increasing from the early 1990s, and exponentially increased after the year 2000. Research as measured in terms of quality established by agencies such as the Australian Business Deans Council (ABDC), has become the most important component of a faculty member's job description, particularly for early-career academics seeking confirmation or promotion in the system.

CONCLUSION

Neoliberalization and rising managerialism in academic institutions, more specifically in the case of the management education scene, has led to a dramatic change in the career 'fields'. In other words, even if the individual does not move across institutions, the practice and the progress of an individual's academic career are now increasingly determined by the 'output' and career

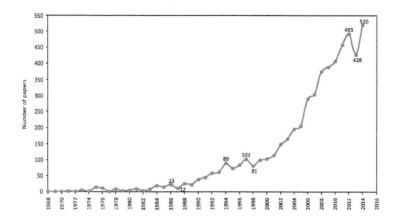

Figure 12.1   Distribution of published papers over years

dynamics of counterparts from across the world. With the career fields and the *doxa* changing, the favourable career capitals are also expected to change. For instance, teaching or consulting were once treated as activities substitutable with research, but in the new career fields, research output is treated as not only necessary but also non-substitutable. These changing practices are a consequence of not only globalization, but also a radically neoliberalized public discourse and a normalization of managerialism in academic institutions.

In the new *field*, one form of 'capital' that is newly relevant is networks in Western academia, and an awareness of what is 'current' among scholars in management in the West. Learning the nuances of the publication game, attendance at relevant reputed academic conferences and access to funding for research projects all contribute to the 'success' of an academic. From an institutional capital perspective, those trained in research cultures and environments that are more oriented towards research and publishing as primary activities (such as typical American universities) are more likely to not only appreciate but also thrive in the new game. Consequently, the disposition or habitus of the new academic is towards looking to begin, manage and complete as many research projects as possible, and treating teaching as an obligation, which is a major shift from how older academics viewed their work life.

Future research in this direction can include the impact of such sweeping changes on work identities, on meanings of work and on the 'productivity' of academics. India is not the only context in which education is increasingly neoliberalized. A comparison of impact of neoliberalization across national contexts on practice of academic careers deserves to be studied.

REFERENCES

Arthur, M.B. and D.M. Rousseau (1996), *The Boundaryless Career*, Oxford: Oxford University Press.

Baruch, Y. (2013), 'Careers in academe: the academic labour market as an eco-system', *Career Development International*, **18**(2), 196–210.

Baruch, Y. and D.T. Hall (2004), 'The academic career: a model for future careers in other sectors?', *Journal of Vocational Behavior*, **64**(2), 241–62.

Bourdieu, P. (1977), *Outline of a Theory of Practice*, Cambridge, UK: Cambridge University Press.

Bourdieu, P. (1984), *Distinction: A Social Critique of the Judgement of Taste*, Cambridge, MA: Harvard University Press.

Bourdieu, P. (1988), *Homo Academicus*, Stanford, CA: Stanford University Press.

Bourdieu, P. (1991), *Language and Symbolic Power*, Cambridge, UK: Polity Press.

Cannizzo, F. (2018), '"You've got to love what you do": academic labour in a culture of authenticity', *The Sociological Review*, **66**(1), 91–106.

Chudzikowski, K. and W. Mayrhofer (2011), 'In search of the blue flower? Grand social theories and career research: the case of Bourdieu's theory of practice', *Human Relations*, **64**, 19–36.

Dany, F., S. Louvel and A. Valette (2011), 'Academic careers: the limits of the "boundaryless approach" and the power of promotion scripts', *Human Relations*, **64**(7), 971–96.

Duberley, J., L. Cohen and M. Mallon (2006), 'Constructing scientific careers: change, continuity and context', *Organization Studies*, **27**(8), 1131–51.

Ehrenberg, R.G. (2003), 'Studying ourselves: the academic labor market: presidential address to the Society of Labor Economists, Baltimore, May 3, 2002', *Journal of Labor Economics*, **21**(2), 267–87.

Fernando, W.D.A. and L. Cohen (2016), 'Exploring career advantages of highly skilled migrants: a study of Indian academics in the UK', *The International Journal of Human Resource Management*, **27**(12), 1277–98.

Iellatchitch, A., W. Mayrhofer and M. Meyer (2003), 'Career fields: a small step towards a grand career theory?', *The International Journal of Human Resource Management*, **14**(5), 728–50.

Inkson, K., H. Gunz, S. Ganesh and J. Roper (2012), 'Boundaryless careers: bringing back boundaries', *Organization Studies*, **33**(3), 323–40.

Jammulamadaka, N. (2017), 'A postcolonial critique of Indian's management education scene', in M. Thakur and R.R. Babu (eds), *Management Education in India: Perspectives and Practices*, Singapore: Springer Singapore, pp. 23–42.

Klikauer, T. (2015), 'What is managerialism?', *Critical Sociology*, **41**(7–8), 1103–19.

Kolsaker, A. (2008), 'Academic professionalism in the managerialist era: a study of English universities', *Studies in Higher Education*, **33**(5), 513–25.

Kumar, P. and D. Israel (2013), 'An exploratory investigation into faculty motivation to publish: a study of business school faculty in India', *The International Journal of Management in Education*, **7**(3), 213–36.

Ojha, A.K. (2017), 'Management education in India: avoiding the simulacra effect', in M. Thakur and R. Babu (eds), *Management Education in India: Perspectives and Practices*, Singapore: Springer Singapore, pp. 55–77.

Pratap, S. and B. Saha (2018), 'Evolving efficacy of managerial capital, contesting managerial practices, and the process of strategic renewal', *Strategic Management Journal*, **39**(3), 759–93.

Sahoo, B.K., R. Singh, B. Mishra and K. Sankaran (2017), 'Research productivity in management schools of India during 1968–2015: a directional benefit-of-doubt model analysis', *Omega*, **66**, 118–39.

Sancheti, N. (1986), *Educational Dependency: An Indian Case Study in Comparative Perspective*, London: University of London Institute of Education.

Sancheti, N. (1988), 'Philanthropy in practice: the case of the Indian Institute of Management, Calcutta', *Compare: A Journal of Comparative and International Education*, **18**(2), 127–38.

Sinha, A. (2017), 'From management institutes to business schools: an Indian journey', in M. Thakur and R. Babu (eds), *Management Education in India: Perspectives and Practices*, Singapore: Springer Singapore, pp. 43–53.

Spence, C., C. Dambrin, C. Carter, J. Husillos and P. Archel (2015), 'Global ends, local means: cross-national homogeneity in professional service firms', *Human Relations*, **68**(5), 765–88.

Thakur, M. and R.R. Babu (2017), *Management Education in India: Perspectives and Practices*, Singapore: Springer Singapore.

Umarji, V. (2016), 'Javadekar hints at greater autonomy, wants older IIMs to scale up', *Business Standard*, 20 September.

Valsan, C. and R. Sproule (2008), 'The invisible hands behind the student evaluation of teaching: the rise of the new managerial elite in the governance of higher education', *Journal of Economic Issues*, **42**(4), 939–58.

Vannini, P. (2004), 'Authenticity and power in the academic profession', doctoral dissertation, Washington State University.

Vannini, P. and J.P. Williams (2009), *Authenticity in Culture, Self, and Society*, Farnham, UK: Ashgate Publishing.

Varman, R., B. Saha and P. Skålén (2011), 'Market subjectivity and neoliberal governmentality in higher education', *Journal of Marketing Management*, **27**(11–12), 1163–85.

Wacquant, L. (2005), 'Habitus', in J. Becket and M. Zafirovski (eds), *International Encyclopedia of Economic Sociology*, London: Routledge, pp. 315–19.

13. The changing nature of academic careers in management education in Western societies

Yehuda Baruch

INTRODUCTION

Recent decades witness the development of the general field of career studies (Inkson and Savickas, 2013) and of academic careers (Baruch, 2013; Kraimer et al., 2019), where the increase in prominence and relevance of such careers for contemporary life is critical. Academe is responsible for education and knowledge creation, both critical to many actors at different levels – individual, institutional and national. Higher education is a growing sector that deserves wider attention, as academic careers are still understudied. Of special relevance for the wider field of career studies is the idea that the academic career model fits well and represents contemporary career theories and developments (Baruch and Hall, 2004) such as the boundaryless career (Arthur, 2014; Arthur and Rousseau, 1996). Within the global labour market, individuals and institutions share the management of academic careers. Moreover, the sector emphasizes individualization of its career systems, with a significant level of self-management. It anticipated a clear shift of responsibility for the career – once dominated by employers – toward employees. This leads to a more individualized career orientation (Gubler, Arnold and Coombs, 2014) where the nature of the psychological contract between the players becomes complex and multilayered (Baruch and Rousseau, 2019).

The competitive form of universities and related institutions (especially private business schools) stems from their ability to attract and develop resources – mostly human resources – in the knowledge-driven industry (Nonaka, 1994). Financing these institutions can be guided by market forces as well as national priorities and processes. Institutions need to acquire and develop human talent to be able to deliver on both research and teaching, and the 'war for talent' causes the academic labour market to be highly dynamic in principle, but less so in practice (Chambers et al., 1998; Waaijer et al., 2018).

The more organizations depend on knowledge for performance, the higher their dependency on people becomes (Baruch, 2013). As a result, the management of people and their careers presents a fundamental human resource management challenge for academic institutions, where knowledge creation and dissemination are the critical tasks, delivered by academic scholars.

The higher education sector is expanding globally, with a dominance of the Anglo-Saxon model. Institutions are challenged by the emergence and flourishing of business schools in many parts of the world. Business education has developed into a multiform and highly competitive industry. International rankings and accreditation by various bodies dictate quality indicators that form practices, leading to individual choices and institutional strategies to reach such accreditations. The academic system is stratified, whereby factors like institutional prestige and influence shape career development and subsequent outcomes (Bedeian et al., 2010).

In most prestigious institutions, the progress of academic careers focuses mostly on research outputs. Rankings have significant influence on the choice of research topics, pedagogical approaches and the wider agenda as expectations change. Scholars are expected to be involved with additional tasks – for example, gaining grant bids on the research side and online education on the teaching side. Academic careers unfold under the influence of individual, institutional and national constraints that bind academic work, science development and teaching (Dany, Louvel and Valette, 2011).

ACADEMIC CAREER IDENTITY IN WESTERN MANAGEMENT EDUCATION

Using Bourdieu's sociological theory of practice (Bourdieu, 1988; Ozbilgin and Tatli, 2005) as well as protean, boundaryless and finally ecosystem career theories, I will explicate the way an academic career in management education is set within the Western context. Unlike the process of institutional mentoring with a leading group that spreads at a national level, as is the case in India (see Chapter 12 by Kommu and Dhiman), the concept of management education started in most places in the West as a vocational system, like the case of the *grandes écoles* in France, but most notably by the creation of specific business schools (Harvard in particular) that trained and educated an elite cadre of senior managers. These institutions served as the role model for many other universities, though not all followed it. For example, Cambridge and Oxford did not introduce business schools until late in the twentieth century. Further, because management education originated from multiple areas, the academic staff who teach in management education come from many disciplines, as well as from industry.

The most prestigious degree was, and still is, the Master of Business Administration (MBA). In the past it was considered as a 'licence to reach the top echelons' in business, but with the expansion of MBA provision its value was diluted and its impact is much subject to the prestige of the granting institution. Still, the MBA is considered the flagship of management education and offers numerous advantages to the graduates (Baruch, 2009). Competing degrees and professional specializations emerged and today many graduate students will be enrolled in MSc programmes, while many other students are enrolled in business management at the undergraduate level. In other systems or in different countries, other management education paths exist, like in the French system, where the education path more firmly defines the future career (Bourdieu, Grignon and Passeron, 1973). There, the completion of formal management education as a 'rite of passage' (Van Gennep, 2013) into leadership roles has evolved throughout the years.

Looking through the lens of the theory of practice of Bourdieu (which is also applied to the Indian context in Chapter 12 by Kommu and Dhiman), it becomes clear that the *field* of management education is broad. Academics in management education can join the discipline coming from different areas and, unlike other academic fields (for example, medicine or life and natural sciences), people from industry can also seek to develop academic careers in the area of management education. Scholars who work in business (or management) schools conduct research in related areas – finance, accounting, strategy, marketing, organizational behaviour/human resource management, operations and others like data analytics, decision-making, information system management, and so on.

Academic careers in the field of management education evolve around and are shaped by the 'rules of the game'– what Bourdieu (1988) termed *doxa* (the original meaning of *doxa* in Greek is common belief or popular opinion). For instance, rankings have a significant role in determining the value of research. In most of Western academia, as well as in other countries, the quality of journals, hence targeting these journals, is evaluated by external bodies. Some measures involve calculated metrics, the best known of which is the impact factor (International Scientific Indexing [ISI] list). Others are based on views from the field, and thus are always partially political and partially reflecting true reputation. Examples of these lists are the Association of Business Schools (ABS) list – originated in the UK, now well accepted globally – the French CNRS (Centre for National Scientific Research) and the FNEG (National Foundation for Management Education) setting the rules in France and other French-speaking countries, and the Australian Business Deans Council (ABDC) list. To develop a career, to publish in highly reputable journals becomes a necessary target for academic staff. There is significant convergence towards this trend in the Western academic career system, but variations still exist. Where the Anglo-Saxon tradition prefers journal papers, books are still more important in many European countries. A new global trend in the Western academic arena, dictated mostly by government and public opinion, is the need to manifest 'impact' – where the research guides policy and practice – for organizations and/or for public bodies. This seeks to address the need for research to be both rigorous and relevant (Pettigrew, 2001), even though the measurement or evaluation of research quality by national bodies might be detrimental to academic freedom (Martin-Sardesai et al., 2017). The actual direct impact of research in business management is debatable, and some say the impact on actual management practice is marginal (Dibb and Quinn, 2010).

The way academics read and internalize these 'rules of the games', is called their academic 'habitus' – or their 'feel for the game' (Nicolini, 2012, p. 55), based on their previous experiences outside and inside the field (Matthies and Torka, 2019). The academic habitus may be regarded as a system of acquired perceptions, thoughts and actions that are typical to the system. Academic scholars develop and devote their commitment, engagement, loyalty and impact-seeking in three arch-categories, which I define as the profession, the institution and the culture (in a wider sense – 'the way we do things around here'). The combination of the three elements is depicted in Figure 13.1, where all three elements influence the way people think and act, their belief and perceptions (that is, their specific habitus).

The academic habitus influences the way in which academics develop their career (Matthies and Torka, 2019) and shows that career aspirations and decisions are neither purely the result of individual agency nor of external structures. This is nicely illustrated by Matthies and Torka's (2019) study among German academics. They identify three types of academic habitus and relate these to career decisions. The first type, the self-fulfilling type, feels an inner drive and is characterized by the need to bring something to fruition. Being an academic is who they are and they feel at the right place in the academic field. The authors relate this to protean careers, in which self-awareness and self-fulfilment are drivers for career decisions. Yet, the increasing pressure for high scientific and societal impact makes some of these academics question whether they should continue their career. The second type, the self-surpassing type, aims for excellence and wants to tackle major questions. They are goal oriented in their thinking, which is often also influenced by their family history (for instance, parents who climbed the social ladder). They have a more strategic orientation in their career thinking and have a boundaryless, that is, interorganizational, career orientation. They show a strong willingness to adapt to institutional changes and to the pressure for scientific and societal impact that fits with their family history and personal experiences. In contrast to these protean and boundaryless career types, the third, self-asserting career

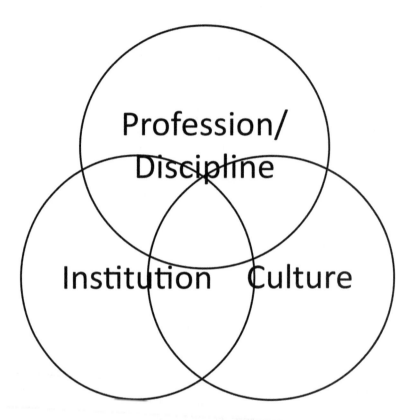

Figure 13.1   The shaping of academic habitus

type, aims for external social recognition. They want to stand out, and often this is also driven by an urge to break out from the environment in which they grew up. They are motivated to seek recognition by adapting to the new rules of the game in academia, even if these are not in line with their own values and thinking.

CAREER ECOSYSTEMS AND MANAGEMENT EDUCATION

The above manifests different ways through which different players interact and influence the career system in place. Like many other career systems, management education operates as a career ecosystem (Baruch, 2013, 2015) where multiple actors interact with each other. An ecosystem constitutes a set of relationships across the actors (Müller, 2005) and was applied for the under-standing of careers and labour markets across national and global contexts (Baruch, 2015; Baruch, Altman and Tung, 2016). The theory of ecosystem was introduced by Moore (1996, p. 9), who defined a business ecosystem as 'an economic community supported by a foundation of interacting organiza-tions and individuals – the organisms of the business world'. A later definition specific to management studies was introduced by Iansiti and Levien (2004), who defined it as 'a system that contains a large number of loosely intercon-nected actors who depend on each other to ensure the overall effectiveness of the system'. An ecosystem is characterized by having multiple actors and offers a wider perspective than other career theories in considering the 'overall health' of the system (Iansiti and Levien, 2004) in which careers develop.

The principal *actors* are individuals, institutions and societal entities. Individuals communicate, act, react and, in the context of careers, make career decisions such as stay, move, develop or undergo career change. Institutions are mostly the employers – universities and other academic entities – that aim to plan and manage the careers of their employees. At the societal level, governments and legal systems set and apply rules for the system (for example, industrial relations and employment law) and develop human capital (for example, through education) at regional and national levels. The actors are *interconnected* via complex structures, coordination and arrangements – for example, both legal and psychological contracts (Rousseau, 1995). Career outcomes are the result of *interactions* between the actors, starting with the basic transactional exchange of labour for wages, as well as a higher level of agreements, for example, regulation of intellectual property, use of knowl-edge – patents, spin-out ventures, and so on – as influenced by policies and strategies at the institutional level. There is a clear *interdependency* across the actors: academic institutions rely on their staff to survive, perform and thrive; nations rely on their human capital to strive; and global moves can inflict brain drain, brain gain, or brain circulation when it comes to winning or losing key individuals.

MANAGEMENT EDUCATION AS A CAREER ECOSYSTEM: A WESTERN PERSPECTIVE

Career ecosystems can be local to a geographic area, or exist within a sector, a region, a country, up to a global career ecosystem with cross-national moves of talent, expatriation, immigration, and so forth. In Western economic devel-oped societies, similar actors carry similar roles and the interactions follow a similar pattern. For example, social boundary-crossing usually takes place through gaining higher education, or alternatively, via acquisition of financial resources. Some countries like India, or countries in Africa, or Eastern Europe, can supply more of the talent, thus suffer 'brain drain', but perhaps benefit later through 'brain circulation'.

Boundaryless or Bounded?

Let us return to the notion of boundaryless careers (Arthur and Rousseau, 1996; DeFillippi and Arthur, 1994) where individuals are seen to exercise greater freedom over traditional barriers to career moves. Taking the term boundaryless literally, the academic career comprises boundarylessness and boundedness elements (Baruch and Hall, 2004; Dowd and Kaplan, 2005). Some elements, like individual agency and the ability to move across institutions and globally (Richardson and Zikic, 2007), reflect a boundaryless system; conversely, the practical lack of realistic options to move to different disciplines represents a relatively strong boundary, as does the partly 'scripted' nature of the system to which people are expected to comply (Dany et al., 2011). While the theory of boundaryless careers is controversial (for example, Inkson et al., 2012), it does draw attention to the volatility of contemporary labour markets. Taken literally, the metaphor of 'boundaryless' is overstretched, and in practice it means that it is more possible and acceptable to cross boundaries that were once considered major barriers. Many of these barriers still exist and are significant in the attainment of academic status. Organizational boundaries are less critical, and it is fairly common for academics to move across universities and other institutions. Other boundaries are still relevant – for example, geographical (Arthur et al., 2005), psychological, cultural (Sullivan and Arthur, 2006) and national (Inkson et al., 2012), where legal considerations like the need for a work permit or a foreign language obligation still exist (Pudelko and Tenzer, 2019). To elaborate on the latter, within the global business realm, as well as in the area of management education, there is the hegemony of the English language. The impact of language barriers on academic careers is critical – most of the reputed journals and books in the field are English written, most global conferences are presented in English, and in many business schools across the globe, the teaching language is English. Thus, lack of proficiency in the English language is a major barrier for academic career success.

Promotion Phenomena or Available Academic Career Paths

There are several paths to follow in academia within the Western context. I will present what may be considered the most prominent.

The most desirable is the 'star' path. This is a career when an individual who seeks an academic career managed to study for a PhD in a leading university is then appointed to the lower rank (assistant professor or equivalent) and progresses to a position of a full professor. This promotion depends mostly on a publication track record and carries global reputation (Beigi, Shirmohammadi and Arthur, 2018). At that time, the academic can opt for several directions; each of them is worthy on its own merit. The basic choice is whether to opt for pure academic leadership (for example, lead a field, be an editor, gain recognition as a 'distinguished professor') or the service leadership (become a head of department, dean, then the managerial ladder up to be the president – USA – or vice chancellor – UK – or whatever the title is in the specific realm).

Yet, very few make it to the top. For the rest, the most common path means reaching a career plateau when the progress stalls along such development. Some remain as associate professor, others may eventually gain a full professor position, but not making a considerable progress beyond that. The early stage is critical, and the university of graduation, supervisor impact and networks can be influential (Baruch, Point and Humbert, 2019). At this stage, chance events can have a lasting impact on the future career direction (Kindsiko and Baruch, 2019). Those who stay, though, typically enjoy their career, and many prefer to work further into normal retirement age (Altman et al., 2019).

Conversely, many just do not make it to a position of research–teaching balanced contract. They find themselves engaged with adjunct work, temporary or short-term contracts, with no job security – for example, being in research assistant roles and not making it to the academic ranks. I term it a 'troubled path': not gaining position, sometimes opting to deliver 'teaching only' in a balanced contract environment or working in a teaching-oriented institution. This can be a fulfilling career for those with a calling for education, but not so for those who wish to be academic scientists.

Career transitions can take place in each of the above paths. As the major identity and commitment may be devoted to the profession rather than to the institution, cross-institutional moves are typical, and can offer a fast path for progression – for example, to gain a full professorship. The availability of sabbaticals encourages cross-fertilization (Carraher, Crocitto and Sullivan, 2014) but can also induce wishes for a career move.

For the more successful scholars in business schools, in many ways, the labour market for academics resembles the competitive sport labour market. The commitment is directed more towards the profession, and institutional prestige is critical in luring strong names. There are many transitions across institutions, as well as cross-border moves, in particular at the equivalent of top leagues, and distinguished professors may gain lucrative jobs.

One of the factors that leads to the similarity to the labour market for footballers is that performance is measurable and open, at least in terms of publications. As in any academic position, the business and management education performance in terms of productivity is measured and evaluated alongside two major dimensions: research and teaching. This measurement is based mostly on the meritocracy system of blind review for research outputs, and skills evaluated by the 'customers' – students – for teaching quality. Moreover, business schools are known to be 'cash cows' (Starkey and Tempest, 2008). They bring significant income to the universities and the universities, in return, wish to improve reputation by having 'big names' working for them. With available monetary resources, salaries can be high, in particular for the higher echelons.

Challenges Within the Academic Career

Academic new agendas – the supply inputs and outputs sides – influence academic careers. Unlike in the past, where the majority of those aspiring for academic careers could become academics, we have many trends. There are many barriers to success: first in the publication realm (Ashkanasy, 2010), where competition increases with the growth of the profession following the high demand for management education; second, in the teaching realm, where fee-paying students consider themselves customers and expect value-for-money from their degree. Academics experience high levels of stress (Miller, Taylor and Bedeian, 2011) but much of it is because these academics are motivated by the prospects of enhancing their own professional reputation through their publication. This follows the desire for leaving a permanent mark on the profession, as well as the practical aims of improved remuneration and having the option for high job mobility.

Publishing, as the major instrumental antecedent of career success in reputable institutions, is difficult and the criteria and 'what needs to be done' in order to succeed are not always clear, as the following quote suggests: 'For many, the process of publishing in the best management journals is an enigma wrapped in a mystery. Even when they are successful, they are never sure why. And too often rejections hurt, but don't provide insight about how to increase the likelihood of success' (Barney, 2016).

Other challenges exist – the need to educate students, as well as academics, for entrepreneurship. With shrinking opportunities in the traditional organizational structures – both production and services – many graduates should be ready to explore the entrepreneurial path. In tandem, universities try to encourage their staff to generate new business ideas, including developing spin-out businesses. With a high level of uncertainty, universities refrain from employing a large number of permanent staff and explore alternative employment arrangements alongside the 'tenure track'.

The Academic Career as an Open System

Figure 13.2 depicts the main processes and interactions that characterize the career system in management education. The figure presents a matrix of influential factors, procedures and processes that take place, and career outcomes.

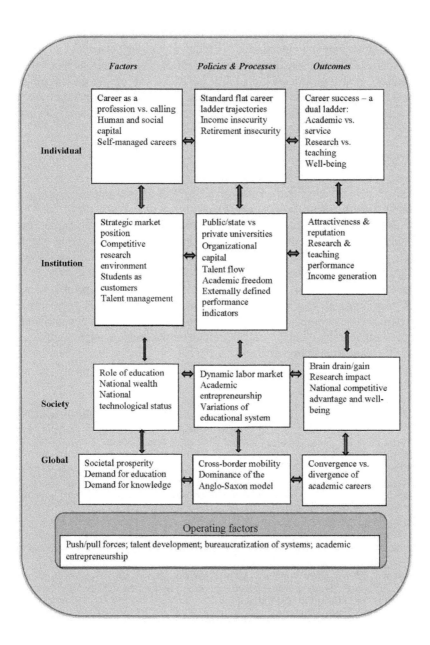

Figure 13.2   Academic careers framework

This is done for each level – the individual, institutional, national and global levels. The interactions take place across the levels and with relations to the inputs, processes and outcomes. This follows from the perspective of careers as ecosystem, with principal *actors*, the individuals, institutions and societal entities – both national and global. The actors are *interconnected* via complex structures, coordination and arrangements, and the career outcomes are the result of *interactions* between the actors, which take place as there is an *interdependency* across the players and the levels.

A FINAL NOTE

The academic labour market and career system are developing in line with contemporary career theories, developed mostly in Western academia. These reflect a trend of globalization, and convergence towards the Anglo-Saxon model. This model is adopted by many but adapted to local constraints and cultures. It remains for the future to see how relevant this model will be for other global locations, in particular the East and the South. The emerging Brazil, Russia, India, China and South Africa (BRICS) economies and many small developing countries are starting to compete in the same market – students and staff – and the competition is global. I hope that this chapter will contribute to our understanding about the way the system works, and how careers are shaped by, but also shape the system.

REFERENCES

Altman, Y., Y. Baruch, P. Zoghbi-Manrique de Lara and M. Viera-Armas (2019), 'Baby boomers at the cusp of their academic career: storming ahead, hanging on, or calling it a day', *Studies in Higher Education*, https://doi.org/10.1080/03075079.2019.1610864.

Arthur, M.B. (2014), 'The boundaryless career at 20: where do we stand, and where can we go?', *Career Development International*, 19(6), 627–40.

Arthur, M.B., S.N. Khapova and C.P. Wilderom (2005), 'Career success in a boundaryless career world', *Journal of Organizational Behavior*, 26(2), 177–202.

Arthur, M.B. and D.M. Rousseau (1996), *The Boundaryless Career: A New Employment Principle for a New Organizational Era*, New York: Oxford University Press.

Ashkanasy, N.M. (2010), 'Publishing today is more difficult than ever', *Journal of Organizational Behavior*, 31(1), 1–3.

Barney, J. (2016), Cover note for T. Clark, M. Wright and D. Ketchen (eds), *How to Get Published in the Best Management Journals*, Cheltenham, UK and Northampton, MA, USA: Edward Elgar Publishing.

Baruch, Y. (2009), 'To MBA or not to MBA', *Career Development International*, 14(4), 388–406.

Baruch, Y. (2013), 'Careers in academe: the academic labour market as an eco-system', *Career Development International*, 18(2), 196–210.

Baruch, Y. (2015), 'Organizational and labor market as career eco-system', in A. de Vos and B. van der Heijden (eds), *Handbook of Research on Sustainable Careers*, Cheltenham, UK and Northampton, MA, USA: Edward Elgar Publishing, pp. 164–80.

Baruch, Y. and D.T. Hall (2004), 'The academic career: a model for future careers in other sectors?', *Journal of Vocational Behavior*, **64**(2), 241–62.

Baruch, Y. and D.M. Rousseau (2019), 'Integrating psychological contracts and their stakeholders in career studies and management', *The Academy of Management Annals*, **13**(1), 84–111.

Baruch, Y., Y. Altman and R.L. Tung (2016), 'Career mobility in a global era – advances in managing expatriation and repatriation', *Academy of Management Annals*, **10**, 841–89.

Baruch, Y., S. Point and A.L. Humbert (2019), 'Factors related to knowledge creation and career outcomes in French academia: the case of the human resource management field', *Academy of Management Learning & Education*, https://doi.org/10.5465/amle.2018.0028.

Bedeian, A.G., D.E. Cavazos, J.G. Hun and L.R. Jauch (2010), 'Doctoral degree prestige and the academic marketplace: a study of career mobility within the management discipline', *Academy of Management Learning & Education*, **9**(1), 11–25.

Beigi, M., M. Shirmohammadi and M. Arthur (2018), 'Intelligent career success: the case of distinguished academics', *Journal of Vocational Behavior*, **107**, 261–75.

Bourdieu, P. (1988), *Homo Academicus*, Stanford, CA: Stanford University Press.

Bourdieu, P., C. Grignon and J.C. Passeron (1973), 'L'évolution des chances d'accès à l'enseignement supérieur en France (1962–1966)' [The evolution of the opportunities to access higher education in France (1962–1966)], *Higher Education*, **2**(4), 407–22.

Carraher, S.M., M.M. Crocitto and S. Sullivan (2014), 'A kaleidoscope career perspective on faculty sabbaticals', *Career Development International*, **19**(3), 295–313.

Chambers, E.G., M. Foulon, H. Handfield-Jones, S.M. Hankin and E.G. Michaels III (1998), 'The war for talent', *The McKinsey Quarterly*, **3**, 45–57.

Dany, F., S. Louvel and A. Valette (2011), 'Academic careers: the limits of the "boundaryless approach" and the power of promotion scripts', *Human Relations*, **64**(7), 971–96.

DeFillippi, R.J. and M.B. Arthur (1994), 'The boundaryless career: a competency-based perspective', *Journal of Organizational Behavior*, **15**, 307–24.

Dibb, S. and L. Quinn (2010), 'Debate: research impact or career progression?', *Public Money & Management*, **30**(6), 326–8.

Dowd, K.O. and D.M. Kaplan (2005), 'The career life of academics: boundaried or boundaryless?', *Human Relations*, **58**(6), 699–721.

Gubler, M., J. Arnold and C. Coombs (2014), 'Reassessing the protean career concept: empirical findings, conceptual components, and measurement', *Journal of Organizational Behavior*, **35**(S1), S23–S40.

Iansiti, M.R. and R. Levien (2004), 'Strategy as ecology', *Harvard Business Review*, **82**(3), 68–81.

Inkson, K.M. and M. Savickas (eds) (2013), *Career Studies*, Thousand Oaks, CA: Sage.

Inkson, K., H. Gunz, S. Ganesh and J. Roper (2012), 'Boundaryless careers: bringing back boundaries', *Organization Studies*, **33**(3), 323–40.

Kindsiko, E. and Y. Baruch (2019), 'Careers of PhD graduates: the role of chance events and how to manage them', *Journal of Vocational Behavior*, **112**, 122–40.

Kraimer, M.L., L. Greco, W.E. Seibert and L.D. Sargent (2019), 'An investigation of academic career success: the new tempo of academic life', *Academy of Management Learning & Education*, **18**(2), https://doi.org/10.5465/amle.2017.0391.

Martin-Sardesai, A., H. Irvine, S. Tooley and J. Guthrie (2017), 'Government research evaluations and academic freedom: a UK and Australian comparison', *Higher Education Research & Development*, **3**(2), 372–85.

Matthies, H. and M. Torka (2019), 'Academic habitus and institutional change: comparing two generations of German scholars', *Minerva*, **57**(3), 345–71.

Miller, A.N., S.G. Taylor and A.G. Bedeian (2011), 'Publish or perish: academic life as management faculty live it', *Career Development International*, **16**(5), 422–45.

Moore, J.F. (1996), *The Death of Competition: Leadership and Strategy in the Age of Business Ecosystems*, New York: HarperBusiness.

Müller, F. (2005), 'Indicating ecosystem and landscape organisation', *Ecological Indicators*, **5**(4), 280–94.

Nicolini, D. (2012), *Practice Theory, Work, and Organization: An Introduction*, Oxford: Oxford University Press.

Nonaka, I. (1994), 'A dynamic theory of organizational knowledge creation', *Organization Science*, **5**(1), 4–37.

Ozbilgin, M. and A. Tatli (2005), 'Book review essay: understanding Bourdieu's contribution to organization and management studies', *Academy of Management Review*, **30**(4), 855–69.

Pettigrew, A. (2001), 'Management research after modernism', *British Journal of Management*, **12**, S61–S70.

Pudelko, M. and H. Tenzer (2019), 'Boundaryless careers or career boundaries? The impact of language barriers on academic careers in international business schools', *Academy of Management Learning & Education*, **18**(2), 213–40.

Richardson, J. and J. Zikic (2007), 'The darker side of an international academic career', *Career Development International*, **12**(2), 164–86.

Rousseau, D.M. (1995), *Psychological Contracts in Organizations: Understanding Written and Unwritten Agreements*, Thousand Oaks, CA: Sage.

Starkey, K. and S. Tempest (2008), 'A clear sense of purpose? The evolving role of the business school', *Journal of Management Development*, **27**(4), 379–90.

Sullivan, S.E. and M.B. Arthur (2006), 'The evolution of the boundaryless career concept: examining physical and psychological mobility', *Journal of Vocational Behavior*, **69**, 19–29.

Van Gennep, A. (2013), *The Rites of Passage*, London: Routledge.

Waaijera, C.J.F., C. Teelken, P.F. Wouters and I.C.M. van der Weijden (2018), 'Competition in science: links between publication pressure, grant pressure and the academic job market', *Higher Education Policy*, **31**, 225–43.

PART VII

Careers in IT

The chapters on this topic address career challenges for employees in the IT sector and look at individual, organizational and institutional factors.

Gunjan Tomer and Pawan Budhwar's chapter is titled 'Flying high in the turbulent skies: managing careers in the Indian IT industry'. They study careers of workers in the highly volatile and fast-growing IT industry in India, which is confronted with high turnover rates. In their chapter, they reflect on career management of IT workers and focus both on challenges for the IT worker and for IT organizations. The Indian IT industry is in the lower segment of IT services and product development. Its workers often perform repetitive work. A concern for IT workers is to obtain challenging work and to stay professionally relevant. For IT organizations, it is essential to effectively manage their technical resources. Many IT organizations are torn between business requirements and individual expectations. The authors discuss implications for management of IT professionals.

Sara Haviland and Jennifer Craft Morgan study IT workers in the US and Canada. In their chapter, titled 'Risk allocation, employer dependence and the welfare state: an investigation of IT workers in the US and Canada', they study how IT worker perceptions of risk are influenced by the welfare regime they live in. The US and Canada are two similar countries that vary in social welfare policies, more specifically the provision of universal healthcare and generosity of retirement benefits. Their qualitative research results show that US IT workers have higher employer dependence than their counterparts in Canada: workers feel more pressured to maintain employment so that they can keep benefits. They also discuss implications for IT workers and the firms that employ them.

Both sectors focus on a similar industry but in different institutional and thus also different organizational contexts. Looking at both chapters separately, they zoom in on different factors: individual and organizational factors in the Indian context and institutional factors in the US and Canadian context.

Looking at both chapters together, they show how career challenges for IT workers are highly context specific. You may reflect on how the IT industry in your country evolves and how that shapes IT careers. You may also reflect on how institutional and organizational practices shape the challenges you face in your own career.

14. Flying high in the turbulent skies: managing careers in the Indian IT industry

Gunjan Tomer and Pawan Budhwar

INTRODUCTION

The information technology (IT) industry has significant implications for various critical aspects of the Indian economy such as competitiveness, economic growth, per capita income and quality of life. IT professionals are core to this industry, given that it is often identified as knowledge driven. The contribution of IT professionals towards the sustained competitive advantage of organizations in the IT industry is now well accepted (for example, Devaraj and Kohli, 2003; Sykes, 2015). Thus, it can be asserted that IT professionals hold a significant position in the overall growth and development of this industry. In this chapter we aim to explore and examine the dynamics of career management of IT professionals in the industry.

What IT professionals expect from their career is a critical concern for organizations regarding both employee turnover rates and the sustainability of growth of this industry (Igbaria, Greenhaus and Parasuraman, 1991; Lo, 2015). The IT industry has also been observed to exhibit a higher attrition rate in comparison to other industries (Budhwar, Luthar and Bhatnagar, 2006a; Joseph et al., 2007; Patel, Budhwar and Varma, 2012). Previous literature suggests that fulfilment of career expectations leads to positive outcomes such as employee commitment and retention, thus strengthening the strategic growth of the organization as well as the industry (Budhwar and Baruch, 2003). In turn, we focus here on two dimensions of career management in the context of IT industry: (1) individual professional challenges; and (2) organizational challenges.

THE IT INDUSTRY IN INDIA

The IT industry in India invites attention for various reasons. According to the Ministry of Electronics & Information Technology, Government of

India, in the last 20 years the contribution of the IT industry to Indian gross domestic product (GDP) has increased from 1.2 to 9.3 per cent in 2018. This considerable growth has also impacted labour markets and the Indian IT industry continues to be a net employment generator, thus providing direct employment to about 3.9 million and promising to create 3 million new jobs by 2025 (NASSCOM, 2019). The significant demand for trained IT professionals influences the career decision-making processes of those concerned. Also, individuals joining the IT profession have a distinct range of aspirations, career orientations and professional and personal alignments (Ahuja et al., 2007; Fu and Chen, 2015). This leads to issues related to the effective management of IT professionals. A series of studies on the key issues facing IT professionals has consistently listed human resource management as a leading concern (for example, Budhwar et al., 2006b). Table 14.1 provides a summary of the Indian IT industry situation.

IT PROFESSIONALS

IT professionals can be seen as an occupational group known for their technical competence. They are expected to acquire proficiency in various software tools and technologies to perform their job requirements. Primarily, they are responsible for the design and development of information systems, though not limited to these tasks. They are responsible for maintaining and updating the information systems by continuously improving the features and the functionalities. Their job description also includes providing technical support to the end users and business partners. Along with the technical expertise, they are expected to possess domain-level knowledge and an understanding of business processes and operations. Their business acumen guides them in designing and developing better-performing information systems (Bassellier and Benbasat, 2004).

IT professionals are also required to acquire interdisciplinary knowledge and skills to be able to work in cross-functional and cross-domain work projects (King and Torkzadeh, 2008). And, since the business and technological requirements are constantly changing, one of the job expectations from IT professionals is to continually learn new skills and technologies to adapt to the uncertain environment. In turn, the existing work environment thus exerts a great amount of pressure among IT professionals, leading to increased stress and turnover (Armstrong, Brooks and Riemenschneider, 2015; Joseph et al., 2007). In the present context, the constrained supply of highly skilled IT professionals has meant the demand–supply gap has been constantly increasing (Zaza and Armstrong, 2017).

Table 14.1   *Indian IT industry, an overview*

Indian advantage	• IT industry has continued to remain a growth catalyst for Indian economy with an immense contribution of 9.3%
	• Share in global software development (GSD) markets stands at 7%
	• Expected sector growth is around 11%
	• Sustained cost leadership
	• Infrastructure expansion, building cities as IT delivery centres
Sector facts	• Annual revenue around US$160 billion
	• More than 15 000 firms, over 1000 large IT firms
	• Over 600 offshore development centres in 70 countries
	• Non-linear growth due to platforms, mobility, automation and product lines
	• Revived IT demand from various continents
	• Increased local ICT adoption in both government and private sectors
Growth drivers	• Emerging vertical-driven growth
	• Social, mobility, analytics and cloud (SMAC) market to reach US$225 billion by 2020
	• Steady increase in R&D investments 100% foreign direct investment (FDI)
Labour market	• Largest private sector employer with 3.7 million jobs, 12 million indirect employment 40% lateral recruitment with over 130 nationalities employed
	• US$1.6 billion spent on workforce training and development. Skilling/re-skilling has emerged as the single most important challenge to fulfil resource requirement
	• Market suffering from lack of skilled labour across high-tech domains such as artificial intelligence and big data

Source: Ministry of Electronics & Information Technology, Government of India (MEITY, 2018).

CAREERS IN THE INDIAN IT INDUSTRY

The software industry relies more intensively upon human capital. This has triggered demand for trained software engineering graduates. The IT industry has been consistently challenged by labour dynamics with regard to: (1) the widening gap between supply and demand of IT personnel; (2) their reported high turnover rates; and (3) low career satisfaction and higher stress (Lo, 2015; Ragu-Nathan et al., 2008).

Considering the high turnover and increasing stress levels among IT professionals, it has become a challenge to keep these professionals motivated. What they expect from their career is one of the critical factors that should be an issue of concern for organizations. Literature suggests that fulfilment of career expectations leads to many positive outcomes such as commitment and employee retention (Greenhaus, Parasuraman and Wormley, 1990; Gupta, Guimaraes and Raghunathan, 1992). IT professionals include a diverse range of individuals with different sets of skills, preferences and desires. This is of serious concern for human resources management of IT professionals (Lo, 2015).

Operations within the Indian IT industry primarily adopt a project management model, where projects are work efforts involving IT infrastructure, information systems or new-technology products. Individuals can gain expertise and experience through working on a project that calls for core technical skills as well as domain knowledge. Some technologies and domains are preferred, based on multiple criteria such as opportunities available in the job market, utilization of skills and career stability. Individuals working on projects of their choice tend to gain more career satisfaction as compared to individuals who are working in non-preferable projects. Due to a large employee base and market uncertainty, individual preferences are not considered while assigning work, thus leading to reduced career satisfaction (Chilton, Hardgrave and Armstrong, 2005; Tomer and Mishra, 2019). Managing preferences for a large number of projects and an even larger employee base is a critical challenge for IT firms. However, it is imperative that organizations understand the internal desires and needs of IT professionals, considering the higher attrition and reported stress among them. These factors not only impact organizational productivity but also incur high costs in talent acquisition and training (Agrawal, Khatri and Srinivasan, 2012).

CHALLENGES OF IT PROFESSIONALS

Given the above overview of the IT industry, let us now look at the challenges for IT professionals.

To Be an IT Professional

Career prospects and risks associated with not getting suitable employment are important factors while making vocational choices. Students joining the computer science/IT programmes may not have strong professional affiliations at entry level, as their interests and capabilities are not the primary drivers (Tomer and Mishra, 2016). This can often influence academic outcomes for students, and in turn affect the need for on-the-job training and the long-duration induction programmes before the first actual work assignment.

My Kind of Work

The Indian IT industry concentrates on implementation rather than research and development. Technologically skilled professionals seek challenge in their work, which justifies their skill utilization. However, due to the Indian IT industry being in the lower segment of IT services and product development, Indian IT workers often perform mundane and repetitive work of coding, testing and maintenance. These product life-cycle stages often involve following a well-documented deliverable, thus limiting the scope for innovation and creativity. As a result, many IT professionals complain of routine monotonous work. During our interactions with IT professionals, many professionals quoted that the work they are doing can be completed by even a school graduate (Tomer and Mishra, 2016). On the other hand, there are professionals who experience exhaustion due to overwork, through working on challenging projects or working at inconvenient hours. Existing research on IT professionals also reports higher levels of dissatisfaction and work-related stress than observed among other professionals (Sykes, 2015).

Moreover, IT professionals are expected to acquire interdisciplinary knowledge and skills to be able to work in cross-functional and cross-domain work projects (King and Torkzadeh, 2008). This accumulated experience allows them to develop work-related preferences such as technologies they want to work in or domains they are more interested in. For instance, an IT professional might like working in a specific technology/domain as he or she perceives his or her best professional contribution can be realized there. Self-efficacy, familiarity with the project/client or prior work experience with the supervisor and team members can be multiple factors that might influence work-related preferences of IT professionals. Along with these, career outcomes can also motivate IT professionals to favour certain projects and technologies. High or low market demand for a particular technology skill set can influence various career outcomes such as opportunities inside and outside the organization, access to better projects and clients, monetary benefits and onsite opportunities.

Considering the large number of employees in IT organizations, it becomes highly complex for an organization to incorporate individual preferences in work allocation. Most of the time, work allocation is driven by business requirements and managers keep rotating IT professionals between projects based on requirements received from business clients. Poor project management, lack of interest of managers in ensuring professional growth of team members and pressure from the clients often lead to suboptimal work allocation for IT professionals (Agrawal et al., 2012). As a result, IT professionals face the challenge to cope up with all kinds of work that come their way, rather than preferences-based work assignments.

Keeping Up with Technology

Since business and technological requirements are constantly changing, one of the job expectations from IT professionals is to continually learn new skills and technologies to adapt to the uncertain environment (Rong and Grover, 2009). To learn and upgrade skill sets, IT professionals often need to put in extra hours and additional effort. During our interactions with IT professionals on past research projects, we discussed in detail their perceptions and expectations of technology. One of the themes was technology uncertainty and we received interesting and often mutually contrasting responses. While there were IT professionals who seek challenge from their work and keep updating their technical skill sets to avoid being professionally obsolescent, we also found another set of IT professionals who perceived technology changes as a threat to their professional existence (Tomer, 2015). Pressure to remain technologically relevant also leads to loss of career stability and security. The existing work environment thus exerts a great amount of pressure among IT professionals, leading to increased stress and turnover (Hunter, Tan and Tan, 2008; Joseph et al., 2007).

Working in a Global Software Development Environment

Working in a global software development (GSD) environment has multiple implications on career management of IT professionals. Apart from the challenges such as coordination and communication, GSD also impacts career prospects and progression of IT professionals. Evidence points to factors such as work–life conflict due to time coordination issues between offshore clients and team members (Krishna, Sahay and Walsham, 2004). Due to communication gaps and cultural barriers, IT project teams – often despite their best efforts – are unable to meet their clients' expectations, thus influencing their performance evaluation. In several incidents, resource allocation for the project leads to issues such as miscalculated man hours or lack of skilled professionals. These communication errors lead to multiple change requests from the client and pressure to meet deadlines (Agrawal et al., 2012). Since IT professionals keep rotating between different projects, sometimes working on multiple projects simultaneously, they experience difficulties in coping with the work pressure and stress due to continuous switching between different kinds of work (Huemann, Keegan and Turner, 2018).

The coordination between onshore and offshore project teams also leads to multiple performance appraisal issues. Research has suggested that due to proximity and visibility of onsite members, clients rate them favourably to their managers and these onsite members are often given more than due credit (Vlaar, Van Fenema and Tiwari, 2008). Due to the rapport they build with the client, onsite IT professionals are often given more opportunities and responsibilities that help them secure a long-duration onsite assignment. Onsite projects offer opportunities to gain global exposure, enhanced domain knowledge and monetary incentives. However, activities like this impact the perception of fairness and equity among the offshore team members. On the other hand, IT professionals returning to India after an onsite assignment perceive a similar breach of trust when their promotion opportunities have been lost, and their salary and perks are not on a par with their offshore counterparts. Thus, the relationships between onsite and offshore team members are characterized by asymmetries in knowledge, experience and rewards, which often become the cause of potential misunderstanding (Vlaar et al., 2008)

CHALLENGES OF IT FIRMS

Diverse Workforce

In the past decade, the Indian IT industry has evolved substantially. Managing the human resource management of highly skilled professionals has become even more challenging, coupled with a diverse workforce. IT professionals are a source of strategic advantage for IT organizations, thus recruiting and retaining the best professionals has become critical. Over the years, work practices have become flexible to adjust and accommodate the expectations of a diverse workforce. Foreign firms operating in India have also influenced the overall working environment and culture (Jain, Mathew and Bedi, 2012). Along with the changing organizational work culture, demographic changes also contributed to increased diversity in the current IT industry. Factors such as an increase in the number of women in the workplace, dual-career families, spouses working in different cities and professionals hailing from all socio-economic strata have contributed to increased diversity (Smith and Gardner, 2007). IT professionals have different aspirations, expectations and career goals and no single approach can ensure satisfaction across segments.

Thus, organizations must realize that career growth paths, incentives, rewards and recognitions need to be tailored as per different strata of the workforce. Despite innovation in human resource management of IT professionals, the challenges of career management of these professionals remain unaddressed.

Gender Disparity

Studies have identified the persisting disparity in gender ratio in the Indian IT industry (NASSCOM, 2017). Industry reports and popular media have also often highlighted the gender crisis prevailing in the IT industry (Srinivas and Bansal, 2018). Lack of women's presence in IT represents a loss of opportunities for organizations as well as individuals to work in a diverse, creative work environment. Organizations are pitching in with new initiatives such as working from home, flexibility in selecting project work and improved maternity leave options. Many organizations have made efforts to become more inclusive of women professionals such as opening lactation rooms, parking space for pregnant employees and daycare centres inside the premises. In many organizations, it is not uncommon to relocate female employees to allow them to stay together with their spouses.

Despite all the inclusive efforts and attempts at diversified hiring, the men to women ratio in the Indian IT industry is almost 70:30. While many organizations claim to hire a 50:50 ratio of male and female professionals at the entry level, gender ratios at higher levels of organizational hierarchy are as low as 90:10. If we look at the data on the top three IT firms in India, Infosys employs the largest percentage of women at 33.4 per cent, followed by TCS 30 per cent and Wipro 29 per cent, and Infosys senior management has only 2 per cent of women professionals. The lower ratios of top management can be attributed to women leaving their careers or having different career expectations. We cannot also rule out the gender bias prevailing in IT industry, specifically because of conspicuous absence of women in top management.

Lack of Skilled Human Resources

The Indian education industry is not able to meet the demand for trained IT professionals. Both the public-funded and the private-funded education programmes are inherently inadequate, and even combined would not be able to meet the burgeoning demands of the Indian domestic and exports industries (Cisco-IDC, 2018).

Leading IT players have devised mechanisms for managing this lack of skilled labour. Many IT export companies in India have created their own training institutes and have begun training new employees. For example, Infosys intends to spend around US$200 million on training in 2018. Wipro has also set up large training centres where 5000 entry-level professionals can be trained simultaneously (Wipro, 2018). Overall, the Indian IT industry may ultimately spend approximately US$1.1 billion – or about 3 per cent of its revenue on training and development of IT professionals.

The lack of skilled resources can be attributed to a poorly designed and executed curriculum of engineering and computer science programmes (Tomer and Mishra, 2016). Most students on these programmes are not exposed to actual industry settings and the curriculum does not fulfil the requirements of a professional programme. Thus, access to on-the-job training is essential to prepare these professionals.

Talent Acquisition and Retention

The high growth rate of the Indian software industry and the high attrition rate have led to it recruiting large numbers on a regular basis (Agarwal et al., 2012). Recruitment by leading IT organizations occurs through institution tie-ups as campus placements (Singh, 2018). The campus placement focuses on evaluating technical, logical and soft skills of the candidates. Once selected, they are trained in a particular technology and domain. Later, based on business requirements, they are assigned to projects. Work assignments meeting the expectations of IT professionals help them realize their career aspirations.

However, often, work pressure on managers does not allow them to accommodate the career aspirations of team members. Uncertainties at market level as well as project level also contribute to the complexity of managing careers of IT professionals. Moreover, individuals joining this profession have a distinct range of aspirations, career orientations and professional and personal alignments. Existing theories, like dual career ladder theory (Allen and Katz, 1986), aim to diversify career paths considering both organizational needs and individual aspirations. The dual career ladder theory proposes two ladders for career progression: a technical career path and a managerial career path (Allen and Katz, 1986). However, literature suggests that it is not a very appropriate way to cater to the intrinsic needs of an individual, as it only categorizes individual orientation into two segments although many other career orientations may also be possible (Baroudi, 1998). Also, IT professionals who are promoted to managerial positions often lack training and managerial acumen. Since they have been star performers, they often compare team members with themselves, and fail to understand the struggles of those less competent and their need to be mentored.

Overall, inefficiencies in project assignments, lack of mentoring and absence of proper career planning of IT professionals are critical challenges IT organizations are currently facing. Career management in IT firms is complex and a continuous exercise in aligning both organizational needs and individual career aspirations.

Market Uncertainty: Disruption and Obsolescence

Market uncertainty concerns change in the standards or specifications of products, which become characterized by rapid obsolescence (Geyskens, Steenkamp and Kumar, 2006). Innovations in the field of cloud computing, artificial intelligence and data management have been changing the very definitions of IT industry operatives. Time to market has shortened and so has the shelf life of these products. Organizations are investing in IT and they are upgrading their information systems frequently. Technologies and technological skills are becoming obsolete faster. All these market-level changes and disruptions have made survival of the IT firm more challenging, driven market uncertainty, and required the firm to become more dynamic and agile in response.

Technology uncertainty (TU) has implications for human resource management within the IT industry. Frequent changes and upgrades in technology lead to acquiring and sustaining the relevancy of technical skill sets. To achieve this, IT firms continuously invest in skill upgradation of their employees through internal certifications and in-house training. TU also leads to hiring of skilled human resources on a regular basis. These market conditions have implications on IT professionals such as compelling them to learn and acquire new technology skills repeatedly and to achieve this often searching for organizations with better learning opportunities.

Managing Resources in Global Delivery Model

The global delivery model poses multidimensional challenges for the organization. Coping with market uncertainty, competition, disruptive technologies and shortages of personnel, IT organizations struggle to meet expectations, standards and deadlines. As a result, project teams are created/modified at short notice in the case of project contingencies (such as changes in client requirements, project members leaving, or scheduling issues) (Mahmood et al., 2017). Higher attrition also leads to movement of professionals from one team to another. Attrition also leads to loss of knowledge and often creates complexities in managing projects efficiently. Fresh graduates are assigned to projects without proper project-related training, or professionals with different expertise are put on the team. These members are expected to learn and work simultaneously, thus exerting additional pressure to cope with work. These incongruent work assignments not only impact the overall performance of the project but also influence how a team member is evaluated and appraised.

While managing shortage of personnel through mismatching work assignments and work rotation, growth aspirations of IT professionals are often ignored.

DISCUSSION AND CONCLUSIONS

Exploring individual and organizational challenges helps us to understand the dynamic landscape of the IT industry in the Indian context from multiple perspectives. We have explored how profession-related and industry-related factors contribute to explaining career perceptions and outcomes of IT professionals.

The most crucial challenge for managing one's career in the IT industry is getting the expected kind of work and staying professionally relevant. Studies have indicated that a mismatch of career expectations and work overload are a source of exhaustion and attrition (Tomer and Mishra, 2019). Since uncertainty is an integral part of the technology industry (Moreno et al., 2012), individuals need to upgrade their technology skills and stay flexible to work across technologies and domains (Armstrong et al., 2015). Organizations can play a significant role in enabling IT professionals to achieve this objective and create a strong connect with employees. For instance, in-house training programmes, strong knowledge management and work flexibility and autonomy are found to be highly useful in increasing positive work outcomes.

On the other hand, IT organizations in India are facing multifaceted challenges to sustain their competitive advantage. Operating in a highly volatile industry, where skilled personnel is the key resource, organizations are stretched to meet all ends. To stay competitive in a market fuelled by cost arbitrage, organizations are adapting strategies to reduce costs and become more effective. Studies have highlighted the role of IT professionals in achieving strategic advantage (Sykes, 2015); however, often, organizations are torn between business requirements and individual expectations. One element of effective management of IT professionals involves satisfying employees' career values and aspirations (Greenhaus and Callanan, 1994). Managing careers of IT professionals within an organization poses challenges in the form of managing varied career aspirations of IT professionals in a highly uncertain market. These aspirations are related to growth needs and future career management.

Considering the significance of skilled technology professionals, IT organizations need to become people oriented and people driven. Also, empowering skilled IT resources would not only increase productivity and effectiveness, it would also create a conducive environment for innovations (Moon and Bretschneiber, 2002). Innovations in processes and products will allow them to move up the value chain and help them become profitable and strategically relevant. Moving forward, we highly recommend a more synergistic relationship among IT professionals and organizations.

REFERENCES

Agrawal, N.M., N. Khatri and R. Srinivasan (2012), 'Managing growth: human resource management challenges facing the Indian software industry', *Journal of World Business*, **47**(2), 159–66.
Ahuja, M.K., K.M. Chudoba, C.J. Kacmar, D.H. McKnight and J.F. George (2007), 'IT road warriors: balancing work–family conflict, job autonomy, and work overload to mitigate turnover intentions', *MIS Quarterly*, **31**(1), 1–17.
Allen, T. and R. Katz (1986), 'The dual ladder: motivational solution or managerial delusion?', *R&D Management*, **16**, 185–97.
Armstrong, D.J., N.G. Brooks and C.K. Riemenschneider (2015), 'Exhaustion from information system career experience: implications for turn-away intention', *MIS Quarterly*, **39**(3), 713–27.
Baroudi, J. (1988), 'Career needs of IS personnel: does the dual career ladder work?', *Proceedings of the Hawaii International Conference on System Science*, 171–80.
Bassellier, G. and I. Benbasat (2004), 'Business competence of information technology professionals: conceptual development and influence on IT–business partnerships', *MIS Quarterly*, **28**(4), 673–94.
Budhwar, P. and Y. Baruch (2003), 'Career management practices in India: an empirical study', *International Journal of Manpower*, **24**(6), 699–719.
Budhwar, P., H. Luthar and J. Bhatnagar (2006a), 'Dynamics of HRM systems in Indian BPO firms', *Journal of Labor Research*, **27**(3), 339–60.
Budhwar, P., A. Varma, V. Singh and R. Dhar (2006b), 'HRM systems of Indian call centres: an exploratory study', *The International Journal of Human Resource Management*, **17**(5), 881–97.
Chilton, M.A., B.C. Hardgrave and D.J. Armstrong (2005), 'Person–job cognitive style fit for software developers: the effect on strain and performance', *Journal of Management Information Systems*, **22**(2), 193–226.
Cisco-IDC (2018), *20 Most Significant IT Roles You Should Consider*, accessed 23 August 2019 at https://learningnetwork.cisco.com/community/it_careers/20-most-significant-it-roles-you-should-consider.
Devaraj, S. and R. Kohli (2003), 'Performance impacts of information technology: is actual usage the missing link?', *Management Science*, **49**(3), 273–89.
Fu, J.R. and J.H. Chen (2015), 'Career commitment of information technology professionals: the investment model perspective', *Information and Management*, **52**(5), 537–49.
Geyskens, I., J.B.E. Steenkamp and N. Kumar (2006), 'Make, buy, or ally: a transaction cost theory meta-analysis', *Academy of Management Journal*, **49**(3), 519–43.
Greenhaus, J.H. and G. Callanan (1994), *Career Management*, Hinsdale, IL: Dryden.
Greenhaus, J.H., S. Parasuraman and W.M. Wormley (1990), 'Effects of race on organizational experiences, job performance evaluations, and career outcomes', *Academy of Management Journal*, **33**(1), 64–86.
Gupta, Y.P., T. Guimaraes and T.S. Raghunathan (1992), 'Attitude and intentions of information centre personnel', *Information and Management*, **22**, 151–60.

Huemann, M., A. Keegan and R. Turner (2018), *Human Resource Management in the Project-Oriented Organization*, Newtown Square, PA: Project Management Institute.

Hunter, M.G., F.B. Tan and B.C.Y. Tan (2008), 'Voluntary turnover of information systems professionals: a cross-cultural investigation', *Journal of Global Information Management*, **16**(4), 46–66.

Igbaria, M., J.H. Greenhaus and S. Parasuraman (1991), 'Career orientations of MIS employees: an empirical analysis', *MIS Quarterly*, **15**(2), 151–69.

Jain, H., M. Mathew and A. Bedi (2012), 'HRM innovations by Indian and foreign MNCs operating in India: a survey of HR professionals', *International Journal of Human Resource Management*, **23**(5), 1006–18.

Joseph, D., N. Kok-Yee, C. Koh and S. Ang (2007), 'Turnover of information technology professionals: a narrative review, meta-analytic structural equation modelling, and model development', *MIS Quarterly*, **31**(3), 547–77.

King, W.R. and G. Torkzadeh (2008), 'Information systems outsourcing: research status and issues', *MIS Quarterly*, **32**(2), 205–25.

Krishna, S., S. Sahay and G. Walsham (2004), 'Managing cross-cultural issues in global software outsourcing', *Communications of the ACM*, **47**(4), 62–6.

Lo, J. (2015), 'The information technology workforce: a review and assessment of voluntary turnover research', *Information Systems Frontiers*, **17**(2), 387–411.

Mahmood, S., S. Anwer, M. Niazi, M. Alshayeb and I. Richardson (2017), 'Key factors that influence task allocation in global software development', *Information and Software Technology*, **91**, 102–22.

MEITY (2018), 'Fact sheet of IT & BPM industry', accessed 2 July 2019 at https://meity.gov.in/content/fact-sheet-it-bpm-industry.

Moon, M.J. and S. Bretschneiber (2002), 'Does the perception of red tape constrain IT innovativeness in organizations? Unexpected results from a simultaneous equation model and implications', *Journal of Public Administration Research and Theory*, **12**(2), 273–92.

Moreno, A.M., M.I. Sanchez-Segura, F. Medina-Dominguez and L. Carvajal (2012), 'Balancing software engineering education and industrial needs', *Journal of Systems and Software*, **85**(7), 1607–20.

NASSCOM (2017), 'Women and IT scorecard – India', accessed on 20 January 2020 at https://www.nasscom.in/knowledge-center/publications/women-and-it-scorecard-%E2%80%93-india.

NASSCOM (2019), *Strategic Review: IT-BPM Sector in India 2019: Decoding Digital*, accessed 26 September 2019 at https://www.nasscom.in/knowledge-center/publications/strategic-review-it-bpm-sector-india-2019-decoding-digital.

Patel, C., P. Budhwar and A. Varma (2012), 'Work group identification, conscientiousness, organisational justice and work outcomes: test of a moderated mediation model within the Indian call centre context', *Journal of World Business*, **47**(2), 213–22.

Ragu-Nathan, T.S., M. Tarafdar, B.S. Ragu-Nathan and Q. Tu (2008), 'The consequences of technostress for end users in organizations: conceptual development and empirical validation', *Information Systems Research*, **19**(4), 417–33.

Rong, G. and V. Grover (2009), 'Keeping up-to-date with information technology: testing a model of technological knowledge renewal effectiveness for IT professionals', *Information and Management*, **46**(7), 376–87.

Singh, A. (2018), 'Campus hiring in Indian IT sector expected to shoot up in 2019', *The Week*, 20 December 2018, accessed 20 January 2020 at https://www.theweek

.in/news/biz-tech/2018/12/20/campus-hiring-in-indian-it-sector-expected-to-shoot
-up-in-2019.html.

Smith, J. and D. Gardner (2007), 'Factors affecting employee use of work–life balance initiatives', *New Zealand Journal of Psychology*, **36**(1), 3–12.

Sykes, T.A. (2015), 'Support structures and their impacts on employee outcomes: a longitudinal field study of an enterprise system implementation', *MIS Quarterly*, **39**(2), 473–95.

Srinivas, A. and S. Bansal (2018), 'Gender gap in Indian formal sector worse than global average, LinkedIn data shows', *Hindustan Times*, 14 November 2018, accessed 20 January 2020 at https://www.hindustantimes.com/india-news/gender-gap-in-indian-formal-sector-worse-than-global-average-linkedin-data-shows/story-yOtfsFNazeMZbOnjGL9a1I.html.

Tomer, G. (2015), 'Person–technology fit and work outcomes: a study among IT professionals in India', paper presented at the 23rd European Conference on Information Systems (ECIS), Münster, Germany.

Tomer, G. and S.K. Mishra (2016), 'Professional identity construction among software engineering students', *Information Technology and People*, **29**(1), 146–72.

Tomer, G. and S.K. Mishra (2019), 'Expectation from technology and career satisfaction: a study among IT professionals in India', *Australasian Journal of Information Systems*, **23**, 1–17.

Vlaar, P.W.L., P.C. van Fenema and V. Tiwari (2008), 'Co-creating understanding and value in distributed work: how members of onsite and offshore vendor teams give, make, demand and break sense', *MIS Quarterly*, **32**(2), 227–55.

Wipro (2018), 'Wipro launches skill enhancement program for undergraduate students', accessed 7 May 2019 at https://www.wipro.com/en-IN/newsroom/press-releases/archives/wipro-launches-skill-enhancement-program-for-undergraduate-stude/.

Zaza, I. and D.J. Armstrong (2017), 'Information technology professionals' turnover intentions: a meta-analysis of perceived organizational factors', paper presented at the International Conference on Information Systems (ICIS), Seoul, South Korea.

15. Risk allocation, employer dependence and the welfare state: an investigation of IT workers in the US and Canada[1]

Sara Haviland and Jennifer Craft Morgan

INTRODUCTION

In the modern global economy, risk is increasingly borne by individuals rather than social collectivities (Beck, 1992; Kalleberg, 2011). While an expansive welfare regime can be costly, the reduction of risk for individuals by institutions or welfare states can potentially free individuals to pursue risky entrepreneurial economic endeavours that have potential for both greater individual reward and contributions to the overall economy (D'Amours and Legault, 2013). IT workers, for example, balance high risk and high reward potential, as their fortunes can be made and lost through rapid innovation (Marshall, Morgan and Haviland, 2010). Small, young companies can offer employees exciting potential rewards, from the chance to help steer the company to the profit that accrues from company sale or initial public offerings. They also offer greater risk of failure than larger, more secure firms through higher potential for layoffs.

This assumption of greater risk associated with small, new firms and rapid innovation in IT can be supported by reducing the risk burden at the societal level through greater social welfare policies, or at the individual level through strategies such as maintaining robust health, savings, acquiring private health insurance, having fewer dependants and delaying or forgoing retirement. Without risk mitigation at one or both levels, employees may find themselves relying on employers to provide fundamental benefits that reduce individual risk. This level of employer dependence is related to individual workers' needs and goals, location in the life course and their societal/state context. Employer dependence has implications for the way that workers navigate employment, and their abilities to take risks that have the potential to reap the greatest rewards. This chapter examines the extent to which social welfare regimes influence IT workers' perceptions of risk and levels of dependence on their individual employers. The focus is on the US and Canada, two countries that are largely similar but have key differences in healthcare and pension benefits. We address the following research questions: (1) What is the societal risk context in which US and Canadian IT workers engage in paid work? (2) Do IT workers in these countries have different risk experiences? (3) How do they perceive that risk? (4) How does perception of risk affect their employment choices?

We hypothesize that individuals will have greater feelings of anxiety in a society where the state bears less of workers' risks and in turn creates high employer dependence. Therefore, in a country with a more privatized welfare approach (US), employees will look to employers as the primary means to meet these needs and have higher employer dependence and less flexibility to pursue high-risk, high-reward work. For a country with more generous social welfare programmes (Canada), the government plays a larger role and dependence on the employer for individual well-being is diminished. This affects the nature of the employment relationship, as workers with high employer dependence face greater pressures to maintain a full-time employed status with benefits. These pressures are not distributed evenly throughout the population and vary by policy context; workers with different life course situations, greater healthcare needs or those nearing retirement age may be more vulnerable and therefore more affected by social welfare variation (Cooke, 2006). This may affect their ability to participate in high-risk, high-reward work.

RISK ALLOCATION AND THE SOCIAL WELFARE CONTEXT

Risk is a value-neutral term related to chance (Lupton, 1999), yet has a negative connotation, typically referring to the chance that something might go wrong (Amoore, 2004; Hacker, 2006). Risk can be distributed in several ways, and different levels of society can bear the burden of risk for individuals in areas such as employment, health and retirement. The approaches examined in this analysis are: the assumption of risk by the individual (micro level), or by the state (macro level), with employers (meso level) serving as intermediaries whose roles vary depending on the micro/macro balance of the welfare regime. Societies typically utilize a combination of these approaches, weighing more heavily toward one end or the other on an individual/state continuum of assumption of risk. The role of the meso level is therefore variable depending on the general balance of risk in societies where there is a strong individualist or micro-level assumption of risk. The meso level can offer an extra buffer (particularly through the provision of health insurance and pension plans) (D'Amours and Legault, 2013). States can also intervene in high-risk industries, as the US does with subsidies for farmers to guard against the effect of weather fluctuations on crops; however, in IT this would be a very unusual practice.

Societies that favour individualist assumption of risk are referred to as the risk societies (Beck, 1992). The pool of workers who enjoy employer risk protection through job security, health insurance and retirement benefits is dwindling, creating a rise in worker-borne risk that not all welfare regimes are prepared to bear. Indeed, many labour policies were built on the premise of stable, long-term employment in firms with internal labour markets and strong benefits (Kalleberg, Reskin and Hudson, 2000). IT workers today face precarious working arrangements, characterized by 'employment that is uncertain, unpredictable, and risky from the point of view of the employee' (Kalleberg, 2009, p. 2). Understanding the role that social welfare policies and firm benefits play is critical to providing a sense of stability for workers and to encouraging societally beneficial risk taking.

Esping-Andersen (1990) defined typologies of welfare regimes. Conservative welfare regimes (typified by Germany) intervene in the market, though with an aim to preserve traditional societal hierarchies rather than to offer more universal benefits. Social democratic nations (typified by Scandinavian countries) are universal in their benefits and the most successful in liberating individual standards of living from the market. The US and Canada, in contrast, are liberal welfare regimes, valuing the free market and offering minimal safety nets for their citizens. Among Organisation for Economic Co-operation and Development (OECD) countries, the US is one of only four nations that do not have universal health coverage (OECD, 2011). According to the World Bank, the US healthcare system is quite expensive, spending approximately 5–7 per cent more than Canada over the last ten years. Canada is much closer in percentage of gross domestic product (GDP) to healthcare spending to other Western European countries but far more than developing economies like India (3.66 per cent in 2016) or China (4.98 per cent in 2016). Given the expense of US healthcare and the lack of a societal safety net, US workers have an increasing incentive to maintain employment relationships that subsidize health insurance plans.

Although the stakes are different, workers in Canada also have reasons to seek out employer-sponsored health benefits. The sizeable private insurance markets in Canada are part of a system where public coverage offers a baseline (universal doctor and hospital visits, without co-payment), but does not cover everything (for example, prescription drugs). In health benefits, the US is clearly the weaker public system, offering state insurance coverage only to a targeted, means-tested population of its citizens. The US is somewhat more generous with respect to public pensions, to which it devotes a larger percentage of GDP than Canada. Still, both countries are below the OECD average spending on public pensions. Given the variations in the state of healthcare and pension systems, we modify Esping-Andersen's welfare states typology to include a subcategory of liberal welfare regimes. We classify the US as a *high liberal* welfare regime and Canada as a *low liberal* welfare regime.

IT WORK: RISKY BUSINESS

The IT industry is constantly evolving alongside technological innovation. IT can be simultaneously exciting and unstable, as evidenced by its notable 'boom' in the 1990s, followed by its 'bust' in the 2000s (Beckstead and Brown, 2005). This instability is even more pronounced for IT workers in companies that are smaller and solely tech-focused. While IT workers might be able to find greater stability and benefits at larger companies in unrelated businesses, often working as technicians, IT workers in small IT companies face the attendant risks of disbanding that come with nascent businesses (Aldrich and Ruef, 2006; D'Amours and Legault, 2013; McMullin and Marshall, 2010).

DATA AND METHODS

Workers' worries serve as markers of the experience of risk at the individual level. We employ data from the Workforce Aging in the New Economy (WANE) project to address the proposed research questions. WANE was an international, cross-comparative study of IT workers, using a case study method to understand the nature of working and ageing in the new economy. Case study techniques are ideal for in-depth, contextualized data and sensitive to complexity (Marshall, 1999; Ragin, 2014). The analysis is based on US and Canadian WANE data, which include 11 and 18 firms, respectively. The data used in this chapter include web-based surveys, which took about 40–60 minutes to complete, and hour-long semi-structured interviews; both methods asked respondents about their personal histories and IT careers, attitudes about work and so on. The WANE study was conducted prior to the Affordable Care Act (ACA) reform in the US (data collection took place from 2004 to 2006), and the snapshot it offers grants insight into the nature of work before the promise of greater universality in health insurance protections and coverage was part of the US collective conscious. Given the Affordable Care Act's tenuous political position, its introduction simultaneously brings greater stability and less certainty to the US health market; during the WANE collection, the ACA was not even a part of the public debate.

To address the research questions, we examine three levels: the welfare regime, the firm and the individual (IT workers). This is centred in two analyses: first, we examine individuals by welfare regime, and second, we examine individuals by firms.

At the welfare regime level, we compare results by country (US and Canada) in relation to the social safety net differences between the two countries – health insurance provision and entitlement programmes. This analysis utilizes two sources of data from the WANE study: surveys of employees in all Canadian and US WANE firms ($N = 107$ Canadian, $N = 139$ US), and qualitative interview data from employees of these firms ($N = 141$ Canadian, $N = 103$ US). Web surveys were processed with SPSS. Interviews were processed in NVivo through an open coding framework, using a grounded approach to theory building (Corbin, Strauss and Strauss, 2015). For a more in-depth discussion of the study methods, please see Jovic, McMullin and Duerden Comeau (2011) and McMullin and Marshall (2010).

Next, we examine how firms could serve as meso-level risk buffers in this high-risk industry. Using the same survey data, we created a worry index that allows us to determine which companies in the WANE sample have the least worried workers and then directly compare interview data from respondents in each country, analysing discussions of worries, risk and stability, with a particular focus on healthcare and retirement. The index is built from the web survey, which featured a ten-item 'worry' series. The series asked respondents to assess how worried they were about different components of life, with responses arrayed on a four-point Likert-type scale from 1 = not at all worried to 4 = worried a great deal. Items addressed concerns at the individual level (worry about ability to be competitive in the market should you lose your job, failing to keep your IT knowledge and skills current, your health, health of family members, juggling work and family/personal life), firm and industry level (worry about future economic success of the company, future of the IT industry, offshoring of IT jobs to other countries) and the country and international level (state of the economy in general, international stability). These ten items were summed into a worry index, with a range of 10–40 (Cronbach's alpha 0.828; Haviland, 2011). A lower value indicates less worry and a higher value indicates greater worry.

We arrayed firms based on the average worry index score of their employees, identifying the four least-worried cases (two per country) for in-depth analysis. Using the same search terms as the welfare-state level comparison, the results are sorted into high liberal firm strategies, low liberal firm strategies, and universal strategies for the alleviation of worry. The interview data allows an exploration of patterns in low-worry firms to ascertain how firms may play a role in diminishing IT worker concerns, and how that role may differ between high and low welfare regimes.

RESULTS

The sample of IT workers is largely young, male and white. Both the interview and web-survey respondent pools skew quite young, with mean ages in the mid- to late 30s (Canadian mean 37.2 years for interviews, 37.4 for surveys; US mean is 40.0 for interviews and 38.7 for surveys; the overall range is 19–63 years). The percentage of male respondents is 76.6 for both interview and survey data in Canada, 73.6 per cent for US interview data, and 69.4 for US survey data. In both countries, most respondents are married (65.9 and 68.1 per cent of Canadian interview and survey respondents, respectively; 80.8 and 71.4 per cent of US interview and survey respondents). More than half of respondents in both countries have children. All but one US respondent in the WANE survey sample reported that they did have healthcare insurance, though sources varied (39 per cent fully paid by their employers; 45 per cent partially paid by their employers). In a country where such a large portion of the population is uninsured, WANE participants represent a privileged group of workers.

Worry Index

There were no significant differences in the total scores on the worry index between the countries. Independent sample *t*-tests showed little variation between the individual items. While the lack of difference on the worry index is surprising at the country level, we examined the variation in the index across firms relative to country context. As these were all currently employed IT workers, perhaps stable employment was bearing the risk at the meso level, thus masking higher individual worries in US firms. We arrayed the average of respondent scores on the worry index by firm, from low to high scores (range 14.7–21.1, median = 21), using this index to orient our firm-level approach to the qualitative data. The firms clustered very tightly on the index; the mean scores by firm were all within six points of each other, at the less worried end of the scale. Given the high level of individual risk in these countries, we were interested in why firms had such unworried respondents and focused the firm-level analysis on the two least worried firms in each country. Table 15.1 shows the data availability for these firms.

Risk and the Social Welfare Context: Comparing the US and Canada

We begin with an overall comparison of the US and Canadian workers in the WANE sample (across all firms). The US is used as a baseline for comparison. Results are organized into two categories: concerns expressed by IT workers

Table 15.1   Data availability for low-worry firms

Location	Case ID	Firm Size (N employees)	Interview Respondents	Web Survey Respondents
US	US509	6	4	4
	US512	41	6	17
Canada	CAN107	11	11	8
	CAN112	14	10	7

about their own healthcare and retirement, and concerns expressed by managers and owners about the provision of healthcare and retirement.

Worker concerns about healthcare and retirement
Put broadly, while Canadian respondents were concerned about supplemental health benefits, US respondents were more concerned about maintaining basic health benefits. Workers in both countries lacked confidence in their retirement plans; although likely due to their younger ages, these concerns were less salient than healthcare.

Healthcare
Healthcare was paramount in the minds of many of the US workers, who were more likely to report that benefits were keeping them in their jobs, indicating a high level of employer dependence. A strong health insurance plan often appeared on lists of reasons why a job was good, and for some it could be the only reason to maintain an employment relationship. Healthcare benefits could be urgent issues for older workers as well. One respondent, an older worker who was putting off retirement for the benefits, described the paramount importance of a strong benefits package, noting:

> I have positioned myself to where we could work for half of my salary and still put money in the bank. So we didn't care about the money. I care about the insurance. Cause that equates to a lot more money under the wrong circumstances. So I'd almost work for free now.

There was plenty to recommend larger firms, benefits-wise. One respondent who had previously worked for IBM described what he perceived to be the illusory nature of security at larger firms, but noted the benefits were much better:

> You know, at IBM I'm not sure you're much more secure than you are at a place like this but you have sort of a what I'll say is a false sense of security. So you have a sense that you're secure, you're probably not … Some of the benefit stuff you feel

a little more exposed here than we did at IBM, which have more of a fuller, more of a sense of taking care of you from a benefits point of view.

While the respondent was acknowledging that even employment with larger firms can be prone to disruption, risk was diminished by the benefits plans; small firm benefits left one 'exposed'.

Although when compared to the US, Canada's state health benefits are more universal and generous, many companies offered health coverage that supplemented the state plans, and several companies offered dental, disability and vision plans despite their small firm size. Discussions of benefits package shortcomings in Canada were about these supplemental plans, and therefore the urgency in language was absent when compared to what US respondents expressed about health insurance.

Retirement

Retirement benefits were offered less frequently than medical benefits in both countries. Retirement planning may have seemed less relevant to such a young workforce, but it was something that many respondents in both countries noted as problematic at their companies. The importance of solid retirement benefits was highlighted by participants who reported the difficulty in taking on retirement investing on their own, as exemplified by one US respondent:

> It's definitely easier to do we think if you got it set up and it comes out of your pay check. And, also for the companies that will like match certain amounts, you know, then that's a real encouragement to add extra amounts. And, we did that while we [were] at the other company, so to be honest right now, I'm really not. I haven't really continued my retirement savings. I'm kind of waiting.

On both sides of the border, some respondents were able to make private investments and plans, but many had similar experiences to the above respondent. With such a young workforce, sometimes retirement did not register as a concern; other times, there was not enough extra personal money to invest or the process seemed remote.

The difficulty workers experienced in taking care of their own retirements became more problematic where companies were not perceived to be committed to helping employees. Experiences with companies who were perceived to have taken advantage of people's commitment and cut them loose before owing full retirement benefits were mentioned, most vividly by one US respondent whose husband had lost his job as he drew near retirement. She noted:

> I think business today, especially big business, is just interested in the bottom line ... And we think that there's a growing trend to get rid of the older workers, and

that cuts down on the bottom line. My husband just lost his job … . He was told in September that his job would go away in December. And it did. And he was a year and 2 months away from full retirement.

The couple had been dependent on their employer for a full retirement pension and were powerless when the firm did not deliver. Examples like these contributed to a perception among some US respondents that businesses were solely out to make a profit and workers were in a position of disadvantage. These stories of companies' lack of commitment were part of a larger landscape of stories about workers left in the lurch when it came time for retirement. Cautionary tales abound in the US firms, though not so prominently in Canadian firms, and inspired anxiety in the workers who told them.

While there were some first-person stories of retirement woes, as in the previous quote, US participants shared stories of people who witnessed the difficult events of others. These lessons of instability experienced by others had an impact on the participants. A respondent worried over a father who had demonstrated tremendous commitment to his company throughout his working life, only to find himself out of luck when the company went bankrupt during his retirement:

My father worked for the same company for 35 years. Five years after he retired, he had retired at the age of 70, that company went [bankrupt], got bought by [another] company. His pension was in the bankruptcy, had nothing. Yeah, so you know my dad's 83 and my mom's seventy-something … And, we mean, gosh, their meds alone they spend $1000 a month. You know on the things that keep them alive.

This anecdote illustrated the particular predicament some US workers apparently found themselves in; the parents in this story were doubly harmed as they were so fully dependent on their former employer for their welfare, and as the healthcare and prescription drugs were so expensive. Stories like these contributed to a general sense that no one was looking out for retirees.

Canadian workers did not share specific stories of retirements gone wrong but were also pessimistic about retirement. Many interview respondents reported that they had no pension plans, although a few companies did offer tax-sheltered Registered Retirement Savings Plans (RRSPs) with matching funds, akin to US 401K plans. Some demonstrated distrust for the state plans, which mirrored the distrust some US respondents have of Social Security. One stated, 'We don't really trust the government that they're going to be there with all of the money we put into the Canada Pension Plan [laughs]'.

Some Canadian respondents were less fatalistic about the need to continue working in their later years but were taking personal action to ensure that they would be able to exit the labour force. Noting the rarity of pensions in private companies and the prevalence of RRSPs that employers did not contribute much to, one respondent stated:

> [Y]ou pretty much are on your own as far as your retirement. So you do … put your own money away and you … do your own … decision-making in terms of … asset mixes and so forth. Some respondents invested in plans privately, and some had other forms of investment (such as real estate or their own companies) to cover expenses.

Risk and the firm

As all liberal regimes allow individual lifestyles to remain tied to the market, workers in these regimes should theoretically be quite concerned about their work and security. We selected the two least worried firms in each country on the worry index for further case study analysis as employees of these firms offer the greatest contrast to expected worry levels, given the high risk burden borne by individuals in this industry and in these liberal welfare states. This may indicate that risk protection for these workers is being offered at the firm level. We wanted to see what firms did to help minimize worry, or to shoulder some burden of risk for individuals. Selected cases are highlighted in Table 15.1, with country identifiers added to the beginning of each firm ID for clarity. These are mostly small firms, which makes their feelings of stability all the more remarkable.

There was no one universal set of criteria that emerged from the qualitative analysis for each low-worry company. Rather, several factors emerged that were duplicated throughout these firms, with each firm possessing a few of these characteristics. These factors were primarily related to firm practices and firm context, and were experienced differently based on individuals' life experiences.

Firm practices

The role of ownership or management practices was notable in several firms, and energetic or high-commitment owners were remarkable in the low-worry firms. For example, one respondent in US509 described a situation where he needed a pay advance because he had no money right after he was hired, which the owner issued on the spot. Owner commitment was also high in CAN107, where one respondent described the efforts of the owner to keep the team together: '[W]orking for [the owner], he has proven that he is as loyal to us as we are to him. So, given some hard times, he should have laid people off but he didn't'. These owners demonstrated a commitment to their employees that was quite strong, and this may in part help ease worries about employment stability.

Another characteristic of these low-worry firms was strong communication of firm goals, values and market contexts. This was the case in firms where business or finance-type personalities were prominent in the company (US512 and CAN112), though not exclusively so. US512 held regular, all-hands meetings to discuss the state of the company, where it was going and how everyone fit into that. In US512, there was a strong push from the CEO to make sure that all products had market applications. The importance of focusing on market applications was reiterated by the owner of CAN112, who mentioned that 'one of the problems that these developers have is they develop stuff that they like … The successful companies will probably have had somebody that's had their feet on the street and know what the market is looking for'. Employees in several firms were able to articulate a consistent company vision, indicating that firm values were being expressed in a consistent manner (US512, CAN107 and CAN112). This is an area where firm size may be helpful; at smaller firms, the employees have more access to leadership than employees of larger businesses would.

Firm context
A history of failure was a theme in several firms, including US512. These firms also had a high tolerance for mistakes. As noted by the US512 CEO: 'We also sort of believe in a culture that being wrong is okay. If you don't do something, that's not okay. You lose your job when you don't do something. You don't lose your job if you make a mistake'. The tolerance for mistakes meant that the employment relationship was more likely to be preserved, a reassuring feature in systems where individual well-being is so strongly tied to that relationship. Some of the low liberal firms were in recovery mode following layoff cycles or downturns, particularly CAN107. This gave the remaining incumbents a sense of stability, having survived the layoff cycles, and the cutbacks were seen as time-limited affairs that were not necessarily indicative of a company spiral. Again, communication was key; layoffs without a clear organizational objective and explanation were dangerous, but those that served to cut 'dead weight' and were explained as such were not. Growth was not the only way a company signalled viability; another was operating in a stable niche. US509, US512 and CAN112 all occupied specialized markets where they had a regional, national, or even international dominance.

DISCUSSION AND CONCLUSIONS

Information technology can be precarious work, characterized by uncertainty and risk (Kalleberg, 2009). However, unlike their low-wage counterparts in other occupations, IT workers in the US and Canada have greater potential for shelter from this risk in the employment relationship, as many of their employers confer health insurance and pension benefits that mitigate risk for the individual. As a white-collar job with great levels of precariousness, the experience of IT workers is instructive.

Looking to welfare state differences, workers in the US were worried about getting and maintaining basic health insurance coverage, while workers in Canada were worried about getting supplementary health plans. For both countries, perhaps because of the young age of the IT workforce, pension worries were of less salience. However, especially in the US, catastrophic stories of loss of pensions and jobs later in life served as cautionary tales and were perceived causes for long-term concern.

Focusing on worry as a manifestation of perceived risk at the individual level, we found that US workers were highly employer dependent and under the greatest pressure to maintain employment relations to keep fundamental health benefits and pension plans. Firms that successfully mitigated worker worries were those that demonstrated high-commitment practices or communicated firm market contexts that heightened individual worker perception of job security. An emphasis on communication from management was universally beneficial, allowing workers to understand the firm goals, values and market context.

The assumption of risks related particularly to healthcare and pensions appears to be more palatable for workers in societies where the state takes a greater role in ensuring well-being, lessening employer dependence. This may have implications for what types of workers can pursue jobs in these high-risk enterprises. Firms can help alleviate these risks, but in the end, even the best employer-dependent protection is something of an illusion. The risk society has inherent problems that can make it cruel to even the most dedicated workers. Catastrophic events such as major accidents or health disruptions can pose a challenge for continued employment, but continuous employment itself is a condition for protection from these misfortunes. It is also contingent upon the employer's continued success and stability and the availability of alternative employment prospects. In good economic times, workers are more able to assume that *an* employer, if not *their current* employer, will fill this role. In looser markets, when job searches take longer, and available positions are quite competitive to acquire, unemployed individuals can find themselves subject to the whims of fate at a vulnerable time. Risk mitigation dependent largely upon employment leaves even highly skilled workers unsheltered and risk averse. This is likely to have deleterious effects on growth and innovation at least from worker groups who have higher perceived individual risk burdens such as older workers, workers with dependents and those managing chronic health conditions.

ACKNOWLEDGEMENT

The work in this chapter was both enabled and enhanced by our late advisor, mentor and friend, Victor Marshall, who served as the Principal Investigator of the US team for the Workforce Aging in the New Economy Project (WANE). WANE was an international collaboration of scholars funded by Canada's Social Science and Humanities Research Council, led internationally by Principal Investigator Julie McMullin, also a former student of Victor's. It is not possible to overstate the influence of his methodological rigor, insightfulness and generosity of spirit on our work and the work of a whole generation of scholars, for which we are ever grateful.

NOTE

1. This work is abbreviated from a dissertation (Haviland, 2011), which was embedded in a four-year multinational research programme, the Workforce Aging in the New Economy Project (WANE) (McMullin and Marshall 2010).

REFERENCES

Aldrich, H.E. and M. Ruef (2006), *Organizations Evolving* (2nd edition), Thousand Oaks, CA: Sage.

Amoore, L. (2004), 'Risk, reward, and discipline at work', *Economy and Society*, **33**(2), 174–96.

Beck, U. (1992), *Risk Society: Towards a New Modernity*, Newbury Park, CA: Sage.

Beckstead, D. and W.M. Brown (2005), 'An anatomy of growth and decline: high-tech industries through the boom and bust years, 1997–2003', *Statistics Canada, Insights on the Canadian Economy*, 11-624-MIE No. 010.

Cooke, M. (2006), 'Policy changes and the labour force participation of older workers: evidence from six countries', *Canadian Journal on Aging*, **25**(4), 387–400.

Corbin, J., A.L. Strauss and A. Strauss (2015), *Basics of Qualitative Research* (4th edition), Thousand Oaks, CA: Sage.

D'Amours, M. and M.J. Legault (2013), 'Highly skilled workers and employment risks: role of institutions', *Labor Studies Journal*, **38**(2), 89–109.

Esping-Andersen, G. (1990), *The Three Worlds of Welfare Capitalism*, Princeton, NJ: Princeton University Press.

Hacker, J.S. (2006), *The Great Risk Shift: The Assault on American Jobs, Families, Healthcare, and Retirement and How You Can Fight Back*, New York: Oxford University Press.

Haviland, S. (2011), 'Age relations in small and medium-sized information technology firms', dissertation, University of North Carolina at Chapel Hill.

Jovic, E., J.A. McMullin and T. Duerden Comeau (2011), 'Methods', in J.A. McMullin (ed.), *Age, Gender, and Work: Small Information Technology Firms in the New Economy*, Vancouver, BC: University of British Columbia Press.

Kalleberg, A.L. (2009), 'Precarious work, insecure workers: employment relations in transition', *American Sociological Review*, **74**(1), 1–22.

Kalleberg, A.L. (2011), *Good Jobs, Bad Jobs: The Rise of Polarized and Precarious Employment Systems in the United States, 1970s to 2000s*, New York: Russell Sage Foundation.

Kalleberg, A.L., B.F. Reskin and K. Hudson (2000), 'Bad jobs in America: standard and nonstandard employment relations and job quality in the United States', *American Sociological Review*, **65**(2), 256–78.

Lupton, D. (1999), *Risk*, London: Routledge.

Marshall, V.W. (1999), 'Reasoning with case studies: issues of an aging workforce', *Journal of Aging Studies*, **13**(4), 377–89.

Marshall, V.W., J.C. Morgan and S.B. Haviland (2010), 'Making a life in IT: jobs and careers in small and medium-sized information technology companies', in J.A. McMullin and V.W. Marshall (eds), *Aging and Working in the New Economy: Careers and Changing Structures in Small IT Firms*, Cheltenham, UK and Northampton, MA, USA: Edward Elgar Publishing.

McMullin, J.A. and V.W. Marshall (eds) (2010), *Aging and Working in the New Economy: Changing Career Structures in Small IT Firms*, Cheltenham, UK and Northampton, MA, USA: Edward Elgar Publishing.

OECD (2011), 'Coverage for healthcare', in *Health at a Glance 2011: OECD Indicators*, Paris: OECD Publishing.

Ragin, C.C. (2014), *The Comparative Method: Moving Beyond Qualitative and Quantitative Strategies*, Oakland, CA: University of California Press.

PART VIII

Opting out or staying in

Both chapters under this heading look at career decisions of women, and in particular at the decision whether to aim for a professional career.

Tania Saritova Rath and Mousumi Padhi's chapter is titled 'Integrating care work for sustainable careers of women: an Indian perspective'. They start from the observation that the labour force participation of educated women in India is declining. In their study, they focus on highly educated women likely to have a greater choice about returning to work and find that many of those women see unpaid work through caregiving as more important than paid work from any job. Traditional accommodations to help women to return to work – maternity leave, flexi-time, working from home, and so on – are just 'minor enablers'. They make a strong case for government and organizations to reconstruct the concept of care work and integrate it with paid work, both to value the work of women and to account for lost income.

In her chapter titled, 'Leaning in: why some women are challenging the opt-out model', Margie J. Elley-Brown looks at the opposite career decision to opting out, that is, staying in. She uses a similar approach to explore the decisions of professional women educators in New Zealand to remain in the workforce. In contrast to previous research results, these educators chose not to opt out at mid-career. Instead they wanted to succeed and achieve career goals and they did so in consultation with their partners. In many cases, these partners took a step back in their own career, as the women took a 'front seat' in their dual-career partnerships.

Both of these studies use the Kaleidoscope Career Model concerned with the dimensions of authenticity, balance and challenge, providing an opportunity to compare Indian and Western approaches. Rath and Padhi report that authenticity, balance and challenge are sought simultaneously in care work rather than paid work, but that care work is also work and should be regarded as such. Elley-Brown also argues that the three parameters of authenticity, balance and challenge overlap and are not mutually exclusive. Yet, more in line with the

Western reading of the Kaleidoscope Career Model, she considers balance to be opposed to challenge and authenticity, so that achieving balance across different life domains interferes with opportunities for challenge and authenticity through work. How will you see the meanings of authenticity, balance and challenge across different cultural settings after reading these chapters?

16. Integrating care work for sustainable careers of women: an Indian perspective

Tania Saritova Rath and Mousumi Padhi

INTRODUCTION

In almost every country in the world, men are more likely to participate in labour markets than women. However, in recent decades, the gender differences in labour force participation rate (LFPR) have been narrowing substantially. When the global average is rising, the declining trend of the female LFPR in India is a matter of concern. Even smaller neighbouring countries such as Bhutan, Bangladesh and Sri Lanka are faring better than India. In India, the female LFPR was 50 percentage points lower than the male LFPR in 2018 (International Labour Organization [ILO], 2018). The declining LFPR of women in India from 42.7 per cent in 2004–05 to 26 per cent in 2018 (ILO, 2018), despite being a growing economy with increasing educational attainment, has generated a lot of curiosity in recent times. According to the Deloitte report (2019) titled *Opportunity of Challenge: Empowering Women & Girls in India for the Fourth Industrial Revolution*, 95 per cent or 195 million women are employed in the unorganized sector[1] or are in unpaid work. In India, a substantially high proportion of educated women report their activity status as attending to domestic duties. This domestic work is not documented in official statistics. Neetha and Mazumdar (2011) reason that this can be a potential explanation for the low female LFPR of India.

The complex sociocultural dynamics predicting the workforce participation behaviour of Indian women continues to amaze researchers. A growing body of research (Chapman and Mishra, 2019; Kapsos, Silberman and Bourmpoula, 2014) on this issue point to three key factors that have limited the role of women in the Indian economy: the role of entrenched gender norms in Indian society, the rising incomes of men (which raises family income and makes it easier for women to quit working) and the lack of quality jobs for women. The latest evidence on regressive attitudes towards women comes from the Social

Attitudes Research, India survey (2016) covering Delhi, Mumbai, UP and Rajasthan. Coffey et al. (2018) in their study found that that many men and women feel that married women whose husbands earn well should not work outside the home. What perhaps is ignored in the labour force participation debate is the continuing contribution of labour by women on the home front or in care work.

The need for further exploration to understand this phenomenon has resulted in the study in this chapter. In the first stage, the study aims to understand how career and empowerment are perceived by highly educated urban women who have chosen not to work or have withdrawn from the workforce. In the second stage, we explore the perspective of women on work and career to gain insights into the factors that drove their decision to drop out of the workforce. The Kaleidoscope Career Model (KCM) (Mainiero and Sullivan, 2005; Sullivan and Mainiero, 2008) is used as a lens to view how Indian women perceive the dimensions of authenticity, challenge and balance in the context of their work.

LITERATURE REVIEW

The review of literature covers the concept of work and economic explanations of the decision of women to participate in the labour force.

Concept of Work

According to the United Nations Statistics Division (UNSD, 1993) activities carried out by individuals in any society can be classified into three categories. The first category is economic activities or SNA (System of National Accounts) activities. Non-economic activities or care work falling outside the SNA production boundary form the second category. Leisure and personal care activities form the third category. It suggests that countries can compile a parallel set of accounts to reflect the care economy that includes household production and unpaid care work. In India, women are responsible for both.

Education and Women's Workforce Participation

While 'economic factors largely determine male participation in employment, the factors that influence a woman's participation in work are varied and include individual, demographic, social, religious and cultural factors' (Srivastava and Srivastava, 2010, p. 50). In most developed countries, increased education causes an increase in women's labour force participation (England, Gornick and Shafer, 2012). Complex socio-economic phenomena underlie the paradox of increasing education and decreasing female workforce participation in India. Abraham (2013) argues that the rising incomes of Indian households have enabled Indian women to withdraw from the labour market. Using unit-level data from the National Employment Survey in urban areas of India, Klasen and Pieters (2015) have confirmed that rising levels of household income play an important role in declining rates of women's labour force participation.

Income and Substitution Effect in a Collective Household Labour Supply Model

In understanding family behaviour and household decision variables on consumption, fertility, labour supply, savings and so on, the economic models used in extant literature have diverged in two directions. The first model is the traditional unitary model of labour supply that views family as a whole as the basic decision-making unit (Crespo et al., 2013). A second model, the collective household labour supply model proposed by Bourguignon and Chiappori (1992), is gaining popularity (Bloemen, 2019; Blundell et al., 2007; Cherchye, De Rock and Vermeulen, 2009; Donni, 2003). In this model, the family is considered as a group of individuals characterized by their own preferences who interact with each other when making their decisions. Its growing usage is because the traditional unitary model ignores the underlying role of the household members who may influence labour supply decisions. In the Indian context, the collectivistic nature of the society makes it more pertinent to use the collective household labour supply model for understanding the preferences of women and explaining their workforce participation.

Quantitatively, the decision on household production is assumed to be an income maximization problem (Xu, 2007) where investment continues till the marginal rate of return equals the marginal cost. The study in this chapter looks at the experiences of women who according to the traditional literature on labour supply can be viewed as non-participating (Bloemen, 2010; Blundell et al., 2007; Donni, 2003; Vermeulen et al., 2006).

In this chapter, we study some of the assumptions of the quantitative economic models. In extending the assumptions, the chapter more specifically explores and finds out what the cost is vis-à-vis the return the women get who choose to drop out of the workforce. While the quantitative studies look at the cost and return quantitatively, this chapter looks at it qualitatively to more specifically understand how loss of real income by dropping out of the workforce is substituted by the gains or return that the women make.

METHODOLOGY

As stated above, we aim to add to the quantitative body of research documenting the decline in female labour force participation in India. We conduct a qualitative study to dig deeper into the reasons behind this decline. To do so, the study uses the interpretivist paradigm to understand the phenomena of career and work through the meanings that women assign to them (Boland, 1985; Deetz, 1996; Orlikowski and Baroudi, 1991). Researchers who are using the interpretivist paradigm seek experiences, understandings and perceptions of individuals to uncover reality rather than rely on numbers of statistics. It is also contended that in the absence of insufficient a priori theory, an interpretivist paradigm is often helpful for theory construction.

Narratives have been used to collect data for the purpose of the study. The narratives were collected from 45 technically and professionally qualified women who had dropped out of the workforce or had not joined the workforce at all. The women ranged in age from 25 to 55 years. Snowball sampling was used to identify women who although professionally qualified were not voluntarily working at the time of the study. Technical qualification referred to women who had a BE/BTech and/or MTech degrees. Professionally qualified referred to women who had MBA, MCom, LLB or PhD degrees. In the sample under study all respondents had a bachelor's degree. Eighty per cent of the respondents had worked at some point but were not part of the workforce at the time of study. Twenty per cent of the respondents had never joined the workforce. In addition to a set of demographic questions enlisting the respondent's age, family size, education level and so on, open-ended questions were asked about the respondent's decision not to join the workforce, such as: 'What, who or which factors influenced your decision not to work?'; 'When did you drop out of the workforce?'; 'Was it an individual decision or a family decision?'; 'Who in the family influenced this decision?'; 'What were significant developments in your life after you dropped out?' and so on. Time was given to the respondents to reflect over the questions and narrate. The narrative essays were collected a day later. Narrative essays differ from answers because the respondent chooses the information and orders the relevant issues in order of individual priority and relates the details to the context (Aarikka-Stenroos, 2010).

In the second stage, all 45 respondents were contacted for focus group discussions. Fourteen respondents agreed to take part. They were divided into two groups based on whether they had work experience. Each focus group had seven respondents. Discussions were based on the themes that emerged from the narrative analysis. Additionally, the women having work experience were asked to describe how their manner of living changed before and after they dropped out of the workforce. The discussions were recorded with permission from the respondents. These were later translated into English and transcribed wherever there were some sentences or words in the local language.

To analyse the data, we used holistic-content analysis (Lieblich, Tuval-Mashiach and Zilber, 1998). The narratives were put together and read multiple times to understand the pattern that emerged. The initial observations on the narratives were documented. The narratives were compared for similarities and differences. The different foci and themes that emerged were noted down and were recorded as they occurred in the text. The effects of background variables such as age, family size and so on and differences and similarities in pattern were noted. The explicit content in the stories were categorized according to theme. The researchers went through the narratives individually in the first phase and then compared notes and looked at the narratives jointly.

FINDINGS

The findings point to individual, sociocultural and organizational factors explaining the decision-making behaviour of Indian women with regard to participating in the labour force. These factors help explain why women decide to drop out and why as a consequence the LFPR of women in India continues to decline.

Individual Factors

Career aspirations
It was interesting to find that nine of the 45 respondents said that they had always been a top-ranking student throughout their academic career. Another 26 women reported that they were not top rankers but considered themselves as reasonably good students in their academic career. It was all the more intriguing to note the career aspirations of these women when pursuing their education. A majority of the women aspired to be career women who would succeed in their chosen fields. Some desired to be CEOs, some to be successful managers, some to be bankers, some Indian Administrative Service officers. Some were specific in their response and very focused regarding their career aspirations, whereas others were generic. For example, Shriya,[2] a 32-year-old mother with two children said: 'I topped my group in BTech. I wanted to be an automobile engineering designer right from my 12th grade'. Reena's response was more generic when she said: 'I wanted to become successful in my career, to work in different places, to get a lot of exposure and travel to different countries'. She, an engineer, had dropped out of the workforce after she had her son. Whether their responses were general or specific, without exception all women as they studied dreamt of having a career.

Marriage and family
A factor that came out predominantly was that the respondents stayed away from the workforce to be with their family. Some simply put that it was the need to move with their husband to a different city when he got transferred.

Sudha, an MBA, said she had always been a good student and wanted to become the CEO of a company. When she graduated, she had the option of joining a leading company in the fast-moving consumer goods sector. She joined and worked there for some time but 'I had to let go because my husband was moving to another city and I wanted to move with him'.

It is apparent that, for some, the family took precedence over their career choices. In some cases, the life event of marriage was reason enough for women to take a break. For instance, Anita says: 'I had got married and wanted to take a break because I was completely burned out in job life. That was the first break I had taken for six months'. The fact that her husband worked and was in a well-paying job could have been an additional factor for taking the break. She added: 'My husband was in a very well-paying job and I just wanted to be home to look after my home'. Anita had been working since she had completed her education and had never taken a break. The fact that her husband earned enough to look after them both motivated her to drop out of the workforce. Care work done at home and the return from it in the form of simple pleasure of looking after a home and husband outweighed the cost of leaving her job that she had been doing for a long time. It is noted that women can drop out of the workforce just to look after their home and husband.

Social perception on gender roles

In some cases, women also reported that what kept them away from the workforce was 'family conditions' or 'having a joint family'. A joint family system is a characteristic of the Indian social system where elderly parents, their married adult children and grandchildren live under the same roof and cook meals in the same kitchen. This is surprising because there is availability of more help in the house and more support with care work in a joint family system. But some of the narratives mentioned that in a joint family it meant 'more meals to be cooked, more cleaning to be done and more care work' and as the daughter-in-law of the house, the responsibility for these tasks were on them. Socialized into the gendered role of a primary caregiver, this is also not questioned by many and they naturally drift into this role taking on the responsibilities from their mother-in-law. Women also feel proud of the fact that the family depends on them. They take pride in their roles as order-keepers and caregivers in the house. The sense of power and control they derive from their economic independence and roles in the workplace becomes insignificant when compared to their roles in the household. As one respondent said:

> I cannot think of going back to work now. Even one day that I am not there my kids cannot manage. I even go to my mother's place when they have their vacations. Once when I had to go for the marriage of a cousin, the whole household was

topsy-turvy. Not just my kids, my husband also find it difficult to coordinate with the maids and issue simple instructions on what is to be cooked for each of the kids.

Bina, who dropped out of her consulting job when her son was six months old, said: 'I wanted to be with my son when he was young – a choice that I made and am proud of'.

Sociocultural Factors

Security and care of children

It was also found that in a majority of instances, it was concern for the security of the child that kept the women away from the workforce. Leaving children alone or with a maid is not considered safe enough. Increasing reports of child abuse is a matter of concern. As Sarla put it:

> This friend of mine left her two-year-old with her maid to go to work. One day the child was crying for some reason and the maid put sugar in her mouth to stop her. But she had put so much sugar in her mouth that the child choked and died. I am afraid if something happens to my child due to me not being around, I won't be able to forgive myself.

Organizational Factors

It was found that organizational factors such as lack of flexibility, inadequate policies for work–life balance, a hostile culture and pressures to fit in keep women away from the workforce (Rath, Mohanty and Pradhan, 2016). As Mita said 'The 24/7 work culture in my organization makes it difficult for me to have a life of my own'. Ramya said: 'The pressure to fit in to male style of working and environment alienated me'. Bina said: 'I had taken maternity leave, which I am legally entitled to, was perceived as a break in service and I was bypassed for promotion'. Anita said: 'My manager used to sit for long hours and expected the same from me. Although I was able to submit the deliverables in time and wanted to leave for home by 6:00 p.m., he was sceptical about employees going home before him and it affected my annual appraisal adversely'. There is a gap between stated policy and practices of the organization.

Factors That Would Enable Joining the Workforce

The women also pointed out factors that might enable them to participate in the labour market. We could identify individual, sociocultural and organizational factors. Table 16.1 consolidates these factors.

Table 16.1   Thematic analysis for joining the workforce

Individual Factors	Organizational Factors	Socio-cultural Factors
Person–job fit: 'I just took up managerial job commensurate to my years' of experience. In terms of salary and the actual profile I wanted to work for, I have compromised'	*Job security:* 'Always wanted a job that provides security'	*Domestic support:* 'Availability of reliable domestic help would facilitate joining workforce'
Scope to use skill: 'Go back if opportunity to use my skills'	*Job satisfaction:* 'Most of the time the working conditions are not satisfying. I would like to rejoin if the organization considers and respects my various roles and define job conditions accordingly'	*Family support:* 'Cooperation of family members and husband would have been helpful to reconsider rejoining'
Pay package: 'High salary commensurate with my education is a consideration'	*WLB policies:* 'Flexible work hours and part time work options, family-centric policies are important'	*Social infrastructure:* 'Availability of high-quality childcare infrastructure or professional help'
	Organizational support: 'I would prefer a crèche at office premises, playroom for kids to rejoin'; 'I would like to rejoin if the organization provides such infrastructure support'	*Cultural acceptance:* 'Acceptance of my work responsibility in society as important and recognition of both parents as primary caregivers for children would encourage me to join workforce'

The respondents have noted a strong support system for childcare and professional help as major factors that would motivate them to consider joining or rejoining the workforce. Staying with family is another important consideration. For example, one of the respondents noted that she could work in a bank as per her convenience. She needed to travel with her husband and hence refused promotion offered by the bank. The bank in the USA considered and allowed her to rejoin whenever she wanted at the existing level as a bank teller.

Quantitative Value for the Care Work

It was found through the focus group discussion that the women perceived their compensable amount for the work they did to be worth a value in the range of INR 500–1,000 per day. When translated into monetary terms for a 30-day month, it would mean a sustenance allowance of INR 15,000 to 30,000 per month. Integrating care and productive work by regarding all work as productive was a widespread concern for women respondents to this research. Greater flexibility from either male spouses or those male spouses' employers could in turn help provide the greater flexibility the women sought in their careers.

DISCUSSION

In this chapter, we started from the collective household labour supply model and studied the labour supply decision of one family member, namely the woman. We added to the mainly quantitative studies on this topic and conducted a qualitative study to get more insights into the reasons behind Indian women's decision not to join or rejoin the workforce. The results show that for the Indian women we interviewed, the work at home is equally valuable whether it is care work or paid work. This is in line with Kossek and Lautsch's (2012) findings that women are 'dual-centric' (equally high identity with family care and paid work). Employed women's use of flexibility and virtual multitasking to blend work and unpaid work roles can be an issue, as integrating work and family may lead to a higher percolation of work into the family domain or vice versa and lead to greater work–family conflict due to lack of separate time and space. Such coping strategies may lead to greater stress and opting out of the workforce (Kossek, Su and Wu, 2017).

The Indian women's perspective on work can be explained with the help of the KCM model developed by Sullivan and Mainiero (2008; see also Mainiero and Sullivan, 2005). This model is also used as a theoretical lens in Chapter 17 by Elley-Brown on careers of women in New Zealand. The KCM uses a kaleidoscope as a metaphor. The adjustments and shifts modelled by a kaleidoscope with its rotating tube and mirrors enabling the glass chips to fall into changing and complex patterns, reflect the distinctive pattern an individual creates during their career. The KCM distinguishes three parameters that influence career decisions: the need for authenticity, balance and challenge (Mainiero and Gibson, 2018). Authenticity is the need to act in accordance with one's true self. Balance is the need to balance both work and family domains. Challenge is the need to grow and develop one's skills and do intrinsically motivating work. According to this model, one of the three parameters dominates the two others and this may change throughout a woman's career. Elley-Brown (Chapter 17) contends that individuals work towards balance or challenge or authenticity to achieve a good fit between demands and constraints of work relationships and values.

Our results shed a different light on the notions of authenticity, balance and challenge. They show that Indian women strive for balance, challenge and authenticity, giving priority to their family care work responsibilities. In that sense, balance, authenticity and challenge are all looked for in care work along with paid work. This idea is interesting and different from the more Western reading of the KCM, in which balance is opposed to challenge and authenticity based on the idea that striving for balance means less opportunities for challenge and authenticity through work. This is also demonstrated in the study by Elley-Brown (Chapter 17).

Implications for Practice

To stimulate labour force participation of women in India, organizations as of now are only providing minor-enablers in terms of flexi-time, work from home, leave facilities, including sabbaticals as well as maternity leave. This only reinforces the gender role of the women and is in no way helpful for defeminization of care work. It is not surprising that women stay out, take career breaks and drop out of the workforce. Researchers (Carlson et al., 2006; Frone, Russell and Cooper, 1992; Padhi and Pattnaik, 2013, 2017) argue that work-to-family interaction can be bidirectional. From a sustainable career perspective, reconstructing the concept of work by valuing care work and integrating it with paid work and time for leisure is the need of the hour (Rath, Mohanty and Pradhan, 2019).

In India, professionals get non-practising allowance for not taking up similar responsibilities outside the organizations they work for. For example, doctors working in government-owned hospitals are provided an allowance for not carrying out private practice. A non-practising allowance could be given to these highly educated professional women for not joining the workforce, of, for example, of INR 1,000 per day, thus INR 30,000 per month. This is not being encouraged by family, government or society because it will take away from the value system of the family, where tendering, nurturing and care work is natural to a mother. Paying money for it would be tantamount to demeaning this. Further, the mother figure is like an owner-partner and therefore owner of half of the family resources. This also reaffirms the collective household labour supply decision.

It is found that for various reasons there is a strong emphasis placed on care work by educated women who stay out or drop out of the workforce. From a sustainability angle, care work sustains others in the family by ensuring the well-being of all, including the earning member. Paid work implies a better lifestyle and status for the family as well as sustains the self by deriving satisfaction from work. Personal time for leisure and relaxation sustains the self. Organizations need to understand this perspective of Indian women and devise policies accordingly to attract and retain them.

Limitations

The limitations of the study refer to the sample chosen. The sample is from urban middle class. It is likely that the findings could have been influenced by the respondents in the study who had spouses in high-paying jobs. In the future, a wider sampling would be required. A sampling across a more rural setting in India could bring out different sociocultural factors affecting the workforce participation of rural women. Cross-country samples can also help to test the model from different contextual perspectives.

CONCLUSION

The study explored various factors that women consider for their labour supply decision. These may influence their decisions to join the workforce or drop out of it. It reinforces the view of the role of family members in labour supply decisions, and in a social context that is collectivistic in nature it leads to extenuating the findings. The importance given to care work from individual, organizational and socio-cultural perspectives makes it pertinent to include care work in measuring the productive work for a country. Future research can further explore to what extent the sense of power and control that women derive in their roles in the household exceeds their desire for joining the workforce in the changing context of work that regards all types of work as productive.

NOTES

1. 'The unorganised sector covers most of the rural labour and a substantial part of urban labour. It includes activities carried out by small and family enterprises, partly or wholly with family labour. In this sector wage-paid labour is largely non-unionised due to casual and seasonal nature of employment and scattered location of enterprises. This sector is marked by low incomes, unstable and irregular employment, and lack of protection either from legislation or trade unions' (Ministry of Labour & Employment, Government of India, 2009).
2. All names changed while citing quotes to ensure anonymity.

REFERENCES

Aarikka-Stenroos, L. (2010), 'The contribution and challenges of narrative data in interorganizational research', paper presented at the IMP2010 conference, Budapest, Hungary, accessed 2 August 2019 at https://www.impgroup.org/uploads/papers/7553.pdf.

Abraham, V. (2013), 'Missing labour or consistent de-feminisation?', *Economic and Political Weekly*, **48**(31), 99–108.

Bloemen, H.G. (2010), 'An empirical model of collective household labour supply with nonparticipation', *Economic Journal*, **120**, 183–214.

Bloemen, H.G. (2019), 'Collective labor supply, taxes, and intrahousehold allocation: an empirical approach', *Journal of Business & Economic Statistics*, **373**, 471–83.

Blundell, R., P.A. Chiappori, T. Magnac and C. Meghir (2007), 'Collective labor supply: heterogeneity and nonparticipation', *Review of Economic Studies*, **74**, 417–45.

Boland, R.J. Jr (1985), '10 phenomenology: a preferred approach to research in information systems', in E. Mumford, R.A. Hirschheim, G. Fitzgerald and A.T. Wood-Harper (eds), *Research Methods in Information Systems*, Amsterdam: North-Holland, pp. 181–90.

Bourguignon, F. and P. Chiappori (1992), 'Collective models of household behavior: an introduction', *European Economic Review*, **36**(2–3), 355–64.

Carlson, D.S., K.M. Kacmar, J.H. Wayne and J.G. Grzywacz (2006), 'Measuring the positive side of the work–family interface: development and validation of a work–family enrichment scale', *Journal of Vocational Behavior*, **68**(1), 131–64.

Chapman, T. and V. Mishra (2019), 'Rewriting the rules: women and work in India', *ORF Special Report No. 80*, New Delhi: Observer Research Foundation.

Cherchye, L., B. De Rock and F. Vermeulen (2009), 'Opening the black box of intra-household decision-making: theory and non-parametric empirical tests of general collective models', *Journal of Political Economy*, **117**, 1074–104.

Coffey, D., P. Hathi, N. Khurana and A. Thorat (2018), 'Explicit prejudice: evidence from a new survey', *Economic and Political Weekly*, **53**(1), 46–54.

Crespo, C., P.E. Jose, M. Kielpikowski and J. Pryor (2013), '"On solid ground": family and school connectedness promotes adolescents' future orientation', *Journal of Adolescence*, **36**, 993–1002.

Deetz, S. (1996), 'Describing differences in approaches to organization science: rethinking Burrell and Morgan and their legacy', *Organization Science*, **7**(2), 191–207.

Deloitte (2019), *Opportunity or Challenge? Empowering Women and Girls in India for the Fourth Industrial Revolution*, accessed 26 July 2019 at https://www2.deloitte .com/content/dam/Deloitte/in/Documents/about-deloitte/UNGCNI_black_final   v6 web high res.pdf.

Donni, O. (2003), 'Collective household labor supply: nonparticipation and income taxation', *Journal of Public Economics*, **87**, 1179–98.

England, P., J. Gornick and E.F. Shafer (2012), 'Women's employment, education, and the gender gap in 17 countries', *Monthly Labor Review*, **135**, 3–12.

Frone, M.R., M. Russell and M.L. Cooper (1992), 'Antecedents and outcomes of work–family conflict: testing a model of the work–family interface', *Journal of Applied Psychology*, **77**(1), 65–78.

International Labour Organization (ILO) (2018), 'India labour market update', accessed 1 October 2018 at https://www.ilo.org/wcmsp5/groups/public/---asia/---ro-bangkok/ ---sro-new_delhi/documents/publication/wcms_496510.pdf.

Kapsos, S., A. Silberman and E. Bourmpoula (2014), 'Why is female labour force participation declining sharply in India?', *ILO Research Paper No. 10*, Geneva: International Labour Organization.

Klasen, S. and J. Pieters (2015), 'What explains the stagnation of female labor force participation in urban India?', *Policy Research Working Paper No. WPS 7222*, Washington, DC: World Bank Group, accessed 26 July 2019 at http://documents

.worldbank.org/curated/en/539141468186871615/What-explains-the-stagnation-of
-female-labor-force-participation-in-urban-India.

Kossek, E.E. and B.A. Lautsch (2012), 'Work–family boundary management styles in organizations: a cross-level model', *Organizational Psychology Review*, **2**(2), 152–71.

Kossek, E.E., R. Su and L. Wu (2017), '"Opting out" or "pushed out"? Integrating perspectives on women's career equality for gender inclusion and interventions', *Journal of Management*, **43**(1), 228–54.

Lieblich, A., R. Tuval-Mashiach and T. Zilber (1998), *Narrative Analysis: Reading, Analysis, and Interpretation*, New Delhi: Sage.

Mainiero, L. and D. Gibson (2018), 'The Kaleidoscope Career Model revisited: how midcareer men and women diverge on authenticity, balance, and challenge', *Journal of Career Development*, **45**(4), 361–77.

Mainiero, L. and S. Sullivan (2005), 'Kaleidoscope careers: an alternate explanation for the "opt-out" revolution', *The Academy of Management Executive*, **19**(1), 106–23.

Ministry of Labour & Employment, Government of India (2009), 'Unorganised sector', accessed 19 January 2020 at http://www.cbwe.gov.in/training-activities/unorganised
-sector.aspx.

Neetha, N. and I. Mazumdar (2011), 'Gender dimensions: employment trends in India, 1993–94 to 2009–10', *Economic and Political Weekly*, **46**(43), 118–26.

Orlikowski, W.J. and J.J. Baroudi (1991), 'Studying information technology in organizations: research approaches and assumptions', *Information Systems Research*, **2**(1), 1–28.

Padhi, M. and S. Pattnaik (2013), 'A typology of work family research: perspectives from literature', *Vilakshan: The XIMB Journal of Management*, **10**(2), 83–98.

Padhi, M. and S. Pattnaik (2017), 'Role of integration-segmentation on work–family interface of insurance sector employees in India', *International Journal of Manpower*, **38**, 1114–29.

Rath, T.S., M. Mohanty and B.B. Pradhan (2016), 'Career progression of Indian women bank managers: an integrated 3P model', *South Asian Journal of Management*, **23**(3), 143–69.

Rath, T.S., M. Mohanty and B.B. Pradhan (2019), 'An alternative career progression model for Indian women bank managers: a labyrinth approach', *Women Studies International Forum*, **73**, 24–34.

Social Attitudes Research, India (SARI) (2016), 'Social Attitudes Research, India (SARI) data is available!', accessed 16 August 2018 at https://riceinstitute.org/blog/social-attitudes-research-india-sari-data-is-available.

Srivastava. N. and R. Srivastava (2010), 'Women, work, and employment outcomes in rural India', *Economic and Political Weekly*, **45**(28), 49–63.

Sullivan, S. and L. Mainiero (2008), 'Using the Kaleidoscope Career Model to understand the changing patterns of women's careers: designing HRD programs that attract and retain women', *Advances in Developing Human Resources*, **10**(1), 32–49.

United Nations Statistics Division (UNSD) (1993), *System of National Accounts 1993*, accessed 24 July 2018 at https://unstats.un.org/unsd/nationalaccount/docs/1993sna
.pdf.

Vermeulen, F., O. Bargain and M. Beblo et al. (2006), 'Collective models of labor supply with non-convex budget sets and nonparticipation: a calibration approach', *Review of Economics of the Household*, **4**, 113–27.

Xu, Z. (2007), 'A survey on intra-household models and evidence', *MPRA Paper 3763*, accessed 3 October 2018 at https://ideas.repec.org/p/pra/mprapa/3763.html.

17. Leaning in: why some women are challenging the opt-out model

Margie J. Elley-Brown

INTRODUCTION

Lisa Belkin first coined the expression 'opt-out' in her ground-breaking article 'The opt-out revolution' published in *The New York Times* on 26 October 2003 (Belkin, 2003). Belkin described how highly educated women were leaving the workforce in mid-career rather than continuing to seek career advancement, a phenomenon that quickly attained media popularity. In response, Lisa Mainiero and Sherry Sullivan developed their Kaleidoscope Career Model (KCM) in 2005 that provided a means to describe and explain the reasons for the exodus.

The KCM offered a way to explore career patterns and is based on three parameters premised to guide career decisions – authenticity, balance and challenge. The three parameters are argued to be distinctive and virtually non-overlapping, with one dominating at any given time. The KCM spurned numerous research studies (for example, Cabrera, 2007, 2009; Sullivan and Mainiero, 2007) that resulted in the emergence of distinct gendered patterns: predominantly, women demonstrated careers characterized by interruptions (beta career pattern) of challenge, followed by balance, then authenticity; in contrast, men pursued careers in an alpha career pattern: challenge, authenticity, then balance. The assumption of men's career pattern as the benchmark is implicit in the use of the 'alpha' label.

This chapter describes recent empirical research that used the KCM model as a means of investigating the careers of New Zealand professional women educators. The research sought to examine women's lived experience of career and what career means to them at different career stages. Results diverged from previous KCM research in that these women did not opt out in mid-career but continued to seek challenge. The three KCM parameters melded together; authenticity was a potent theme in their career stories. Rather than follow a 'beta' pattern that involved a move to balance in mid-career, women pursued an 'alpha' career pattern, a pattern followed by many men in previous KCM studies. In later career, these women tended to 'lean back' as a desire for balance curbed their need for authenticity.

This chapter reflects on how changes in gender roles influence women's career decisions to 'opt in' rather than out of the workforce. It uses excerpts from women's career stories across the lifespan to explicitly talk back to KCM research and its three-stage model for careers.

CONTEXT FOR THIS STUDY

This research was conducted in Aotearoa (Māori name for New Zealand), a sovereign island country in the South Pacific of approximately 5 million people. New Zealand is a developed country that ranks highly in international rankings: quality of life, education, health, civil liberties and economic freedom. Authority is vested in an elected government with executive political power exercised by the prime minister.

New Zealand's status as the first country to award women the vote in 1893 is well known. As the country celebrated its 125th anniversary of universal suffrage it also celebrated the announcement of the pregnancy of Prime Minister Jacinda Ardern who gave birth during her first term in office in June 2018. This significant political moment was widely documented by domestic and international media, Ardern being only the second prime minister to give birth during office, the first being Pakistan's Benazir Bhutto in 1990. Ardern's rise to power was attended by an instantaneous and significant jump in the polls and huge public and media reaction – now widely known as the 'Jacindamania' effect (Fletcher, 2018).

Timperley (2018) comments that Ardern's pregnancy and motherhood status has been a significant digression for international as well as domestic politics despite not being related to either governance or policy. However, it is noteworthy in terms of presence: politically and relationally, and I suggest socio-culturally. Ardern's career pathway provides a template and inspiration for many women careerists in Aotearoa New Zealand and potentially more widely. She is an unmarried mother in high office, with a long-term partner. Ardern and fiancé Clarke Gayford share the parenting of their daughter, with Gayford taking time out of his work to be the primary caregiver once Ardern returned from six weeks leave of absence. McFadden (2018) reported that Ardern as New Zealand's prime minister 'serves as a role model for working mothers'.

WOMEN'S CAREERS

In contrast to New Zealand's 'trailblazing' recent events, global research on women's careers has tended to focus on how women's multiple caring responsibilities constrain their career progression. Interdependence and fluidity have been shown to characterize women's careers (O'Neil, Hopkins and Bilimoria, 2013), with some feminist perspectives focusing on difference theory, spurning alternative career notions but risking essentialist gender viewpoints (Arthur, Inkson and Pringle, 1999; Cabrera, 2007).

To date, strongly gendered career options that view women and men as equal but different pervade the career ideologies in some countries such as the Arab Middle East. In these countries, social and cultural practices that discriminate and disadvantage women in the workplace still pervade and women's participation rate is amongst the lowest globally. Work–family conflicts and lack of equality initiatives in organizations hinder career advancement (Hutchings, Lirio and Metcalfe, 2012).

In other developing countries such as India, the participation rate of women has decreased over 10 per cent in the past decade, despite economic growth and increase in women's educational attainment. In Chapter 16, Rath and Padhi report that a substantially high proportion of educated women identify their status as 'attending to domestic duties', a statistic not documented officially and potentially a reason for the low participation rates of women. They note the need to understand the 'complex factors' behind this trend of how educated women drop out, or indeed 'opt out' of the workforce.

However, discernible shifts are taking place in some Western countries, with demographic trends indicating dual-income households now predominate over the traditional male breadwinner role (Santos and Cabral-Cardoso, 2008). This chapter provides evidence of these shifts.

DUAL CAREERS AND CROSSOVER EFFECTS

Dual careers are established as a new norm for professional couples and are no longer an atypical pattern (Santos and Cabral-Cardoso, 2008). Such couples can potentially achieve flexibility in work–life arrangements between partners and successfully manage not just individual but shared career–life goals. Fluidity and interdependence, characteristics previously used to describe only women's careers are now becoming a pattern for careers in general (Clarke, 2015; Elley-Brown, Pringle and Harris, 2018), and both women and men have been shown to 'lean back' rather than 'lean in' and to seek increased flexibility at work (Major and Burke, 2013).

Support from a women's partner has received focus in the career literature, alongside which has simmered a continuing debate as to whether women and men are 'allies or adversaries' in balancing work and family demands. Men who are allies are described as men 'who get it'; they become supports rather than impediments to women's careers (Major and Burke, 2013). Litano, Myers and Major (2014) proffered their answer to the debate and argue that key to becoming allies is the extent to which synchronicity of women's and men's efforts to juggle work–family conflict can be attained.

When women and men are allies and together work to balance work and family as a couple, positive 'crossover' effects in their work–family boundary occur. Research into crossover effects investigates the transfer of either positive or negative states of well-being from one partner to the other. When positive well-being is created, it initiates 'an upward spiral of positive transfer' in both work and family spheres (Litano et al., 2014, p. 372). Essentially, both partners are more likely to thrive both at work and at home.

In addition, gender role orientation – the strength with which a person observes societal traditional gender roles – can further intensify crossover effects, for instance: husband as breadwinner and head of the family and wife as submissive caregiver for both household and children (Kailasapathy, Kraimer and Metz, 2014). If one partner, of either gender, adopts a traditional gender role orientation, this tends to intensify work–family conflict for the other partner, negative crossover is increased and the couple risk becoming adversarial. In contrast, assuming non-traditional gender beliefs means both partners attach equal value to career and co-providing roles and a woman's partner who adopts a more egalitarian role willingly takes on caregiving and household tasks (Kailasapathy et al., 2014). Thus, a positive crossover effect intensifies as work–family conflict is reduced for both partners.

KALEIDOSCOPE CAREER MODEL

In the KCM, three career parameters are used to explain how individuals make career decisions, defined as follows (Mainiero and Sullivan, 2005, pp. 113–14):

- Authenticity: can I be myself in the midst of all of this and still be authentic?
- Balance: if I make this career decision, can I balance the parts of my life well so there can be a coherent whole?
- Challenge: will I be sufficiently challenged if I accept this career option?

The metaphor of a kaleidoscope is used to describe the KCM. The adjustments and shifts modelled by a kaleidoscope with its rotating tube and mirrors enabling the glass chips to fall into changing and complex patterns, reflect the distinctive pattern an individual creates during their career. One of the KCM's three parameters takes precedence over the others at any time in an individual's career as their career pattern shifts and changes. In this way, individuals work towards balance or challenge or authenticity to achieve a good fit between demands and constraints of work relationships and values.

Both qualitative and quantitative empirical research was conducted to initially validate the KCM (Cabrera, 2007; Sullivan and Mainiero, 2007); this revealed gender differences in career enactment. The career pattern men tended to follow was described as 'alpha' – challenge followed by authenticity followed by balance, whereas women followed a pattern of challenge, then balance, then authenticity, described as a 'beta' career pattern. Further research confirmed these patterns and established that men typically followed more linear pathways; many women rejected these traditional pathways, due to career interruptions, the contextual nature of their decision-making and their relationship responsibilities (Cabrera, 2009). In later career, women have been shown to exhibit links with all three KCM parameters but with distinct meanings to authenticity and to a lesser degree to balance (August, 2011; Elley-Brown, 2011).

However, more recent research incorporating KCM parameters revealed different findings from these earlier studies and showed that strictly gendered career patterns are less predominant and are being usurped by other less clear-cut patterns, connected not just with gender but with other factors. For example, Cohen's (2014) 17-year longitudinal study with women who opted out of organizations showed that although challenge did dominate initially for women in early career undergirded by a desire to be authentic, the latter parameter was apparent between the interviews and 'provided a coherent thread' (Cohen, 2014, p. 113). Once established, authenticity was linked to both challenge and balance. Further, at mid-career, Cohen's results varied from Mainiero and Sullivan's (2005) in that a shift to balance was not an obvious component of the data. The three parameters fused together at various times in the women's lives rather than being sharply delineated and distinct.

A qualitative study with 18 Gen Y dual-career couples in Australia (Clarke, 2015) that used the KCM also found a subsuming of the gendered KCM patterns. Other factors such as motivation and career aspirations predominated, and the Gen Y couples' career choices rather than constrained by gender stereotypes were surpassed by their desire to have a combination of challenge and balance.

A further qualitative study in New Zealand researched the careers of female CEOs in sport management (Shaw and Leberman, 2015). Authors argued for a graduated approach to capture the career experiences of the women working in sports' gendered environment and suggested, for example, subthemes of passion and relationship-building under authenticity. Such extensions ensure progression of the KCM but only if validated by further findings such as those from this research study.

Although the KCM has its roots in positive career outcomes, Baruch and Vardi (2016), in an evaluation of recent career constructs, comment on the shadow side of contemporary career experiences and warn that these experiences can lead to disillusionment. Career transitions and challenges can be appealing for some careerists, yet others may find the intense transitions lead to anxiety and decreased confidence; career change can be daunting and contribute to burnout and disengagement. Baruch and Vardi (2016) warn that authenticity might well be suppressed for most people as they simply struggle to make a living.

The focus now moves to the research study that sought to question whether the KCM's gendered patterns continue to be followed in the careers of professional women educators.

THE RESEARCH STUDY

The research used purposive sampling with participants selected guided by the research question and to satisfy two primary criteria of having experienced a career in education and being willing to talk about their lived experiences of career and what having a career meant for them. Historically and currently, education has been a substantial sector for female employment in New Zealand as in other Western countries (United Nations Statistics Division, 2012).

A total of 14 New Zealand women were recruited, their ages ranged from 34 to 61 years, and all were currently employed in education at primary, secondary, or tertiary level. Their educational qualifications ranged from diploma to doctoral level. All women had a partner and all but one had children. The methodology used was hermeneutic phenomenology in order to gain a subjective view from the 'inside' (Van Manen, 2016). As with all phenomenological research, the questions asked concerned participants' meaning of lived experiences.

Each participant was involved in an interview of approximately one hour that was conversational in nature. The researcher used prompts and probes to encourage the participant to reflect on and interpret her own experiences. This kind of interview is distinctive in that the data analysis process begins in the interview itself, as the researcher engages with the participant and works alongside her to make meaning of her experiences. The interviews were audio-recorded and once transcripts were made these were analysed for pertinent incidents and stories (Van Manen, 2016).

From these incidents, phenomenological anecdotes were composed that contained interpretive meanings as opposed to descriptive narrative data. The product of this process was a total of four to eight 'stories' for each participant; these were returned to the participants for review. Data analysis did not proceed further until all participants had given their approval. The process then continued to uncover the broad themes of experience. In this way, a composite description of the phenomenon of a woman's career was created (Van Manen, 2016).

FINDINGS AND DISCUSSION

The research findings are now introduced, illustrated with excerpts from the phenomenological anecdotes. These are arranged chronologically – early (less than ten years), mid- (between ten and 25 years) and late career (over 25 years) – and related to KCM research, with two women chosen to represent women from each stage.

Early Career Women: Jackie and Libby

At the time of interview, Jackie and Libby were both aged 34 years. Both had worked in education for ten years: Jackie as a secondary maths teacher with management responsibility and Libby as a primary school teacher, also with a management position.

Mainiero and Sullivan (2006, p. 119) describe how at this stage of their career, 'men and women equally pursue the thrill of the hunt' as they seek to achieve early career goals. Jackie and Libby are both passionate and enthusiastic and want to keep learning and advance in their careers. They have families and are negotiating the demands of full-time work and study or have just completed postgraduate qualifications.

Jackie's interview involved the vivid retelling of a 'road of Damascus' event while travelling in the African country of Mali. At the time she was working in marketing and describes how an epiphany brought her to teaching:

> I knew then, I wanted to do ground-breaking work for low socio-economic kids who are so bright, yet no one has picked apart what makes them learn ... I want to write materials for these kids so that they can succeed, so I can die saying, 'I've done something good'. That's what drives me.

Libby had returned to take on a management role after six months' maternity leave, a role she knew would be demanding but desired so she could continue to invest in her career development:

> I grabbed it (the role). The last year has been challenging, returning to work, with a young child, wanting to carry my career on at exactly the same rate. It's very busy but I'm happy ... I like seeing myself amongst the decision makers. I want to further develop my leadership skills.

Jackie and Libby were energised and challenged by future possibilities, but also determined to be true to themselves: to be authentic (Hall and Mao, 2015). Statements such as I feel 'called to make a difference' (Jackie) and 'I've found my niche' (Libby) indicate that, as with women in Cohen's (2014) study, both challenge and authenticity are to the fore in their careers. Their decisions

included actively seeking promotion and continuing to pursue academic qualifications during this career phase.

Tina and Amanda: Mid-career Women

For mid-career women in this study such as Tina and Amanda, it was typical
to be involved in a dual-career partnership, in fact they described themselves
as having the 'front seat' or 'wearing the pants'. Tina, an associate professor,
and Amanda, a tertiary lecturer, described how their partners took an equal or
major share of childcare and household tasks so that they could work or study
as required. They considered this was the 'normal' way to manage work and
home commitments. Their partners' non-traditional gender role orientation
and egalitarian gender role ideology and support resulted in positive crossover
effects and reduction of conflict (Kailasapathy et al., 2014).

A feature of mid-career women in other KCM studies is that they had
withdrawn from their careers to 'make room for the more relational aspects of
their lives'. Rather than continue to pursue challenge and career advancement,
women followed a beta career pattern with a movement toward balance. In
this present study, only one woman pursued a beta career pattern, choosing to
spend protracted time at home with preschool-aged children.

Amanda observed that in deciding to marry her husband she thought care-
fully about the roles that they might both play in their partnership:

> My husband's not a career man ... he doesn't have that (high career) stress.
> I thought of that when I was dating. I thought if I had somebody who was putting on
> a business suit every day and maxing out at night, there's no life for me. Having his
> down-to-earth approach gives me the freedom to decide on my next step.

Tina's husband encouraged her to apply for roles wherever she wanted, saying
that he would fit in. Tina comments on the value of his unmitigated support:
'Being in academia there's limited places you can go; you have to have
someone who can fit around you. All the decisions I made when I came back
to work were mine. I talked with my husband about them, but they were all
driven by me'.

When decisions were required that affected both themselves and their
partner, for Amanda and Tina it was their own career that took precedence.
Having a partner who was an 'ally' for their career meant Tina and Amanda
experienced the freedom to seek further challenge in mid-career but also to
maintain perspective on their lives (Litano et al., 2014). They experienced positive 'crossover effects' and increased well-being in their relationships, benefits revealed through comments such as 'The other thing that keeps me going
is I've got a wonderful man who says to me, "Don't take it all too seriously"'.

Balance was explicitly mentioned but melded together with authenticity and challenge rather to the fore. Tina enjoys that her career gives her reputation and identity: 'I like having my own reputation; otherwise you get pigeonholed as the mother or the wife of so and so. "Oh, you're the person who always talks about such and such on the radio". Without my work I wouldn't have that'. Yet, she has a realistic appraisal of what she can achieve at this career stage:

> I want balance. I'm happy being internationally recognized for some things but not being that sort of world-class person that travels every month to speak at some conference. My family would not cope if I did all that travelling. So, I never want to be that person. I used to think I'm never going get there and be a bit depressed, but now I'm happy.

The stories of Tina and Amanda reveal that authenticity, balance and challenge are all visible in their career patterns as they seek challenge throughout mid-career. Both these women, typical of women in this study, exhibit the alpha career pattern that Mainiero and Sullivan (2006) described as characteristic of most men and single career-driven women, as opposed to a beta career pattern with a move away from challenge and toward balance.

Tina and Amanda have purposefully enacted an individual career pathway from the outset of their career, one that was authentic and where they continued to progress. For these women, challenge and authenticity were mutually apparent during mid-career as they work while raising children; there was minimal evidence of them 'pulling away' to balance their relational facets of their lives. This stands in contrast to the beta career pattern that involves a search for career authenticity and identity for women once they are 'freed from balance issues' in later career (Mainiero and Sullivan, 2006, p. 131).

Late Career Women: Helen and Sally

Sally and Helen, both senior managers in a secondary school and a tertiary institution respectively, were in late career, having worked for well over 25 years. Recent challenges for these women included layoffs and restructuring. Their response was to seek to achieve more balance in their lives for self-care and to re-evaluate. Helen remarks:

> I'd actually like to just be at home, making bread and knitting my dishcloths, reading and growing plants … I'd love that. I'm sick of working. Not much chance of that I'm afraid … What I would like, thank you very much, is a lovely 65-year-old who's extremely well off and says: 'Darling, you can retire, we need to do a bit of travelling'. That would suit me fine. I'd be out of here. I think about that next transition and how I would do it. I think about it all the time.

Helen is weary after a 40-year career in education and wants more balance in her life and time for herself; she mirrors the preferences of many men in Mainiero and Sullivan's (2006) sample. She has been the major breadwinner in her relationships, and for her, work has taken its toll and lost any sense of challenge or thrill.

A workplace restructure resulted in a new role for Sally:

> I said, 'I'll put my head on the block'. I'm usually a fighter and could have forced things ... but I went on my terms. I was pretty stretched from being a deputy principal, and I wanted to be able to survive somehow until I was 65 [usual retirement]. I didn't want to go out in a box.

Sally was content to take on a less challenging role that meant she could achieve balance in her life, a relief to her, but she considers she has been true to herself as she achieved it on her 'own terms'.

Being involved in a restructuring process that resulted in a layoff were described by other late career women as 'extremely brutal', 'a nightmare', and 'a personal attack'. Women in late career described their work in early and mid-career as filled with meaning and purpose where they enjoyed career satisfaction and fulfilment (Hall and Mao, 2015) but by late career they had experienced some significant times of vulnerability; at these times being true to themselves was not easy. Hall and Mao (2015) comment that it is questionable how much of a person's 'true self' she should bring to work. Sally discovered this when a trusted colleague betrayed that trust, she remarked, 'she was my friend ... she knew the dagger that would pierce me'.

Statements such as this reveal a sinister side of career experiences (Baruch and Vardi, 2016). These women lack enthusiasm for their work, they are disillusioned and their need for authenticity is subsumed by their need for balance and self-care. Stress, burnout and a lack of well-being have predominated in recent years, and they are keen to achieve more life balance as they contemplate the last years of their working lives; they choose to 'lean back' (Major and Burke, 2013). Still, there is no sign of a need to find their own identify, and they follow more of an alpha career pattern along with single career-driven women and many men in KCM studies.

DISCUSSION

Several points are apparent in these findings. First, the three KCM parameters of authenticity, balance and challenges overlapped rather than remained mutually exclusive at various points of these women's lives; they sought authenticity and were clear about a need to seek feedback and to gain insight from their past actions (Hall and Mao, 2015). From the outset, the stories they told indicated a desire to be authentic: this was an undergirding facet that continued throughout their career progression into mid-career. Authenticity was melded with balance and challenge – this persistent search for authenticity trademarked their careers (Cohen, 2014).

In mid-career, rather than opting out they opted in. They described themselves as driven, pushing themselves to succeed, to achieve career goals they questioned 'What is my next thing?' They maintained a focus on challenge and remained engaged in their career, seeking promotion and the chance to upskill through further study. There was evidence that they did seek balance, yet a supportive partner who adopted egalitarian behaviour was key to maintaining perspective.

The pattern these women showed was a clear alpha career pattern of challenge coupled with authenticity in early career; a pattern was maintained in mid-career. Although they were involved in a female-dominated occupation they displayed a typically male career pattern.

Their accounts revealed they existed in a web of relationships so that their decisions were contextual (O'Neil et al., 2013). However, they managed their relationships with skill, and were not constrained by them – to the contrary, these relationships provided positive spirals of positive well-being (Litano et al., 2014). They took a 'front seat' role in their partnerships, with decision-making processes that gave predominance to their own careers. Their partners adjusted their own expectations and took a large share of responsibilities – there is some evidence that their partners career followed a beta career pattern.

For these women, their partner was an 'ally' to their career progression (Litano et al., 2014) and supported them through various mid-career challenges; relationships were a help rather than a hindrance to career progression. Their ability to strongly pursue an individual pathway in mid-career was not diminished or constrained as were women who evidence a beta career pattern.

However, in late career, transitions such as layoffs and restructuring had been experienced, and women's continued search for authenticity coupled with greater work–life balance meant they were working in different roles than previously in mid-career. Findings reveal the 'dark' side of career where authenticity can be curbed by the stark reality of making a living and getting through to retirement age (Baruch and Vardi, 2016).

CONCLUSION

Phenomenological research has the power to uncover details and to obtain a subjective view in a process that produces a composite description of the phenomenon. Study findings have the potential to be applied in different settings, but country specifics may limit the application to other Western countries. It would be unwise to make far-reaching generalizations from a study of this size; however, this study adds to other research that extends the body of knowledge on women's careers and addresses important questions about the changing nature of gendered career patterns.

There is no doubt that more research to determine whether the convergence between women's and men's careers is growing, yet this study indicates that there are indeed subtle shifts to gendered patterns such as the KCM. This research forms part of recent work that extends and critiques our understanding of women's careers using KCM concepts (Clarke, 2015; Cohen, 2014; Shaw and Leberman, 2015); it behoves further research to determine the long-term effects on 'alpha' women as to how they can maintain focus on career challenge. Generational needs should be considered in future research, with studies into both partners in dual-career couples and same-sex couples, as the growing complexity of careers affects theory development for both women's and men's careers.

REFERENCES

Arthur, M.B., K. Inkson and J.K. Pringle (1999), *The New Careers: Individual Action and Economic Change*, London: Sage.

August, R.A. (2011), 'Women's later life career development: looking through the lens of the Kaleidoscope Career Model', *Journal of Career Development*, **38**(3), 208–36.

Baruch, Y. and Y. Vardi (2016), 'A fresh look at the dark side of contemporary careers: toward a realistic discourse', *British Journal of Management*, **27**, 355–72.

Belkin, L. (2003), 'The opt out revolution', *The New York Times Magazine*, 26 October 2003, accessed at 2 October 2019 at www.nytimes.com/2003/10/26/magazine/the-opt-out-revolution.html.

Cabrera, E.F. (2007), 'Opting out and opting in: understanding the complexities of women's career transitions', *Career Development International*, **12**(3), 218–27.

Cabrera, E.F. (2009), 'Protean organizations: reshaping work and careers to retain female talent', *Career Development International*, **14**(2), 186–201.

Clarke, M. (2015), 'Dual careers: the new norm for Gen Y professionals?', *Career Development International*, **20**(6), 562–82.

Cohen, L. (2014), *Imagining Women's Careers*, Oxford: Oxford University Press.

Elley-Brown, M.J. (2011), 'The significance of career narrative in examining a high achieving woman's career', *Australian Journal of Career Development*, **20**(3), 18–23.

Elley-Brown, M.J., J.K. Pringle and C. Harris (2018), 'Women opting in? New perspectives on the Kaleidoscope Career Model', *Australian Journal of Career Development*, **27**(3), 172–80.

Fletcher, M. (2018), *Developments in Social Legislation and Policy in New Zealand: 'Jacindamania' and a New Government*, accessed 2 October 2019 at https://www.mpisoc.mpg.de/sozialrecht/publikationen/detail/publication/developments-in-social-legislation-and-policy-in-new-zealand-jacindamania-and-a-new-government/.

Hall, D.T. and J. Mao (2015), 'Exploring authenticity in careers: implications for research and practice', in S.G. Baugh and S.E. Sullivan (eds), *Searching for Authenticity, Volume 2*, Charlotte, NC: Information Age Publishing, pp. 1–23.

Hutchings, K., P. Lirio and B.D. Metcalfe (2012), 'Gender, globalization and development: a re-evaluation of the nature of women's global work', *International Journal of Human Resource Management*, **23**(9), 1763–87.

Kailasapathy, P., M.L. Kraimer and I. Metz (2014), 'The interactive effect of leader–member exchange, gender and spouse, gender role orientation on work interference with family conflict', *The International Journal of Human Resource Management*, **25**(19), 2681–701.

Litano, M.L., D.P. Myers and D.A. Major (2014), 'How can men and women be allies in achieving work–family balance? The role of coping in facilitating positive crossover', in M.D. Myers and D.A. Major (eds), *Gender in Organizations: Are Men Allies or Adversaries to Women's Career Advancement?*, Cheltenham, UK and Northampton, MA, USA: Edward Elgar Publishing, pp. 365–84.

Mainiero, L.A. and S.E. Sullivan (2005), 'Kaleidoscope careers: an alternate explanation for the "opt-out" revolution', *The Academy of Management Executive*, **19**(1), 106–23.

Mainiero, L.A. and S.E. Sullivan (2006), *The Opt-Out Revolt: How People Are Creating Kaleidoscope Careers Outside of Companies*, New York: Davies Black.

Major, D.A. and R.J. Burke (2013), *Handbook of Work–Life Integration Among Professionals*, Cheltenham, UK and Northampton, MA, USA: Edward Elgar Publishing.

McFadden, C. (2018), 'New Zealand prime minister serves as role model for working mothers', *NBC Nightly News*, 17 April 2018 [video], accessed 2 October 2019 www.archives.nbclearn.com/portal/site/k-12/browse?cuecard=115093.

O'Neil, D.A., M.M. Hopkins and D. Bilimoria (2013), 'Patterns and paradoxes in women's careers', in M. McMahon (ed.), *Conceptualising Women's Working Lives*, Rotterdam: Sense Publishers, pp. 63–82.

Santos, G.G. and C. Cabral-Cardoso (2008), 'Work–family culture in academia: a gendered view of work–family conflict and coping strategies', *Gender in Management. An International Journal*, **23**, 442–57.

Shaw, S. and S.I. Leberman (2015), 'Bringing the pieces of the puzzle together – using the Kaleidoscope Career Model to analyze female CEOs' career experiences in sport', *Gender in Management: An International Journal*, **30**(6), 500–515.

Sullivan, S.E. and L.A. Mainiero (2007), 'The changing nature of gender roles, alpha/beta careers and work–life issues: theory driven implications for human resource management', *Career Development International*, **12**(3), 238–63.

Timperley, C. (2018), 'Jacinda Ardern: a political presence', in S. Levine (ed.), *Stardust and Substance: The New Zealand General Election of 2017*, Wellington: Victoria University Press, pp. 339–50.

United Nations Statistics Division (2012), accessed 2 October 2019 at http://unstats.un.org/unsd/demographic/products/indwn/.

Van Manen, M. (2016), *Researching Lived Experience: Human Science for An Action Sensitive Pedagogy*, New York: Routledge.

Index